The *Iliad* and the *Odyssey*

To Professors Pat Easterling and Lorna Hardwick, for a lifetime of inspiration.

For Fred, Matthew, Imogen, Rosie, Family, with gratitude.

The *Iliad* and the *Odyssey*

The Trojan War: Tragedy and Aftermath

Jan Parker

Pen & Sword
MILITARY

First published in Great Britain in 2021 by
Pen & Sword Military
An imprint of
Pen & Sword Books Ltd
Yorkshire – Philadelphia

ISBN 978 1 52677 993 9

Typeset by Mac Style
Printed and bound in the UK by CPI Group (UK) Ltd, Croydon,
CR0 4YY

MIX
Paper from
responsible sources
FSC
www.fsc.org   FSC® C013604

Pen & Sword Books Limited incorporates the imprints of Atlas,
Archaeology, Aviation, Discovery, Family History, Fiction, History,
Maritime, Military, Military Classics, Politics, Select, Transport,
True Crime, Air World, Frontline Publishing, Leo Cooper, Remember
When, Seaforth Publishing, The Praetorian Press, Wharncliffe
Local History, Wharncliffe Transport, Wharncliffe True Crime
and White Owl.

For a complete list of Pen & Sword titles please contact

PEN & SWORD BOOKS LIMITED
47 Church Street, Barnsley, South Yorkshire, S70 2AS, England
E-mail: enquiries@pen-and-sword.co.uk
Website: www.pen-and-sword.co.uk

Or

PEN AND SWORD BOOKS
1950 Lawrence Rd, Havertown, PA 19083, USA
E-mail: Uspen-and-sword@casematepublishers.com
Website: www.penandswordbooks.com

Contents

Note

This book explores both the *Iliad* and the *Odyssey*; telling rich stories and opening up the questions in both epics that challenged the original audiences and still challenge us today. Each of the *Iliad* book sections starts with an outline of that book's story, in italics, and is followed by an exploration of the themes, narrative structure and Greek ideas about heroic bonds, values and psychology (fully explored in two special 'key word' sections).

Translations are from my copy of the Greek text, by now heavily marked up with question and exclamation marks and underlinings! Although commentaries have many different conventions about the spellings of Greek names, I have used standardized spellings.

Artist Trisha Kelly has reimagined characters and scenes in the text from those illustrated on Classical Greek Black Figure and Red Figure Vases, from descriptions in the text and – with the map of Odysseus' adventures – from Odysseus himself.

I've been so fortunate in sharing my love of Homer and Greek literature with generations of Cambridge and Open University students and those coming to 'Open the Text' with me on day and summer schools.

I hope that this book will similarly open Homer to readers who may come to share my passion for this extraordinary work.

Odysseus' Travels

Foreword

Why Read Homer?

by Paul Cartledge (A.G. Leventis Professor of
Greek Culture emeritus, University of Cambridge.
Commander of the Order of Honour (Greece))

We classicists and ancient historians have long been amused by the potential confusion – and the resulting jokes – between our Homer and that character made world-famous by Matt Groening, creator of *The Simpsons*. Reading the original Homer is no laughing matter – though neither is it deadly serious; rather, it is exhilarating and enlightening – but it does take the breath away to think that two very long poems, each composed in a verse language never spoken outside the context of a recital of epic poetry, represent the very start of world literature; the oldest literature to have been written down, memorized, recited, continuously, for almost 3,000 years. This makes Greek the longest tradition of continuous poetic language in the whole wide world.

Which means that those two poems, the *Iliad* and the *Odyssey*, must have something, something very special, going for them. I am going to be unashamedly personal in these few remarks: it was a reading of Homer, when I was aged just 8, that set me on my life's course – as a classicist, as a historian and as a perpetual student of the ancient Greeks. Of course I didn't then read them in the original ancient Greek: that had to wait until I went to university, when I read the whole of both of them, all forty-eight 'books' and almost 30,000 lines of verse. I soon found that the more one read at a go, the faster one's reading speed and the greater one's enjoyment (some 300 lines an hour, if memory serves).

That was just about a decade after my first introduction as an 8-year-old. Then – and I still have the two little books – in the mid-1950s I read them both in 'Told To the Children' versions beautifully moderated by Jeannie Lang, daughter of the famous 'Butcher and (Andrew) Lang' duo well known to older and adult classical readers and scholars. And they came with a bonus, one that I learned to appreciate fully only much later – illustrations in full colour by a certain William Heath Robinson (yes, the Heath Robinson, so famous for his drawings of highly complex machines and mechanical devices that he has given his name to a saying – a 'Heath Robinson' effect).

In my mind's eye, I can always still see how Heath Robinson conjured up the *Iliad*'s greatest hero, Achilles, resplendent in the shining new suit of armour that his goddess mother, Thetis, had commissioned from the lame Olympian armourer-god Hephaestus. It didn't occur to me then to wonder how Hephaestus had managed to get the dimensions and the fit just right. But of course it was all done by magic – the magic, not least, of the epic poet's brilliant description. As a boy, the derring-do of Achilles, especially in his fatal duel with Trojan champion Hektor, was what most caught my attention and fired my imagination.

Even more impressive to my impressionable younger self, though, was the magical mystery tour of the *Odyssey*, and – if for different reasons at different stages of my life – my all-time favourite of Homer's many characters, who was and is the divine (in more senses than one) lady Calypso. She somehow contrived to keep the eponymous hero Odysseus with her on her small island for more than two-thirds of the ten years it took him finally to get back home – from the once-mighty, destroyed city of Troy overlooking the Hellespont/Dardanelles strait to his small rocky island kingdom of Ithaca off mainland Greece's west coast.

Calypso's name would, to an ancient Greek reader or listener, have instantly conveyed secrecy, something 'hidden' or 'covered up'. But her secret was known to all-seeing Zeus on Mount Olympus, who sent the divine messenger Hermes to order her to let Odysseus go; to let him go home to his faithful Spartan wife, Penelope, who had never given up hope of his eventual return, and done all she possibly could to fight off the attentions of no fewer than 108 suitors, all equally keen to get their hands on Odysseus' (presumed) widow and kingdom, and to dispossess her barely adult son Telemachus.

After a series of travails (whence comes our word 'travels'), Odysseus does at last, three years later, find himself back on Ithaca – but, thanks to his guardian goddess Athene, in disguise, as a humble mendicant. However, although his disguise did the intended job of fooling any humans he encountered, it did not deceive one of Odysseus' oldest friends, a four-footed one, his faithful hound Argos. By the time Odysseus ventured to approach what had been his palace (we are now in Book 17 of the *Odyssey*'s twenty-four books), Argus – aged 20 or over – was in a sorry state, a truly pitiable condition. How different, 'beggar' Odysseus was told, from the state in which his master had last seen him! Then, he'd been the finest and fastest of all Odysseus' hunting hounds – but now he lay, almost blind, flea- and tick-ridden, amid the kitchen and other waste matter piled into a midden outside the palace's back door, ignored and dishonoured by the suitors. Odysseus, remembering, is deeply moved and sheds a (silent) tear.

Yet by one or other of his remaining senses, Argus somehow sees through his master's disguise and is filled with joy at his *nostos* (return – whence our 'nostalgia'). Only the effort of recognition is too great for him, and by the time Odysseus moves on to enter the palace, the great dog has died. In Chapman's famous translation:

> And [Odysseus] left poor Argus dead; his lord's first sight
> Since that time twenty years bereft his light.

At which point of Jeannie Lang's 'Told to the Children' version, I simply broke down and wept, for a full half-hour. In retrospect, I can see that it was also a tipping point in my own life's trajectory.

Adult vision (or re-vision) brings with it different and deeper, less personal reflections. Homer's epic poems of war and suffering and reunion can still speak to us of the role of destiny in life, of cruelty, of humanity and its frailty. They are the original 'classic' literature, in the sense that whenever one reads them or hears them, one learns something new and valuable. Do please therefore add this book to your bucket list of works of literature that absolutely have to be not just read, but immersed in and internalized.

Part I

The *Iliad*

Aristeia

Introduction: Exploring the *Iliad*

Layers

'I have looked on the face of Agamemnon,' said Heinrich Schliemann, lifting the fabulous gold mask off a figure excavated from the Mycenae shaft grave. When excavating Troy (modern Hissarlik in north-west Turkey), he dressed his wife in 'Helen's treasure'. Schliemann devoted his life to uncovering – in all senses – the heroes of the *Iliad*: so much so that he was incapable of discriminating between the perhaps nine phases of Troy's citadel, digging through until he found fortifications that matched those he found described in Homer's poem.

Potsherds

Editions of Alexander Pope's *Iliad* had fold-out maps so that readers could explore the landscape and remains of the Trojan citadel and the Greek camp, literally treading in Agamemnon's and Achilles' footsteps. However, careful research by archaeologists, oral historians and textual scholars has peeled away earlier and later traditions within our text, distinguishing material culture and cultural practices of the Mycenaean or Bronze Age from those belonging to later Dark Age, Dorian or early pre-Classical cultures.

Chariot Fighting

The text contains some splendid indicators, direct references for example to Bronze Age tower shields, a valuable (being exotic and precious) prize of a lump of iron, 'Dendra'-type armour, the use of chariots from which to fight and the boar's tooth helmet inherited by Odysseus:

Meriones gave Odysseus a bow, a quiver and a sword, and put a cleverly made leather helmet on his head. On the inside there was a strong lining on interwoven straps, onto which a felt cap had been sewn in. The outside was cleverly adorned all around with rows of white tusks from a shiny-toothed boar, the tusks running in alternate directions in each row. Odysseus' grandfather Autolycus stole it when he robbed the Thessalian chief Amyntor's house. He in turn gifted it to his guest, who passed it then to his son Meriones to wear, and now it was Odysseus' head it guarded. (10.265–71)

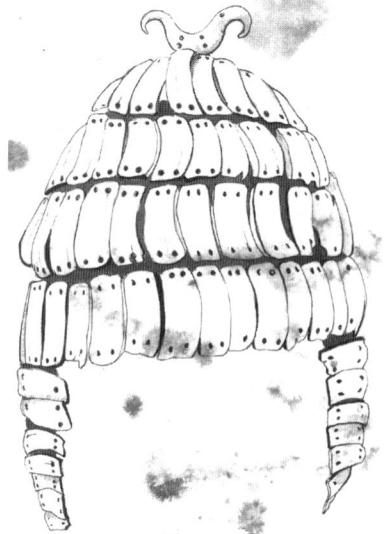

Boar's Tusk Helmet

We have the archaeology of Mycenaean and Dark Age Greece and many references, in the records of the mighty Hittite Empire lying to the east of Troy, to Wilusa (which gives us Ilion) and a Prince Aleksandru who 'has a claim to the throne despite being son of a concubine'. We start to see through the *Iliad* to a Mycenaean world of palaces, empire and a Prince Paris Alexander who certainly went on 'missions' to Phoenicia (Hecuba offers the goddess Athene a Phoenician robe Paris had brought back) and whose actions in Sparta would definitely contravene Hittite regulation of client kings' marriage treaties. This Mycenaean world has a northern trade route past Troy up through the Dardanelles/Hellespont to the Black Sea, which made Troy a valuable area to control.

Origins

We, like Pope's travellers, can look for the real Paris Alexander of (W)ilion and reconstruct from other stories the real Helen who was crown princess of Sparta, a patron goddess in whose honour girls' games were held in Sparta, where thousands of offerings to her have been found. We can go to Agamemnon's Mycenae and look at Near East treaties and trade with Greece for the indications of punitive and restorative expeditions. And in Pylos we can look for the revered Nestor – with his references

Potsherd

to exploits of when he was young, when men in those days could lift one-handed stones that a group of weaklings of today would not be able to raise; who in Book 11 of the *Iliad* offers Patroclus a cup reminiscent of one Schliemann found in grave circle A, shaft grave IV, in Mycenae.

But if we focus only on finding what is left of Troy VII (or whichever), we might miss the important questions explored throughout this book: challenges about what is recognizable, what rings true and what disturbs in a text formed over years of retellings.

In the years of re-performance by the 'Sons of Homer', travelling professional storytellers combining their own and others' cycles of stories about those who went to Troy, these 'rhapsodes' or stitchers-together of songs, interwove other layers than of history and material culture: layers of understandings of and

challenges to heroic and social values, the natural world, psychology, the cost of war and the value of human life.

Hektor, for example, defending his wife, baby and elderly parents, is set against a Paris Alexander who not only cannot be shamed but who sees from outside, unimplicated, what his fellow-Trojans are fighting and dying for. Meanwhile, Helen looks down on the battlefield, towards the two men whose fight for her should settle at least the pretext for the war. This is a Helen who reflects on her position as 'Helen of Troy', seemingly aware of her double-edged position as *Frau Welt*, as the most vilified and the most beautiful, the most fascinating while most destructive woman of all time. This battlefield is the site of heroic duels and bloody, wasteful deaths; heroes, who advance 'glittering in armour like Zeus' thunder-flash', face each other 'like opposing lines of reapers cutting swathes through some rich man's field', but end with chariots up to their axles in gore.

The *Iliad* gives us not historical and archaeological layers, sequences to be peeled away, but a weaving, finally cut from the loom and bound up in the sixth century BCE. (When it was finally 'canonized' and stabilized, it was for performance to Athenians trained to defend their city and fellow citizens, each man's shield protecting his neighbour's fighting arm, with no place for individual 'heroics'.) The storyteller-weaver crafts the strong threads of the stories – of Achilles' anger, of Agamemnon as summoner of forces, of Menelaus and Paris as rivals for Helen, of Hektor as Troy's defender but also as rejector of sound advice, and of those others with stories of their own – Diomedes, the Ajaxes, Odysseus, Aeneas…

But their stories are interwoven with the dark threads of history, of Zeus' will, of their own doom and those of the narrator's own voice: judgments on those who go against the shape of things, the victims whose only immortality is to be their death and a brief biography recording their tragically short life and the effect on those still to hear the news.

Lighter threads are woven through: the gods, unimplicated and irresponsible; the beautifying similes that stop the action and take us to a farmstead or mountainside, from a falling body to a felled tree being trimmed to make a well-wrought, elaborately crafted chariot.

It is this setting of Hektor's story against that of Paris; the 'heroic values' of a Sarpedon against those of a Diomedes; Achilles' and Hektor's combat within a narrative of a doomed city and a doomed man; and all against the viewpoint of those looking down with interest or indifference from Mount Olympus, that places the great set-pieces within a multi-shining texture.

Heroes and warfare: recognition and disturbance

Major-General James Wolfe, 'the most celebrated British hero of the eighteenth century' (National Army Museum) who martyred himself in taking Quebec, reputedly went into that fatal charge quoting Sarpedon's address to Glaukos on the duties and privileges of a hero. Many of the classically educated young officers of the First World War took the *Iliad* with them into the trenches and 'over the top'.

Perhaps conversely, Jonathan Shay, the seminal professor of psychiatry of the Veterans Improvement Program, recognizes in Achilles' wrath many facets of the stories and psychology of those veterans he treats for post-traumatic stress disorder (PTSD).

Many who turn to the *Iliad* see things that they recognize illuminated: grief and rage at the fracturing of values to live by and die for; the fragility and beauty of life at the edge; the strength and importance of human bonds. But others are troubled by the *Iliad*: by those very 'heroic values', its violence, the dark psychology of its heroes. Contemporary poets like Christopher Logue and Alice Oswald, among many others, have been drawn to make their own versions disturbed by some of its layers: by its attempt to memorialize, by its unsettling binding together of threads of elegy with epic.

This book is interested in reflecting on some of the universally and iconically recognizable threads – the striving for excellence, the poppy, the plight of Briseis and the women of Troy, the death of the unequivocally sympathetic Sarpedon and Patroclus, the heart-stopping grief as well as rage of Achilles – while exploring the rich, various and thought-provoking particularities of the narration in which the stories are embedded.

The process of 'composition' is much discussed, but has been beautifully illuminated by Greg Nagy's image, from the Harvard Center for Oral History, of oral poetry as coming together in the same way as butter in a churn: in every rotation, more becomes solid and less fluid. Every 'turn' here is in performance where the 'solids' are the memorable scenes that the oral performer works up, to which audiences look forward: the arming scene, Helen and Priam looking down on the Greek camp from Troy's citadel walls, Hektor saying goodbye to Andromache and his baby son, Diomedes' day of pre-eminence (*aristeia*), Hera seducing Zeus, the death of Sarpedon… Each performance polishes up and may re-site these shining scenes: each performer crafts the scenes into a multi-layered whole, perhaps buffing up the patina of the antique, perhaps voicing a very modern reflection on problematic individualism or the glory of war.

The result is a various, and also variously affecting, whole.

The different parts, for instance, of Sarpedon's great speech affect us differently:

Why do we hold the most honoured seats in our homeland; the choicest meat at the feast; the ever-brimful wine-cups? There they treat us as divine! Ours are the vast estates along the river Xanthus too, the tracts of orchard and the rich plough land. So now we must stand in the front line and lead the fight, so that the well-armed Lycians can say: 'No ordinary men [without *kleos*, fame] these our Lycian kings. Theirs are the fattest sheep and honey sweet fine wines, but theirs the finest courage too.' (12.315–21)

Here is the inspiring heroic contract, honour and reputation, acknowledgment of pre-eminence that has to be upheld on the battlefield. It is not surprising that the great British hero should quote it going to his greatest conquest – and death – at Quebec. But somehow these lines came together with a different sentiment:

Oh, my dear, if we could come through the battle and live ageless and immortal, the last thing I would do is fight in the frontline or send you into the glory-giving fighting.

And finally:

Now, as now the thousand-fold spirits of death are all around, inescapable, let us go out to either give the victory shout, or be some other's victim.

How do these three sentiments go together? How did they sound to a classical citizen hoplite audience, told by Pericles that the greatest glory belongs to Athens, not to any individual (in a speech over Athenian war dead buried with all honour but without name). How do they sound to us?

Whatever the answers, those three sentiments sound and resound differently, and perhaps differently from each other, because of their crafting over time and to different audiences. The layers of the *Iliad* voice different perceptions, put different questions and at different times focalize and embed different value systems. Is *kleos* (fame) worth fighting and dying for? Is anything worth fighting and dying for? What can assuage Achilles' anger? What recompense is there for the death of Patroclus? These are potentially disturbing questions. The *Iliad* can be read, can be heard, as an exploration of Sarpedon's *raison d'être*: the reason for being, for a human life.

The story

The *Iliad* starts with the rage of Achilles, the greatest fighter, the 'best and first of the Greeks', which brought down so many heroes. It ends with the making of the grave mound of Hektor, the sole defence of the women and children of Troy.

The two have extraordinary stories: Achilles, for whom heroic values are absolute, the only framing for his life and so his death; Hektor, a leader and

pre-eminent fighter, but whose story is told with the foreshadowing of fate – Troy will fall.

This *Iliad*, one of the stories of Troy (*Ilion*), is set in the last year of that iconic war, fought for Helen, the most beautiful woman in the world, queen of Mycenaean Sparta, carried off from her palace by the irresistible Paris, prince of Troy, a rich trading city set strategically on the route up the Hellespont, the Dardanelles, to the Black Sea.

From Book 2's catalogue of Greek and Trojan forces – summoned by Agamemnon and Hektor respectively from all over the Greek mainland and islands, Thrace, the Black Sea and Asia Minor – we see the epic scale of this war. Euripides' chorus in his *Iphigenia in Aulis*, performed at the end of the fifth century BCE, are a group of girls who have travelled from a neighbouring island to admire the Greek heroes, the mighty figures of legend gathered ready to embark for Troy. Audiences who came to the performances of the Trojan War epics by the 'Sons of Homer' – the oral poets of the pre-classical age – no doubt came to do the same.

Achilles

The *Iliad* is full of those mighty deeds, of the days of pre-eminence that enable fighters with the sun on their backs to defeat anybody, threatening even the gods who have flown down to play their version of Cowboys and Indians: 'Greeks and Trojans'. The Trojans – and with Achilles out of action, the other Greek heroes – have their times when they are unbeatable, days when they scythe through the opposing forces: their victims falling grotesquely or graphically or tragically, 'their eyes falling in the dust', 'killed by a spear thrust where of all places it is most agonising', like 'a graceful tree felled to be worked into a beautiful chariot' or 'a poppy whose heavy head droops under rain'.

Most of the heroes are not fighting for a cause. Both leaders are reminded that there is no ideological or personal basis to the war, no grounds for enmity or belief in a just cause for which they are fighting. They have come because they were summoned, because as heroes, that is what they do.

These epic encounters are multiply framed, in a narrative coming out of generations of re-performance. Achilles and Hektor know what they are fighting for, but the narrator is scathing about the young man who leaves his bride straight after the wedding to 'win glory': 'Fool!' he says. And the heroes' achievements are set against the gods' perspective: humans are like leaves on the tree, falling in season to nourish the next set. In the epic world of the *Iliad*, the only value that stands up against that bleak vision of the human condition is that of 'immortal, undiminishing reputation'; to perform deeds that will be a subject of song down the generations; to distinguish oneself, to individuate, to have a name that lives on.

The thread running through the narration is that this is a tragic vision: the heroes' victims are given a brief biography that reflects for a moment on what they could have been, what those left behind will suffer when they hear the news. The unforgettable scenes of ordinary life, of nature, of caring for the soil and animals, woven into the text in similes and cast on Achilles' shield, are a constant reminder of the values of life away from the battlefield.

All the famous names whose stories ring out through later retellings and Greek dramas have their place in the narration – figures such as Agamemnon, Menelaus, Ajax, Odysseus and Diomedes.

But there are also those whose voices and fate cut across the narrative. Sarpedon, the Trojan ally who left his home and baby son, against whose impending death even Zeus protests. Patroclus, likewise, over whose body not only Achilles but Briseis and all the women of the Greek camp cry.

Furthermore, there are those whose story form the *casus belli*: Paris and Helen. They have stories of their own. Helen relates the pain of being brought into Paris' story, of leaving her daughter and companions, her home as queen of Sparta. Though the *Iliad* we have is set in the male heroic world, Helen carries her own story, that of the Mycenaean princess through whom the throne passed; in the *Odyssey* she has semi-divine powers, and there are traces of the marriage games at which she was 'won' by Agamemnon offering a huge dowry to make his brother Menelaus king of Sparta. (The much-travelled Paris – there are references to presents he has been given when on diplomatic missions – may have brought back not just a beautiful woman but a claim to the throne of Sparta.)

If Helen's dislocation is sensitively described, reflected in her response to Priam – who 'was always kind to her' – when he asks her to describe the Greek forces below the walls, Paris' disengagement is shown by his very occupation (an archer, who fights from afar) and total disregard for his proper role in this fight. His response to Hektor's demand he leave Helen's bedchamber and fight, and his return to it, would be blackly comic were the consequences not so terrible.

Whereas Achilles is a single and singular figure, who burns through the narrative with frightening force, Hektor is nearly always surrounded, enmeshed in bonds of loyalty and responsibility. Even in the heat of battle, he is conscious of the watching Trojan women; his exploits as a hero on an epic battle landscape are framed by the cautious strategic advice given him as leader and defender of the Trojans.

Whereas Achilles and the other Greeks fight in their own persons, to 'win glory or give glory to others' (Sarpedon), every action of Hektor is doubly, and tragically, ironized. At the end of Book 1, Zeus accedes to Achilles' mother's supplication that he help the Trojans so that the Greeks perceive what Achilles' absence has cost them in daily deaths, daily territory retreated from. The Olympian gods being an unruly lot, it is not until Book 8 that 'Zeus' will' becomes evident, but it means that Hektor's advances seem overshadowed, his victories ironized by Zeus' invisible tilting of the scales. In Book 8 there is a major change in the geography of battle: the Greeks build a wall to protect their ships. There is now a zonal marking: if the Greeks can storm the walls of Troy or the Trojans cross the protective wall and fire the Greek ships, the war will be decisively won.

Hektor's advance takes him straight up to and, despite advice, over the Greek wall. But it is here that the narrative constructs him as going too far – that Greek fault of faults. For whatever Zeus promised Thetis, whatever the gods' will, there is an overarching shape to the cosmos, to his and his city's destiny: Troy is fated to fall. So Hektor is seen to be heedlessly flying in the face of history, rashly challenging Fate.

When he last leaves his wife and baby son – a touchingly lovely scene – he foresees what their fate will be if he is killed. Andromache piteously laments him 'though he was still alive', says the narrator disapprovingly. But their fate is to be exactly what he foresaw; it forms one of the greatest and most played tragedies of all time, Euripides' *The Trojan Women*.

The story of the 'wrath', the overwhelming rage of Achilles and its consequences – his refusal to be reconciled, his disastrous agreement to allow Patroclus to fight in his armour in his stead – was also dramatized by Aeschylus in a lost play, *The Myrmidons*, Alexander the Great's most precious text. The *Iliad* similarly vividly dramatizes each stage of this tragedy; each scene is played out between the main actors but also seen from the perspective of the likes of old Nestor, canny Odysseus and critical Ajax; and seen by the gods, looking down from Olympus.

The *Iliad* is full of words for battle fury, for the necessary psychology for adrenalized precision-killing and how it is incited and aroused in fighters. Achilles' wrath – *mēnis* – is of a different order. How it came to rule Achilles and how it fed into his emotions and vengeance after Patroclus' death is sensitively and recognizably tracked through to Book 24. It can be recognized today, for example, by those treating war veterans with post-traumatic stress disorder. But it is recognizable also to anyone who rebels against the sentiments expressed by Hera when Zeus considers rescuing his and our beloved Sarpedon: she says that the only and proper end for a mortal is burial, the only 'compensation', sufficient material correlate, for a death is a grave memorial. At the start of Book 24, Achilles is still trying to take sufficient vengeance for the death of Patroclus; the rest of the book is a moving and profound exploration of what brings closure to the story of his wrath … and to him.

Warp and weft

The story starts in the tenth year of the war to take back Helen and her dowry and to punish the rich trading city of Troy. There have been nine years of stalemate, the evenly balanced sides retreating at night back to their respective camps by the Greek ships and the gates of Troy.

This story 'about Ilion' (Troy) is of the wrath of Achilles, roused by a rupturing of the bond of agreement between Agamemnon and those who have come to his aid. Achilles, outraged, feels that he cannot fight now that the 'heroic exchange' – of dangerous exertion for fame and honour – has been nullified.

Achilles' mother Thetis goes to Zeus to ask that her son's importance is validated by his absence, leading to the Trojans gaining the upper hand. Her visit results in a parallel falling out on Mount Olympus, but that is resolved in minutes – unlike that between Achilles and Agamemnon, which, as the *Iliad*'s opening words tell us, brings the death of many heroes.

In Book 2 we have a detailed retrospect of the setting out of the Greek forces, coming from all over the Greek world to win 'everlasting fame', or *kleos aphthiton*. (For more on some of these key Greek terms, see the sections 'Heroic Psychology' and 'Heroic Values', below.) There are glimpses of other Iliads, other heroes' stories available to be stitched together by the 'rhapsodes'.

In later books we have dramatic scenes of fighting that could potentially finish the war. There is an agreement that Helen's two 'husbands', Menelaus and Paris, fight one-to-one. A formal agreement is sworn, with terms and penalty clauses, but the gods intervene. Aphrodite flies Paris away to Helen's bedchamber. The war goes on.

Later, as if this is a different kind of war, each side elects a champion – Ajax and Hektor – to fight to the death. But this truly heroic duel is so evenly matched that both sides agree that, literally, honours are even.

The daily fighting follows various heroes' days in the sun, their times of *aristeia*: in Book 5, Diomedes is so pre-eminent that he has to be shown the gods in disguise! In Book 8, the archer Teuker has his *aristeia*, unexpectedly as archers are usually regarded as less than heroic. His victims, expertly dispatched, are mostly anonymous, but one is memorable: 'peerless Gorgythion, Priam's mighty son, born of lovely Castianeira, goddess-like in form, whom Priam once married. His head, weighed down by the helmet, fell to one side, like a garden poppy heavy with seed and spring rain.' The poppy – fragile, beautiful – is a symbol of the pathos of the death of young men in war that resonates through the ages and was exactly translated by Virgil in his *Aeneid*, reflecting on the price of war and value of the poet's tragic memorializing. Gorgythion's biography slows the action momentarily while we remember that all these heroes have family elsewhere: the pathos is there for us immediately, but there is grief to come for others.

From Book 8, the fighting becomes charged: it is no longer described as individual trials of strength, victors and victims, the shouts of triumph and death agonies, random events and young men meeting their doom. The Greeks have built a wall and protective ditch round their ships, and Achilles' absence has allowed Hektor and the Trojans to advance beyond the neutral zone and threaten the Greek defences. Zeus' promise to Achilles' mother in Book 1 frames the narrative, but for the first time there is an end in sight: if the Trojans attack the Greek wall, they can fire the Greek ships; if the Greeks push back and can beat the premier Trojans, they can render the citadel defenceless.

A tragic narrative begins. Hektor is the best, the *aristos* of the Trojans and summoner of their allies. The Lycian leader Sarpedon reminds him that he, Sarpedon, has left his home and baby to help defend Hektor's home and family. We see Hektor amid his dependants, organizing his errant brother Paris Alexander and setting the women to make offerings to the gods. He is characterized by, and from now on perhaps inhibited by, his sense of responsibility, his sensibility and his sense of shame and proper respect (*aidōs*).

The middle books follow two sympathetic figures: Sarpedon and Patroclus. When eventually Sarpedon meets his doom, even the heavens weep. Amid the ongoing vicissitudes of the battlefield, there is the gathering sense of tragedy as Hektor pushes to fire the Greek ships: in the light of history he is 'going too far', going against fate. When Achilles' gentle comrade Patroclus returns from seeing their fellow Greeks' wounds and danger, he makes a suggestion that is doom-laden from every perspective. Indeed, the narrator calls him out on it: 'Fool! For it was his own doom and death he was begging for.'

Throughout the *Iliad*, there are times when the narrator makes this kind of direct comment about the combatants' values:

Nastes came to the war all covered in gold, like a girl, FOOL! [Greek: *nēpios*: someone wet behind the ears, infant; someone who has no idea of the world he is entering, what it values and demands.] His gold was no help at all in saving him. He came to the battlefield dressed in the gold [that marked him out to be a target and so doomed him] he was killed by Achilles who carried off the gold.

[Of Polydorus] His father Priam had forbidden him to fight, being his youngest and dearest son. He was a champion athlete but like a fool [*nēpios*] showed off his running along the front line, where swift-footed Achilles caught him with a cast of his spear as he shot past.

Suddenly we see a simple answer to some of the big questions that run through the *Iliad*, about the worth of fame, of the heroic venture. The boy killed by Achilles, after leaving his bride on their wedding night to go to win glory at Troy, is a 'Fool, for he had paid a large price for her!' Of the valiant fight to bring back Patroclus' body for burial we are told: 'Fools! Since many lives were torn out over a corpse!'

Shortly after Gorgythion is killed 'like a poppy', Hektor arrogates to himself the narrator's omniscience: he calls the Greeks 'fools' for thinking that Zeus is with them, vaunting that the Trojans will easily leap over the Greeks' flimsy defences. But Hektor is more properly aligned with the narrator when he calls Patroclus *nēpios* for thinking he could take Troy. Both Patroclus and Hektor are being bound into ironizing judgments, by arrogating to themselves a quasi-narratorial understanding of what the Greeks called *moira*: simultaneously the shape of things, the shape of history and the shape of the narrative. In so doing, they seem to be not just vaunting but to be making tragic mistakes: mistaking both Troy's and their own destiny, since their heroic deeds are framed by and judged within a tragic framework.

Epic, elegy, tragedy … the story of Achilles' wrath takes all and none of these forms. What are the rights and wrongs of the rupture of the 'heroic exchange' that gave rise to it? Should Achilles have heeded the bonds of *philia* (alliance, comradeship) and *aidōs* (respect) earlier? When and how does the wrath end, and what kind of closure is effected by that end?

This book will explore these questions. There is one place, however, when we hear answers from Achilles himself:

Fool [*nēpios*], do not talk to me of ransom, make me no speeches! Before the day of fate overtook Patroclus, I had a mind to spare you Trojans.

Many I took alive, selling them far away. Now not one shall keep his life, of all those that the gods send to my hands before Troy not one solitary Trojan, and least of all the sons of Priam.

You too, my friend, must die: why so sad? Patroclus, a far better man, has died. Or look at me, how big and fine I am, my father is a great man, and a goddess bore me, yet death and remorseless fate await me too, either at sunrise, evening or midday, some man in battle will strike me with his spear, or pierce me with an arrow from his bow. (21.99–114)

This is a direct answer to the question of Achilles' psychology.

But from this *aristos*, first or best of the Greeks, who cares more than any other hero for the heroic code, for the absolute and singular importance of *kleos aphthiton*, everlasting fame, does this finally answer or problematize the question roused in all readers of the *Iliad*: is it worth it?

Achilles

Briseis

Agamemnon

Book 1

The Wrath of Achilles

The trouble starts with a girl. The Greek commander Agamemnon is reluctant to give his prize, the beautiful Chryseis, back to her father, Phoebus Apollo's priest. When Apollo forces his hand by sending a plague on the Greek camp and he has to give the girl back, he angrily demands compensation from his chiefs. He takes Achilles' girl, Briseis, against all propriety. This rouses Achilles' destructive anger, the theme of the poem, not just because he cares for the 'bride of his spear'. Achilles is incensed by the injustice of losing his prize, given to him as a mark of his exertion and risk-taking in a battle fought to get back someone else's wife – Helen. Achilles is checked by Athene from killing Agamemnon, but neither she nor wise Nestor can persuade him to heal the rift. All he sees is that to continue to fight would be to continue to bring honour to the man who insulted him.

There is a parallel falling out among the powers that be on Mount Olympus, where Hera, queen of the gods, accuses Zeus of dallying with Achilles' mother Thetis. But the quarrel among the gods is quickly resolved by the clowning of their crippled son, Hephaistos.

The story of the 'rage of Achilles, the destruction of many, many heroes, giving their bodies to the dogs', starts in the tenth year of the Trojan War with an argument over a girl, the beautiful Chryseis – the golden one – allotted to the Greek commander-in-chief, Agamemnon.

Her father, a priest of Apollo, offers Agamemnon a 'shining ransom' and the assembly of heroes demands that he respectfully send the girl back, a proper, honourable exchange, as befits the commander. Agamemnon, however, harshly refuses: Chryseis will grow old as his slave, at the loom and in his bed; if her father returns, he will be beaten. Answering his priest's prayer, Apollo sends a deadly plague on the Greek camp. Achilles takes the lead in finding a remedy and protecting the prophet Calchas if he speaks out … even from Agamemnon.

From all over the Greek world, Agamemnon has summoned the best fighters with their retinues to take part in the great East–West clash between the Mycenaean kingdoms and the Dardanelles-controlling Troy. Agamemnon's position is of 'summoner of forces' to his brother Menelaus' cause: to get back his wife, Helen, now the Trojan prince Paris' lover, and to punish and destroy the rich Asia Minor trading city which has shielded them. As such, his role and responsibility are to enable, to respect the bonds which keep the force together, overseeing fair distribution of validating praise and reward. But the scene is set for a very personal and very damaging rift between the two pre-eminent Greeks, one the supreme commander and the other the supreme fighter.

A dramatic scene follows in the assembly, where the heroes come together in debate and where daily awarding of rewards for distinguished fighting takes place. Agamemnon does indeed threaten the prophet, refusing absolutely to give up Chryseis, whom he says he prefers to his wife; however, if he is forced to give her back, he will demand compensation from his chiefs, saying in effect that 'it's not fair that everyone has a prize but me'. The brewing conflict between commander and his greatest fighter now boils over: 'prizes' are precious tributes to exceptional heroic acts and aren't commodities just lying around. Achilles leads the outcry against this assertion of power and perverting commodification of the honour system, and threatens to leave with his ferocious Myrmidons. In return, Agamemnon outrageously claims Achilles' girl, Briseis. This is intolerable, not just because Achilles cares for the 'bride of his spear': he is incensed by the injustice of losing his prize, given to him as a mark of his pre-eminent exertion and daily deathly risk-taking in a battle fought to reclaim someone else's wife.

The Exchange

The gods are watching this critical scene. Achilles is checked by the goddess Athene from killing Agamemnon – a rupturing act in the assembly – but neither she nor wise 'third-aged' Nestor can persuade him to heal the rift. For Agamemnon, the issue is one of power: Achilles has challenged his dominance. All Achilles sees is that to continue to fight would be to continue to bring honour to the man who insulted him; he swears a solemn oath that he will no longer fight for him and prophesies that the day will come when Agamemnon will beg him to come back. He withdraws to his tent. Agamemnon says he can do very well without him, but of course he cannot – Achilles is the best fighter among the Greeks and his stature can be demonstrated by how badly the war goes without him.

Achilles appeals to his goddess mother, Thetis – the third female now tragically involved in Achilles' story – and explains more in sadness than in anger why Agamemnon has made it impossible for him to continue to fight: she bore him to have a short life but a glorious one. He uniquely does not have the choice of every other hero – ordinary long life or short heroic one – so the only course now open to him is to wait while his worth is re-established, in metres of ground lost to the Trojan front line. Thetis shares his tears, Achilles lamenting for the 'fair-girdled' Briseis, she for the bitterness of his fateful birth. She agrees to intercede with Zeus, whose domain is the shape of the cosmos, the shape of history and the underpinning structures of society (oaths, supplication, guest-rights, sanctity of heralds etc).

The scene now shifts to Mount Olympus, where there is a parallel falling out among the powers that be. Hera, queen of the gods, with the dreadful

Zeus

presence of a pre-Olympian mother goddess, accuses Zeus of consorting with Achilles' mother, Thetis. (Thetis has come to him to beg for the gods' help in demonstrating the Greeks' need for Achilles and, in ritual supplication, has thrown her arms round Zeus' knees.) There is a pettishness and bluster similar to Agamemnon's about Zeus' assertion of authority when he is in the wrong: 'Nothing escapes you, dear wife! But do not try to inquire into things that are too complicated for you.' But when he blusters, the mountain shakes – the king of the gods may not have moral authority, but he has tremendous power.

The insult to Achilles' honour brings death and tragedy to Greeks and Trojans alike. It is literally a deadly insult. But the insult to Hera can, by contrast, be quickly resolved. For the gods, being immortal, nothing has lasting or grave consequences.

Book 2

The Greek and Trojan Forces

Attack!

Agamemnon is shown up in Book 1 as forgetful of the responsibilities of command and of his duty to keep together and reward the forces he has summoned to avenge, as Achilles pointed out, a domestic wrong. He is exposed further in Book 2. Having received a 'deceitful' dream from Zeus that he is, after nine years' vain effort, about to capture Troy, he decides to test the army by reporting that the dream advised flight. The army delightedly takes up the proposition that they return to their homes and families, and it needs all the guile and oratory of Odysseus to dissuade them from setting sail.

This book gives the background to the main story of the Iliad *– the baneful wrath of Achilles and the sorrows and heroic deaths it caused. There is, unusually, a sense of the ordinary men, those 'without a name', who have become caught up in their chiefs' feud. Their concerns are voiced by the base Thersites, but also by Agamemnon and Odysseus. There is a strong evocation of the past nine years of fruitless effort, of wear and tear on men and equipment, of the wives and children waiting back home.*

There is another invocation to the Muse to sing of Achilles, whose claim to be best is borne out in the Muse's reckoning: 'Great Ajax for strength surpassed all while Achilles was away, but he excelled him far.'

The scene then shifts to Hektor at Troy surrounded by the pre-eminent leaders of the allies, finishing with Sarpedon and Glaukos who are the major and sympathetic characters on the Trojan side.

The heart and importance of Book 2 is the detailed description of the forces involved in this 'world war' between Greece and Asia Minor. But before this 'catalogue of ships' there are a series of multi-layered representations of the state of the war in the various Greek leaders' persuasive or delusive speeches. In the catalogue of forces there are also glimpses of other

Iliads, other stories that would have been part of the Trojan War cycle of poems, and of other poets. The poet's shaping of the narrative is also clearly visible in this book, as he narrates Zeus' sending of a false dream and Agamemnon's false reporting of it. This play of ironies is framed by a narratorial comment:

> Fool, he thought that very day he would take Priam's city, not knowing Zeus' plans.

The poet knows both Zeus' purpose and the outcome of the war. From his perspective, he can criticize those with more limited vision. The poet is the servant of the Muses, who are all-knowing, all-seeing, all-recording. He is the 'servant of fame' – of heroic report – in several senses. He is dependent on the tradition passed down through generations of poets, shaping, adding and refining the stories. He is also the servant of fame in being the one channel of immortality available for the heroes on both sides of the Trojan War – immortality of fame in epic song.

First, Zeus, given the difficult task of helping the Trojans, as he promised to Achilles' mother, decides to delude Agamemnon into a last push to take Troy. In his turn, equally incomprehensibly, Agamemnon decides to test the resolve of his troops by announcing a withdrawal in terms which are all too persuasive: 'after nine years, our ships are rotten, the cables broken, our children grown.' A stampede for the ships breaks out, described as a tsunami. Then 'there might have been a homecoming beyond fate' for the Greeks, shaken 'like a field of corn when the west wind blows', had not the gods intervened, encouraging 'wily' Odysseus to stem the tide. His message, 'It's only a ploy to test you: are you going to be caught out and punished by Agamemnon as a coward?', does something to restore order, although it is difficult not to agree with the shrill abuse Thersites, a spokesman for the ranks, heaps on Agamemnon. He asks the reasonable question: why do they stay to fight for someone whose only concern seems to be to amass spoil? Odysseus wins back the assembly, tellingly acknowledging that nine years of absence from home is hard, but enjoining patience and the acknowledgment of the shame if they were to go home empty-handed. With the wisdom of Nestor, some retraction by Agamemnon and Athene's inspiration, the reinvigorated Greeks form up to fight: the light shimmering off the massed bronze helmets vividly likened to 'when the forest fire leaps along a ridge and the flare lights up the skyline'. They march to the Trojan river plain, 'as when the echoing river plain is filled with clashing flocks of migrating geese, cranes and swans, proud of wing', and take their position in the blossoming river meadow 'like a swarm of insects over the sheep's milk splashing out of the pail'; their leaders ordering them 'like the herdsmen who separate their goats to take them to pasture'. These are just a few of the heart-stopping images of the ordinary life that few will survive to experience.

With an invocation to the Muse who 'knows all things' to help in the superhuman task of recording the great expedition, this introduces the catalogue of the Greek forces, described as on their deployment at first, the leaders with their men and ships, and with epic formulas – 'x held rocky y with z black ships'. The forces are described with their distinguishing armour and weapons:

> Those who held sacred Euboia [today's Evvia], the fury-breathing Abantes with long back hair, their long ash spears ready set to rip open the enemy's corselets.

There are also many glimpses of others' stories, such as 'Briseis of the lovely hair': in a reference to the backstory to the *Iliad*, we have a mention that Achilles took Briseis after sacking her home. After the entry for 'Tlepolemos, leader of nine ships with the proud men of Rhodes who fought in three divisions', we hear that he was born after his father Herakles had similarly 'sacked many cities', was raised in a well-built stronghold, but that he was exiled for killing his great uncle and that though he came as fugitive to Rhodes with his followers, they settled and flourished in three areas.

We are also given glimpses of other epics that could be sung on another occasion: Philoctetes the great bowman's seven ships crewed by men all skilled with the bow, 'though Philoctetes had been marooned on an island after a water snake's putrid bite left him in agony. But the Greeks who had abandoned him were to remember him.' This is the story told later in Sophocles' play, when the Greeks heard that Philoctetes and his special bow were needed to finish the war.

There is similarly mention of a hero Protesilaus, one of many suitors of Helen whose story was told in a lost 'Iliad' – the epic cycle *Cypria* quoted by later travel writers and poets. The catalogue has:

> Those who held flowery Pyrasos, precinct of the goddess of fertility, Demeter, and Iton, mother of flocks, and Antron, hard by the sea, and Pteleos, couched in grass, had as leader warlike Protesilaus, while he lived, though now the black earth held him fast, and his wife, lamenting and tearing her cheeks, had been left behind in his half-built house; he had been killed by a Trojan as he leapt from his ship, the first to land. Led by his brother Podarces, they nevertheless longed for the noble man they had lost.

Later references tell more of his story: that a prophecy said that the first man to land in Troy was fated to die, the sacrifice needed to bring victory that is a traditional story in myth and military history. Major-General Wolfe is said to have done the same at the siege of Quebec, while quoting Sarpedon's words in the *Iliad* Book 12, in Pope's translation:

> Brave tho' we fall, and honour'd if we live,
> Or let us glory gain, or glory give!

Protesilaus' wife, Laodameia, is the heroine of many later stories: in Ovid, she is the loving wife doomed by her husband's omen and famous for refusing to live after news of her husband's death.

After the catalogue, two final lists finish the book. One is of 'the best and bravest' among both the horses (intriguingly) and the men. *Aristos*, being first, is the gold standard that survives in today's use of 'aristocrats': literally those who rule by being first and best. The scene then shifts briefly to Hektor at Troy surrounded by the auxiliary leaders 'of special excellence', including especially Sarpedon and Glaukos, but with the listing darkened by mention of burial mounds.

Finally, there is one of the rare moments when we hear the poet directly. At the very end of the list comes Nastes, never again mentioned, who is given a brief biography that serves both as his epitaph and his pathetic, momentary fame:

> Nastes came to the war all covered in gold, like a girl, FOOL! [*nēpios*: an infant; someone who has no idea of the world he is entering, what it values and demands.] His gold was no help at all in saving him: he came to the battlefield dressed in the gold [that marked him out to be a target and so which doomed him] he was killed by Achilles who carried off the gold.

We suddenly remember what Achilles, 'the best of the Greeks', is best *at*.

Book 3

Helen in Troy: Paris and Menelaus Fight for Her

Troy

*As Book 1 gave a character sketch of the main characters in the Greek camp –
Achilles caring for his honour above all; Agamemnon weak and egotistical;
Nestor old, respected, drawing on the past – so Book 3 introduces the telling
characteristics of those on the Trojan side. This book introduces the cause of the
war, the beautiful Paris, who seduced Helen away from her Spartan home. He
is set against his brother Hektor, the brave leader of the Trojans. Hektor is ever
vigilant about his own honour and that of his allies; part of his job as war leader
is to sting his leaders' heroic consciousness, spurring them on. Paris is, however,
one person untouched by others' sense of him, by others' heroic values or by his
brother's reproaches. He is unwilling to face Menelaus, the wronged husband,
though it was his abduction of Helen (his reward for awarding Aphrodite the
goddesses' beauty prize) that started the Trojan War. Menelaus spies Paris
lounging and makes for him like a lion coming on his prey, but Paris reacts like a
man coming on a venomous snake.*

*We also meet Helen of Troy, the face that launched a thousand ships. Unlike
Paris, she does have a pronounced sense of responsibility for her coming to Troy.*

She looks down from the walls of Troy to see her fate decided, picking out for King Priam those Greek fighters who are left after nearly ten years, and is stricken with anguish.

Menelaus challenges Paris to a duel to the death – a simple settlement of the war. Menelaus prays to Zeus as protector of marriage and guest bonds; he wounds Paris, but not seriously, then his sword breaks and he takes Paris by the throat. Aphrodite breaks his grip and wafts Paris from the battlefield to Helen's bedroom. The proper, dignified solution has been frustrated by the gods. With extraordinary and outspoken human defiance, Helen refuses to be a pawn, refuses to go to Paris' bed and suggests to Aphrodite that she herself goes instead. But the gods cannot be defied.

B ook 3 starts with an evocative yet exotic image of the two sides engaging. The Trojans attack like hunting cranes massing for migration and drawing blood from the Pygmies; the Greeks move in silent unity, the dust of their march raised 'like the mist over the mountain scattered by the south wind'.

We also have the first encounter between Helen's warring 'husbands', Paris Alexander and Menelaus. Whereas Menelaus is 'like a hungry lion coming on a carcase of a stag settling to eat despite snapping hunting dogs', Paris Alexander is more complexly portrayed. The story of the Trojan prince's stay in Menelaus' Spartan palace and his running off with the king's wife has been told and retold: as the iconic outrage to the

Paris

guest–host bond; as the mythical prize offered Paris by the gods in the contest of goddesses; as the romantic outcome of the queen of Sparta's meeting with the exotic Trojan prince; as the *casus belli*, the pretext for a trade war between the militaristic Mycenaeans led by Agamemnon and his brother Menelaus, and the city that controls the Dardanelles.

We get a shimmeringly diverse portrait of Paris here. He presents as a charismatic challenger, in a leopard's skin with bow and sword, and shaking two bronze javelins. But whereas Menelaus sees red when he catches sight of his enemy, Paris shrinks away, 'like a man who nearly steps on a snake on a mountain path, jumps back, pale and shivering', and hides himself among the Trojans.

Throughout the epic there is the tradition of 'hectoring' by the commanders of their main fighters, accusing them of cowardice, rousing their fighting spirit and expecting the response: 'I'll show you how brave I am!' Hektor goes further, reproaching Paris for hiding when he was so full of his prowess when enchanting Helen, and pointing out that all around are fighting because of him, fighting to defend his home. Bitterly, he rips into Paris as a laughing stock, Troy's shame, wishing he had never been born. If he were to stand up to Menelaus, he would learn something of the man whose beautiful wife he had stolen; his lyre-playing, lovely locks and gorgeous body will not save him when he is trampled in the dust! But Paris, uniquely, is unimpressed: he wafts Hektor's barbed words away, saying basically, 'yes, you are right but you do go on!':

> You have scolded me, with reason. But you are ruthlessly, shrilly single-minded: like a skilled shipwright working on a piece of hard wood, the saw driven with all his strength back and forth. And do not disrespect my god-given beauty. However, if you insist, I will fight Menelaus for Helen and her dowry.

Helen

Helen of Troy is portrayed as many things: the most beautiful woman in the world, the gift of the Goddess of Love as a bribe to be awarded the golden apple; the queen of a Mycenaean palace; the pretext for a trade war for control of east–west and north–south trade through the Dardanelles; and the 'destroyer' (Helen's name is played on in a choral ode in Aeschylus' *Agamemnon* as signifying 'Destruction of men, ships, cities'). Here in Book 3, we meet the woman in three very moving scenes. First, she hears that the two men she has belonged to and may have loved are to fight for her in a decisive duel. Second, in what became an iconic scene, Priam, 'always gentle with her', asked if she would come to a viewing place on the walls and look down on the Greek leaders, telling him their stories:

> Helen shining among women, answered Priam in respect and reverence. 'How I wish that rather than following your son, leaving my family, my growing child and my lovely girl companions, I had killed myself. But it

did not work like that, so I am worn out with weeping. But, I will do as you ask.'

This is a very moving picture of Helen, treated kindly by Priam, sensitive to the harm she has caused. But as she goes up to the citadel walls, she moves gracefully past a group of old men, sitting in the sun and gossiping 'like cicadas'. Who could blame anyone for carrying her off, they say admiringly, extraordinarily beautiful as she is.

The 'scene from the walls', as this came to be known, is famous for its poetry and its pathos, as Helen looks down, supposedly for the first time since she left, on the men who are fighting to get her back. First, she identifies Agamemnon and Menelaus, strong leaders, once her kinsmen, calling herself a shameless bitch.

We get portraits of the main characters of the epic. There is Odysseus, shorter and broader than Agamemnon, ranging like a ram through his flocks. Helen identifies him as Laertes' son, the various-minded, crafty hero, who grew up in the backwater of rough Ithaca where he developed tricks and stratagems to get by. Priam's counsellor, Antenor, reminisces about when he entertained the Greek embassy: Odysseus looked boorish and fidgety beside Menelaus, a man of concise, lucid speech, but when he started to speak, with his powerful voice, the words drifted down like winter snows and no-one could resist him.

Then comes the mighty Ajax, 'the bulwark of the Greeks', who sometimes seems a simple soul. Helen is moved to see all the prominent Greeks whom she remembers entertaining in Sparta. But she is concerned that she can't see her brothers, the twins Castor and Pollux; the pathos is that Homer's audience would have known that they were already dead, fighting to reclaim her. 'The teeming earth already covered them,' as the narrator says.

The scene shifts to the preparations for this, surely final, duel for Helen. Agamemnon has always referred to Paris' carrying off of Helen as a rupture of the sacred bond of *xenia* – the reciprocal obligations of host and guest. Now he sacrifices to Zeus as 'Upholder of Oaths' to oversee the exchange of oaths: that if Paris wins, the Greeks will leave, but if Menelaus wins, Agamemnon – ever conscious of material gain! – will extort 'exemplary damages'. The scene is set, the protagonists present, and this feels like a crisis point, against a background of troops who have suddenly imagined that they were free to go home.

The protagonists arm – 'greaves with silver straps, chest fitting corselet, bronze sword with silver studs, great shield and horse hair crested helmet, honed, smooth-grip spear' – and the duel begins. Paris' spear strikes Menelaus' round shield and lodges fast; Menelaus' spear likewise, but it pierces Paris' intricately wrought corselet, tears through his tunic and would have pierced his side if he had not turned aside. Menelaus pursues his advantage, but (miraculously?) his sword breaks. In frustration, Menelaus lunges and seizes Paris' horse-hair crested helmet – but again is frustrated by the chin-strap breaking.

The viewpoint shifts from this crucial duel to the gods: to Aphrodite, whom Paris claims as his patron. We see not Paris escaping despite everything Hektor said to him, but a story of his charmed life and the emotions of those impacted by it. Aphrodite, watching closely, intervenes to break the embroidered chin-strap, so the helmet comes away empty in the hand of Menelaus, who angrily flings it away and turns, determined to kill his man. But Aphrodite picks up Paris and wafts him to – where he belonged, rather than on the battlefield! – his perfumed bedchamber; and, shockingly, summons Helen from the viewing platform to go to serve him.

This double viewpoint, making events explicable at both the level of human psychology and as scenes from the gods' point of view, is called 'double determination', a double narrative of why events happen. It is a technique of epic, but social psychologists talk of the actor–observer effect, whereby the actor attributes autonomy to his/her actions but the observer sees a pattern that the action fits into – the psychologist's or perhaps the gods' view!

Helen, summoned from watching her and her men's fate, is told by Aphrodite to go to Paris, lying waiting for her in the bed.

Menelaus v Paris

In an extraordinary, human and tragically sympathetic act of defiance, Helen, in her third scene in this chapter, says, in effect, that if Aphrodite is so enamoured of Paris, *she* can go to him. But mortals cannot defy the immortals: Aphrodite takes her by the hair and drags her inside.

Aphrodite

Book 4

Battle is Joined

Book 4 opens on Mount Olympus with Zeus asking, over a cup of nectar, whether the gods should plant terrible war and the din of fighting or lasting alliance between the two sides. With Hera and Athene, the losers, still feuding with the winner of the Judgment of Paris, Aphrodite, the vote is for continued war. The chilling deal is that Zeus will allow Troy to be destroyed provided he can destroy Hera's favourite cities next time he has a mind to.

On the ground, the melee continues, once the gods tempt an all-too-vain Pandarus into breaking the truce. The history and the craftsmanship of the bow he uses is described in loving detail, a haven of pastoral calm before the fateful arrow hits. The skin wound it inflicts on Menelaus is likened to the delicate staining of precious ivory – from a visual similarity, a glowing miniature is painted of a very different world.

The rest of the book follows Agamemnon, seen in a more sympathetic light, as he cares for his brother and puts heart into his troops. Battle is joined, like rivers in spate. Men die, after a short biography – such as Simoisius, whose parents' marriage and his birth are celebrated. In dying, he is likened to a poplar trunk, lying with curly leaves by the fen, felled by a wheelwright. He is given his moment in the history, his death graced by a telling image before he becomes like all the others, a victim to be despoiled, a victory to be vaunted.

Zeus

Book 4 starts on Olympus, setting the vivid account of individual death or glory duels in a framework of history. The gods are interested in the course and conclusion of this war only as it concerns them personally, and their viewpoint is like that of a news channel that only sees and reports the events that concerns their party's champions.

The gods sit in a gold-floored council chamber, drinking nectar from golden goblets, toasting each other as they look down on Troy. Zeus is first introduced as a sheepish husband somewhat cautious about Hera's sensibilities: Zeus may be king and father of the gods, but Hera is a mother goddess and her anger is blighting. Zeus decides to needle her, reminding her of her rival Aphrodite's support for Paris and setting as the agenda for discussion what to do now she has vitiated the duel: whether to settle matters by declaring victory and Helen for Menelaus and allowing Troy to go back to peacetime trading. This solution displeases Athene and Hera, both holding on to their long-worked-for revenge on Paris, his city and people. Zeus' literally inhuman decision is that they be allowed to destroy Troy in return for allowing Zeus to raze the next city that offends him. Hera agrees terms, even if he decides to destroy one of the three cities 'nearest her heart'. The upshot is that Athene is instructed to arrange a breaking of the truce in a way that implicates the Trojans in the oath-breaking.

Then, like a lightning bolt there is a flash between the heavens and the earth below. What has been agreed on Olympus is translated into human psychology, as the idea occurs to an archer that if he were to let fly against Menelaus and kill him, Paris in particular would reward him generously.

At this crucial moment, the poet pauses to describe Pandarus' bow that is to fire the fatal shot: made of horn from a wild goat he had shot after lying in wait in a hide, bound, burnished and finished with gold wire by a master bowyer. The treaty-breaking act is described in heroic terms: Pandarus, with a prayer and promise of an offering to Apollo the archer god, draws both the grooves and the ox-hide bowstring and bends the great bow into a hoop, the bow aching to release the arrow, the arrow furiously longing to fly and wound. That it does not kill Menelaus is seen as Athene's guardianship,

Athene

Menelaus

who 'brushed the arrow away as easily as a mother brushing away a fly from her sleeping child'. The arrow lands where the gold belt buckles the corselet through the elaborately woven war-belt, and wounds Menelaus in the thigh. The spreading blood is likened to the delicate craft of staining ivory with royal purple: 'to make a cheek-piece for horses which is so precious that it is stowed away in a treasure chamber'.

We get a first sympathetic picture of Agamemnon, shaken and terrified at his brother's wound, imagining the horror of the Trojans glorying over the corpse while he has to return to his Mycenaean kingdom, defeated, in life-long grief. Reassured, he calls for the healer Machaon, son of the fabled doctor Aesculepius, to apply anaesthetizing salves.

From here to the end of Book 5, we have an extended period of Trojan War fighting. First, Agamemnon rouses his fighters and sets his leaders on. Leaving his gleaming bronze chariot and his horses, he strides through his troops, encouraging the eager and reproaching the others: 'Why are you standing like bewildered young deer looking round helplessly at the end of the chase?'

The first 'heroic address' is to Idomeneus, setting him in the epic feasting hall where the cup is always filled with the best wine and where boasts have to be made good on the field of battle. Idomeneus replies in due form: I need no spurring, go elsewhere. Next he goes to the two Ajaxes: Agamemnon looks down at them surrounded by their fighters 'as a goatherd watches a cloud blacker than pitch, moving across the sea driven by the west wind, and moves his goats into shelter'. Then it is the old war horse, Nestor, 'wise in fighting from of old', organizing his young troops with anecdotes of former prowess, and on to Odysseus, whose response is rather more vigorous than polite! Agamemnon for once takes his insult in good part.

Next he moves to Diomedes, whose *aristeia*, time of pre-eminence, will come in the next book:

Agamemnon

Diomedes, breaker of horses, why are you skulking away from the front line? That was not your father's way, always in the front line. [A long anecdote follows.] That was your father, but it seems his son is better at talking than fighting.

Diomedes

Diomedes accepts the reproach as proper from a leader, and goes into battle in his clanging bronze armour. Simile after simile recreate the sound and impact of the fight – the Greeks in terrible, well-ordered silence, the Trojans with many different languages driven on in terror. The Greeks' advance is like when the thundering surf crests and breaks, smashing against the rock, while the Trojans are like sheep in the fold waiting to be milked, hearing their lambs bleat.

The two shield lines meet, like rivers in spate crashing thunderingly together. One warrior is speared through the forehead, falling like an undermined tower, his body fought over by both sides like wolves. A second, Odysseus' companion, is killed with a thrust through the groin; Odysseus, fired to revenge, strikes one of Priam's many sons through the temple. One is brought down by a stone smashing the tendons of the ankle and finished off by a spear through the navel; another is speared through the chest into the lungs and finished by a sword thrust through the stomach.

But the death that means most in this book is that of Simoisius, a short-lived young man born by the River Simoeis, killed by Ajax with a spear thrust up through the chest and out at the shoulder:

He fell like a black poplar lying hardening on a great marsh, felled by a chariot-maker's shining axe, all the side branches trimmed, due to be shaped into the wheel of a finely crafted chariot.

The resonant image stops the narrative of the kill and turns to the natural transformation of living tree to worked wood, shaped and bent to be part of a crafted treasured chariot. The corpse, however, is dragged off.

Book 5

Diomedes' Day of Pre-eminence

Book 5 is the book of Diomedes' pre-eminence – his time for glory both on the battlefield and in the epic. The fights, almost filmic in their detail, are woven into a tapestry of encounters, challenges and reflections, of vaunting victories and fearful defeats. Diomedes thinks it ignoble to shrink back from fighting two major Trojan fighters; rather he sees them, and especially their horses, as an opportunity to win the two assets that establish the status of the hero – 'exquisite prize' and 'great fame'. Diomedes sometimes seems a very straightforward hero!

The tapestry weaves in the participation of the gods: Athene grants Diomedes the special vision to recognize immortals fighting on the battlefield so that he can avoid them or, in the case of the gods of war and love (Ares, Aphrodite), take them on. Others, without it, attribute to some god or to luck/fate the chance happenings of battle: Pandarus, sure of his aim, attributes his failure to hit Menelaus to divine intervention.

The spotlight is on Diomedes – it is his day of pre-eminence, being more than human, until warned by Apollo that he has gone too far and is encroaching on the gods' realm far above. Far above, possibly, but not more dignified – Ares lets out an unmartial bellow when stabbed by Diomedes.

The gods, in disguise, play at Trojans and Greeks. When they get tired or hurt, they can go home to have everything made better. The gods represent humans free of the human condition: war without any of the cost. Not for gods the pain, suffering, heroism or bravery of risking death, the sacrifice of leaving, as the sympathetic Sarpedon has done, home and family – everything that makes life worth living – in order to respond to a call to arms.

Diomedes

Book 5 is a fascinating, multi-faceted, almost filmic account of a special day's fighting, of a hero's day of pre-eminence (*aristeia*). Details of duels, challenges, thrusts and kills are interwoven with snapshots of those whose life-narrative stops here, with details of the family – noble, ordinary or extraordinary – who will now hear of their death. The spotlight is on Diomedes but pans out to see the consequences of his action and to take in other encounters, other emotions, including those of the immortals, who represent larger-than-life characters free of the responsibility of counting the cost of their actions.

The book starts with Diomedes' day – a day on which a fighter feels, and is, invincible. He is everywhere on the battlefield, like a river in spate overflowing containing dykes. The simile, like the details of the encounters, goes beyond vivid description to the cost inflicted: 'The river charges on over the retaining banks into a beautiful orchard, destroying the hard work of many young men' (who will now, one cannot but reflect, be on the battlefield).

First comes a chariot charge by sons of a 'blameless, bountiful priest': one son's spear misses but Diomedes' return cast strikes him full in the chest, toppling him backwards out of the chariot, which with his horses becomes a prize for Diomedes to have taken back to his tent. After the row over Chryseis and Briseis in Book 1, we are reminded that together with the chariots used at times to fight from and at others to transport fighters or the wounded, prizes like armour and horses are worth capturing.

Chariot Fighting

Later in the book we hear about the Trojan arch bowman Pandarus' sadness at leaving his precious horses back home. Characteristically, Diomedes refuses the warning that two major Trojan fighters with divine horses, 'the finest under the sun' (their pedigree is given in detail), are approaching, seeing them rather as a prize opportunity!

Not that Diomedes is invulnerable. Pandarus' fine shot sends an arrow right into Diomedes' shoulder. The bowman calls out to the Trojans to seize the moment now the foremost fighter has gone down, but Diomedes merely gets his charioteer to pull the arrow right through and out, 'a great spurt of blood spattering the fine tunic', and prays he can be avenged against the bowman! Likewise, two god-born heroes, Tlepomenos son of Herakles and Sarpedon son of Zeus, come 'heroically' together in conflict – with a challenge to live up to their begetting – but the outcome is vividly human. Simultaneous spear casts strike Tlepomenos straight through the throat, 'and darkness mantled his eyes', while Sarpedon is hit in the thigh: 'the spear smashed straight through in fury scraping the bone'. Telling details bring the day-to-day bloody business to life. The narrator upbraids the companions who, caught up in the fighting, 'not one of them thought to pull the dragging spear out'. Sarpedon appeals to Hektor: Hektor has asked for help for essentially a family matter, and yet where are the family now? Sarpedon reminds Hektor that he himself has left his beloved home and baby son far away and drives his men on, though there is nothing of his own here. It is a strong statement: Greeks and Trojans are each bonded together as answering the call of the commanders, but they do not fight for a cause, for something of their own, that personally concerns them. Indeed, Hektor rushes past: 'Sarpedon's companions laid him under a lovely spreading oak tree and pushed the spear straight through and out of his thigh; the mist mantled his eyes …' but on the blast of the North Wind he literally got his breath back, the breath he had gasped out in agony.

The kills continue, with another two felled from chariots, speared between the shoulder blades; another right through the shoulder; another screaming, having been stabbed through the buttock, up into the bladder; another through the neck muscles on through the tongue, falling 'into the dust, his teeth gripping on the cold bronze'; and yet another struck in the shoulder with a sword thrust that severed the whole arm. This last, like the others, is given a brief biography, enough to know who cared for him: here a priest honoured throughout the country, earlier a bastard who was nevertheless raised with love by his father's wife.

Everyone on this iconic but bloody battlefield has an epic glow cast on them, by the manner of the telling but also, all too mortal though they are, by being placed in the sight of and in relationship to the immortals. One victim was an expert huntsman, taught and appreciated by the goddess of the hunt, Artemis. Similarly, Athene inspired Phereklos, expert in all crafts, who is targeted by Menelaus because he was the shipwright who made the ship that took Helen to Troy with Paris. Diomedes himself, when wounded, is strengthened by Athene.

Reinvigorated, Diomedes re-enters the battle with proper battle fury – *menos*, strength – 'like a shaggy lion grazed by the shepherd's spear newly angered leaping into the flock of penned sheep'. He kills efficiently, leaving fathers too old to replace their only heirs.

But on this special day, the veil between the mortals and immortals is rolled back for Diomedes, who as a hero is threatening to exceed what is proper for humans. Athene allows him to see the gods play-fighting in disguise so that he can avoid them – all except her rival Aphrodite, whom she sees as fair game!

Like the scenes on Mount Olympus in Book 1, Diomedes taking on the immortals must have been a showstopper! Pursuing Aeneas' prize divine horses, Diomedes cripples him, 'easily taking up a rock such that now two men would have trouble lifting' – a reminder of what a hero is – and 'smashing his hip socket, breaking the tendons on both sides'. But Aeneas is divinely born; his mother, Aphrodite, 'took her beloved son in her white arms and using her shimmering robe to protect him, took him out of the fighting'. Diomedes follows her in hot pursuit, knowing that of all the terrifying goddesses, she is the softest of targets:

Diomedes v Aeneas and Aphrodite

his spear goes through the robe woven for her by the Graces. Giving a great shriek, she drops her beloved son (!) and is flown away to Olympus by the rainbow goddess, Iris. On the war god's gold-bridled horses, she sobs in her mother's lap, needing her wound to be kissed better. Immediately healed, she is told by the martial gods Athene and Ares to leave war to them and focus on her own domain … sex.

With gods concerned with their sons and their preferred side, the narrative fragments into different encounters on and off the battlefield. Apollo takes over protecting Aeneas, Diomedes – strengthened by Athene – presses on, and Ares hectors Hektor to put new heart in the Trojans to stand against him.

Aphrodite

Athene

Battle is rejoined, the Greeks' advance raising the dust like that from the threshing floor. Two youthful champions like young mountain lions preying on fat cattle are brought down by the restored Aeneas, and other major figures challenge each other, fight, kill and strip the bodies for prize armour. The gods continue to intervene. The pro-Greek Hera and Athene (the losers to Aphrodite in the fabled beauty contest) arm for battle – Athene like her statue with her golden horned helmet, worked with hundreds of fighting men, and terror-striking aegis with the gorgon at the centre, Hera in a golden chariot. They fly through the golden gates that open and close the sky and, arriving on Mount Olympus, appeal to Zeus to allow them to stop the 'maniac' god of war!

What follows continues the delightful set piece of gods playing Greeks and Trojans. Athene goes straight to Diomedes, who 'delights her heart', spurring him on to challenge Ares and leaping into his charioteer's position. She lends her strength to Diomedes' spear thrust into Ares' belly; his bellow shakes the battlefield and, sorry for himself, he flies complaining to Zeus, showing his wound and saying, in effect, 'Make her stop!':

> Zeus, the cloud-gatherer, turned on him angrily: 'Stop whining, you're pathetic! You're as bad as your terrible, ungovernable, pig-headed mother [his wife Hera!].'

But this is Olympus:

> So saying, he ordered the Healer god to heal him, spreading soothing ointment on the wound: he healed the fierce god as swiftly as fig-juice thickens milk that curdles when stirred. Then Hebe, spirit of eternal youth, bathed him, dressed him in fine clothes, and he sat down again by Zeus' side, in all his former glory.

Hera and Athene return to great Zeus' palace, having forced Ares to end his murderous progress.

The end of the day is the end of the book, and among the gods all is forgotten. Tomorrow for them is always another day.

Book 6

Inside Troy's Citadel: Hecuba, Hektor and Andromache

Troy

The battle continues, with no sign of Zeus' plan, agreed with Thetis in Book 1, to give the Trojans dominance; a dominance that would make clear to the Greeks how much they need Achilles back. The battle is a matter of individual duels, preceded by the ritual exchange of names and lineage – in battle, as in any contest, the glory of the victor rests in part on the stature and credentials of his opponent. It is the name and lineage that give each individual an identity, to combat the gods' perspective, voiced by Apollo in Book 21, that men are no more worth quarrelling over than leaves that flourish for a time and are then replaced by others.

Hektor goes back to Troy to organize prayers to Athene. The move to the non-combatants' world – old men, women and children – in Troy emphasizes both the bulwark that Hektor is and the price paid by the dependants of those who lose the heroic duels that are going on outside. The non-combatants at this moment include Paris Alexander, who says he has been debating the merits of heroic battle, but will now join in and fight. Hektor wards off the words of his mother and Helen, his dependants, and presses on to find his wife, Andromache. In the most moving scene of the Iliad, he laments the fate that she will suffer, made worse because of her and her captor's knowledge that she was the wife of the worthiest of the Trojans: his heroic stature will, after death, be a matter of suffering not pride to those he leaves behind. He teases his baby son and prays for his glorious future (a heartfelt wish that will be unfulfilled; the conquering Greeks will dash him down from the walls of Troy to crush the seed of Hektor).

Hektor then collects Paris for battle while his household mourns for him beforetimes.

After Book 5's influx of gods' interventions, Book 6 opens with the focus on the grim human to and fro of battle. We have horn and horse-hair helmets, the wounds made by shining bronze spears, beautiful armour stripped from bodies in the dust, an out-of-control chariot colliding with a tamarisk tree...

But we also have so many sidelights from the world that the heroes have left behind to fight in this 'glory-giving' battle, suggesting mini-tragedies: Diomedes cuts down the son of the rich and hospitable Teuthras, 'friend of all humanity', though none of those are here to stand between his son and death. Other victims include twins conceived while the well-born Boukolion was shepherding his flocks, born to a water nymph.

Other biographies come out in the ritual exchange of threats that precede armed combat. There is a truly wonderful dialogue between Diomedes and the Lycian second-in-command, Glaukos, which has an extraordinary outcome. Diomedes asks, 'Who are you who dare to come forward to fight me, me whose spear is all-conquering? Are you an immortal?' Glaukos replies:

> Why ask me about my lineage, since we are all mortals, like leaves on a tree which flourish and then fall to be replaced by next year's leaves. Yet, since you ask ...

The narrative of his forebears includes the fabulous adventures of the Chimaera killer, Bellerophon: after he resisted the wiles of the wife of the King of Ephyra, she (like Phaedra in Euripides' *Hippolytus*) accused him to her husband of rape. And like Phaedra, she engineered his punishment by means of a sealed tablet 'with murderous symbols on'– note that writing is deemed magical and performative in stories located in the mythical past. The murderousness lies in the tasks that Bellerophon has been set – to kill the lion-goat-snake Chimaera, then the Lycians' traditional enemies, the Solymoi, then the Amazons and then local strong men. Overcoming them all, he so impresses his host that he offers him land, rule and his daughter, who becomes Glaukos' grandmother.

But in this long narrative of his forebears, this history that marks Glaukos out as an individual, not just one more leaf on the tree, he unexpectedly establishes common ground with his foe, Diomedes. The meeting ends not in death but with an exchange of armour in token of their discovery of an historic bond of hospitality between them. (It has to be noted that the observance of this bond leads to Glaukos being conned out of his gold armour! As the narrator says, 'Zeus son of Kronos stole away the wits of Glaukos who exchanged armour of gold for bronze, of a hundred oxen worth for nine.')

There are also exchanges of speech as well as of thrusts: appeals, supplications and autobiographies which bring in other stories and other values. Adrestus supplicates Menelaus: 'My father's halls are piled high with treasures, bronze, gold, precious iron: if you let me live, my father will provide a rich ransom.' Menelaus, ever tempted by riches, is about to agree when Agamemnon brings him back to the vicious total war the brothers are pursuing: no mercy for babies in their mothers' wombs.

On this grim reminder of Troy's future, the narrative moves to the city of Troy. Although the leader and inspirer of the Trojan alliance is King Priam's son, Hektor, here as often he needs the wise counsel of his brother, the seer Helenus, who reminds him that he has responsibility for the non-combatants in the citadel as well as the front line. When Hektor gets to the citadel's gate, the wives and daughters run to ask for news, arms outstretched. After the reminder of Menelaus' treating war as despoilation and Agamemnon's pursuit of Troy's devastation, there is both a joyful relief and an implicit tragedy in the move to the

> glorious well-built palace, with polished stone colonnaded cloisters and fifty smooth-laid ashlar bedrooms for the princes, each with his chaste wife, and an inner court with twelve smooth-laid ashlar bedrooms for the princesses, each with her wedded lord.

Hektor refuses his mother Hecuba's offer of sweet wine, but alerts her to the need to appeal to the gods at this crucial time. He tells her to gather the noble women and sacrifice to the hostile Athene:

> Find the most beautiful robe in your palace, the most precious, and lay it on her knees. Vow that you'll sacrifice at her shrine a dozen yearling heifers, unused to the goad, and beg her to have pity on Troy and on Trojan women and children.

Hektor

With her women she went to her sweetly scented store chamber, where she selected the most excellently woven and embroidered of the robes that Paris brought back as guest gifts from Phoenicia (famous for its royal purple dye). But Athene was unmoved.

There is a vivid portrait of Hektor, battle-scarred and battle-weary, turning to his other task in the citadel – to find his fellow prince and brother, Paris Alexander (we have just been reminded of his foreign trips, last time bringing not Phoenician robes but his host's wife, Helen). Hektor finds him, beautiful, in his separate palace, sitting admiring his splendid armour and bow, while Helen is engaged directing her handmaidens. We can almost hear the steam escaping from Hektor as yet again, as in Book 3, he has to remind Paris that he is the sole reason they are toiling away keeping the Greeks away from the walls: 'Shame on you, sulking here while our allies die protecting the city!' Throughout the *Iliad*, leaders reproach their fighters, a standard way of rousing them for battle; and throughout the *Iliad*, the response is along the lines of, 'Who are you calling a coward, I'll show you!' But not from Paris, whom we can just see listening with deliberate, well-practised patience to his older brother, smiling slightly. In a culture where the hero's honour is the only stable value, where any fighter can be roused by accusations of cowardice, Paris is uniquely shameless: 'You are so right and indeed Helen has already been persuasively getting at me; just wait while I get myself ready, putting on my armour. Or you go on and I'll follow when I'm ready.'

Paris

Also characteristically (in the *Iliad*), Helen is sensitively aware of and troubled by her situation:

Oh, brother, how I wish that on the day I was born, some huge gust of wind had blown me to the mountains, or into the waves of the echoing sea, where the waters would have drowned me, and none of this would have come about. But since the gods ordained this fate, I wish that I had a better man for my husband, who felt the reproaches and contempt of his fellow men. [...] Dear brother, come in now and be seated, since you bear the brunt of all this, through my shamelessness and Paris' wickedness. Zeus has brought an evil fate upon us, and in days to come we shall be a song for those yet unborn.

Indeed.

As Helen is so aware, Hektor is weighed down by his responsibilities on and off the battlefield; he won't stay, but presses on to say a brief and, he fears, final farewell to his wife and baby son. What follows is one of the most beautiful scenes ever written:

Helen

Hektor of the glistening helmet went to find white-armed Andromache, but she had left her finely built chamber and run in tears to the battlements when she heard that the Greeks had won a great victory. Retracing his path through the broad streets he reached the Scaean Gate where he met his wife – richly-dowered Andromache, the daughter of brave Eëtion, the ruler of the Cilicians. She ran to her bronze-clad husband; the nurse came after holding her baby son, Astyanax [Lord of the City], Hektor's bright star.

Hektor smiled, and quietly gazed at his son, but Andromache crept weeping to him, clasped his hand and said: 'My dear lord, your fighting spirit will destroy you, and us. If I lose you I would rather die! I have no royal father or mother: Achilles killed my noble father, though he honoured him by sending him to his pyre in his richly ornamented armour, heaping a mound above him, round which the mountain-nymphs planted elm trees. Swift-footed Achilles killed all my seven brothers while they were guarding our lumbering cattle and fleecy sheep. And then he dragged my mother, the queen, off as a prize but accepted a princely ransom for her, only for Artemis to slay her in her father's house. You are my mother, father, brother, husband: take pity on me and your son.'

'My lady,' he said, 'I too am deeply concerned, but everything in me rebels from hiding from the fighting: I would be shamed in the sight of the Trojans and their long-skirted wives. Nor is it who I am: I have always fought for excellence, to be first and best on the battlefield, to win great glory for my father and myself. But deep in my heart and mind I know that the day will come when sacred Troy will fall; but it is not the death of Priam or Hecuba, or my many noble brothers that grieves me to the heart, but the thought of your fate: some bronze-armoured Greek will drag you off, to serve some master's household. And seeing your tears they will say, "There goes the wife of Hektor, who was the first of the Trojans." May I be dead and buried deep in the earth before that happens.'

At this darkest of moments, the helmeted Hektor holds out his arms to take his baby, but at the sight of the dark eye-holes and terrifying nodding horse-hair crest, the baby shrinks back:

His father and mother smiled, and glorious Hektor doffed the shining helmet at once and laid it on the ground. Then he kissed his beloved son, dandled him in his arms, and prayed aloud: 'Zeus, and all you gods, grant

Hektor and Andromache

that this boy like me may be foremost among the Trojans, as mighty in strength, and a powerful leader of Ilium. And some day may they say of him, as he returns from war, "He's a better man than his father", and may he bear home the blood-stained armour of those he has slain, so his mother's heart may rejoice.'

With this he placed the child in his dear wife's arms, and she took him to her fragrant breast, smiling through her tears. Her husband was touched with pity at this, and stroked her with his hand, saying: 'Andromache, dear wife, don't grieve for me too deeply yet. None will send me to Hades before my time: though no man, noble or humble, once born can escape his fate. Go home, and attend to your tasks, the loom and spindle, and see the maids work hard. War is a man's concern, the business of every man in Ilium, and mine above all.'

Their baby cries in fear not at the terrible future but at Hektor's helmet – the horse-hair crest he thinks grows from his father's head. Hektor tenderly reassures and swings him through the air, and Andromache smiles through her tears. He pities her, reminding her that no man escapes his fate (as Chapman):

'and fate, whose wings can fly?
Noble, ignoble, fate controls. Once born, the best must die'

– and that they must both resume their work.

Book 7

Hektor's Challenge

The Encounter

Hektor challenges the Greeks to name a champion to meet him in single combat, ironically envisaging the mound on the shore of the Hellespont as a monument that will stand for all time to his and his victim's heroic deeds. The irony is the poet's, for the Iliad ends with the making of a burial mound – Hektor's. He will be Achilles' victim, and posterity will receive the immortal report of his death in this poem, the Iliad.

The Greeks discuss who to put up; the ranking is plain and is confirmed by the voice of the poet. Nestor scorns them, recalling a similar situation from his youth when he had been the victor though the youngest. In response, nine come forward; the lot chooses Ajax, who speaks the traditional pre-combat words of menace, which Hektor counters by saying that he is not a novice, and by laying out the rules of engagement. It is a good fight, it seems, for when night intervenes, the two separate in mutual respect and exchange of gifts.

*Attempts continue to resolve the issues underlying the war – Paris' flouting
of the sacred bond of guest-friendship and the taking of Helen and her treasures
as 'spoil' – when the Trojan council proposes to give both back. Paris refuses to
return Helen, but will reimburse the possessions with interest. The Greeks refuse.
A truce is arranged to allow for the burial of the dead, and the Greeks build a
defensive wall which offends the gods; Zeus comforts Poseidon by foretelling the
time when it will be obliterated by the sea. The physical survival of landmarks
is, from the gods' perspective, a fragile thing.*

Book 6 ends with tragedy: Hektor's death and Andromache's fate both lamented ahead of time; Hektor's son's future ironically hoped for; Paris' sense of responsibility newly – if all too temporarily! – awakened. The poet and the reader know what will happen; when in Book 7 Hektor challenges the best of the Greeks to combat 'so that in ages to come sailors passing will see the burial mound of the champion that Hektor bested', the irony is deeply painful.

Book 7 has the brothers sweeping out through Troy's gates; the narrative driving forward to that already imagined end.

Helenus, with a seer's insight into the shape of things, proposes that there should be a decisive duel to settle this long-running battle. Here, as often, the poet aligns the shape of the narrative, the psychology of the main figures and the discussions among the gods: the 'double determination', when a crucial decision is described as being dictated by the gods and, simultaneously and independently, thought up by the protagonists. So here, the gods trade insults: Apollo accuses the pro-Greek goddess Athene of delighting in Trojan dead rather than trying to resolve the issue; Athene addresses him by his – here critical – epithet, as 'far-shooting'. Nevertheless, they agree that something should be done; a properly heroic solution: 'Let us rouse the mighty spirit of horse-taming Hektor and let him challenge one of the Greeks to meet him in single combat. Being challenged, the bronze-clad Greeks will choose a champion to fight him.'

There is a sense of going back in time – from the crucial battle for Troy, a strategically important trade city between the Mycenaean and Hittite territories – to a true age of heroes, of trial by combat. Both sides settle on the plain, 'as when a stiff West wind rises and scuds across the waves, darkening the ripples'. The gods literally fly in: 'Then Athene and Apollo of the silver bow in the guise of vultures perched on aegis-bearing Zeus' tall oak-tree, and enjoyed the sight of those warriors in serried ranks, bristling with spears, glittering with helmets and shields.'

The Greeks are cowed by Hektor's defiant challenge (where has Paris gone to, we wonder: there is a felt absence of Helen's lover and the cause of the war), but Menelaus calls them out on their reluctance to fight a Hektor whom we now see as equal in heroic stature to Achilles. *Faute de mieux* (lacking a better alternative), Menelaus offers to meet Hektor, but Agamemnon – brutally or protectively – points out that he is not up to Hektor (note, this is not a battle for Helen but a trial of strength between the best of the Greeks and the best of the Trojans). The sense of a momentous heroic encounter is ramped up by Nestor, ever ready to remind the present generation that they are of a lesser stature to the heroes of his long-ago youth, who tells a David and Goliath story of when he, the youngest, fought and beat the iron club-wielding, Ares-armoured champion. Thus reproached, so many volunteer that Nestor holds a lottery to let

the gods decide the Greek challenger. Ajax's lot leaps out, the lot that all the Greeks hoped for, as Achilles is out of contention. (Note that in this heroic time, an oral culture where writing if referred to at all is seen as an almost magic art, the lots are marked not with a name but with a sign, *sēma*: the lottery is confirmed by Ajax being shown his mark.)

The two step forward, each with their great shields of 'sevenfold leather, worked with the hides of seven strong oxen finished with an eighth layer of bronze'. Their opening dialogue is of a different nature to the usual rousing exchange of insults: these are two pre-eminent fighters who know that simple fighting strength will not be enough to survive this momentous encounter. As Hektor says, this is too important for a descent to playground insults:

Ajax

Noble Ajax, heaven-born son of Telamon, do not try to frighten me, like some young child or an unwarlike woman. I know how to fight and how to kill. I know how to swing my ox-hide shield both to left and to right, and how to use it in combat. I know how to storm the charging chariots with the swiftest mares, and I know how to dance the close dance of the angry war-god Ares.

The exchange of spear casts is described in detail: Ajax's cast piercing both Hektor's round shield and his intricately crafted corselet, cutting his neck but not fatally. They each retrieve their spears and continue 'like raw meat-eating lions'. But the watching heralds and gods alike deem the fight to have been a fair trial and stop them; more like a fencing or boxing match than a battlefield duel to the death – or the settlement of this long and bloody war.

The fight ends honourably with an exchange of gifts – a silver studded sword, highly wrought sheath and belt in exchange for a war-belt dyed with royal purple – 'so that any Greek or Trojan will say of us, "these two fought each other with heart-consuming hate then joined in heartfelt comradeship"'.

This duel is clearly one of the many showpieces of the oral poet, an audience-riveting pause in the narrative of the war. As if to mark this hiatus and re-embed it in time, it is followed in the Greek camp by Nestor proposing that many Greek dead now be honourably buried. This is an honourable get-out which Paris, being Paris, promptly refuses, as we learn from a remarkably phrased speech by the Trojan herald:

> 'The treasure he brought to Troy in his hollow ships, and would he had perished first [!], he is willing to return with gifts of his own, but he will not yield great Menelaus' wife, though the Trojans urged it.'
>
> Aged Nestor whose counsel had often proved so potent offered his thoughts. He addressed the gathering with benign intent, saying: 'King Agamemnon, and all you leaders, many long-haired Greeks have died, their dark blood spilled on the banks of sweet-flowing Scamander, their souls all gone down to Hades. Let us declare a truce at dawn so as to gather the corpses and bring them back here on carts behind oxen and mule. We will burn them not far from the ships, so that each man who returns home may carry the remains of his friends to their children. Let us pile up earth over the pyre in a single mound, and build a high wall from there to protect the ships and ourselves, with strong gates wide enough for our chariots to pass, and a deep trench in front to hold back enemy chariots and soldiers, in case the Trojan attack presses us hard.' So Nestor spoke, and all the leaders agreed.

But the emotions on both sides show through the epic language:

> Now the Sun rising from the calm, deep-flowing streams of Ocean climbed the sky to light the battlefield, as the two parties met. Yet it was hard to recognize the dead, till they had washed the blood-clots from them. Shedding hot tears they loaded them on wagons, but since great Priam had forbidden loud lament, the Trojans, grieving inwardly, heaped the corpses on the pyre in silence, and when the flames had died, returned to holy Troy. The bronze-greaved Greeks likewise wept within, and fed their corpses to the fire, and when the flames had died, went down to the hollow ships.

The book ends with the literal entrenchment of the Greeks in the landscape, to the anger of the pro-Trojan god Poseidon. The building of a defensive wall and trench changes the geography of the battlefield, which until now has been between the Greek (temporary) camp and Troy's citadel; now there are demarcated areas with Greek and Trojan burial sites and a Greek fortified and residential area. But whereas the gods have been quarrelling like toddlers over their chosen toy, the permanence of the new building works brings out the vengefulness of the Olympians when faced with opposition:

Poseidon

> The long-haired Greeks toiled, and the gods seated by Zeus, the lord of lightning, watched the great work of those bronze-clad Greeks with amazement. Poseidon, the earth-shaker, spoke first: 'Father Zeus, have you seen how the long-haired Greeks are again behaving, building a wall to guard the ships, with a ditch around it, and not a single sacrifice to the gods? Surely its fame will reach to the ends of dawn, and men will forget the wall that I and Apollo laboured to build for Hektor's grandfather.'
>
> Zeus the cloud-gatherer was troubled, and said: 'Well now, Earth-shaker, what is this! Some other god weaker in strength of arm than you might share that fear, but rest assured your fame will reach to the ends of dawn. And when the long-haired Greeks have sailed in their ships to their beloved land, shatter the wall, wash it to the sea, and cover the long beach again with sand. So let the work of these Greeks perish.'

Zeus

Finally, the immortals are, exactly that – immortal – and can wait for vengeance.

After this 'long view' from Mount Olympus, the narrative turns to the end of a momentous human day:

> The sun set, and the Greeks completed their task. Then they slaughtered oxen by their huts, feasted all night long and drank the special wine brought from Lemnos, exchanged for bronze, glittering iron, cattle, hides, or slaves. As also did the Trojans and their allies in the city, while through the dark hours Zeus took counsel, plotting evil against them, with ominous peals of thunder. At that sound, they paled with fear, and poured wine on the earth, not daring to drink till they had made libation to mighty Zeus. Then they lay down and enjoyed the gift of sleep.

Book 8

The Trojans Attack the Greeks' Final Defences

Book 7 ends with Zeus' threatening thunder over the Greek camp; Book 8 starts with his terrifying threats to the immortals. He is the strongest of the gods, and his strength will be terrible to anyone who interferes with his newly resumed plan to allow the Trojans to dominate. Gracious when obeyed, he smiles at Athene and sits in triumph overlooking Troy.

The fighting in the previous books has been reported as individual charges and combats, either from the combatants' point of view or from the gods'. Now there is a new sense of the overall geography of the battlefield, with three zones. The first is the city of Troy, with the non-combatants and dependants inside – the Greek goal; the second is the plain in front of the walls, where the day's fighting goes on, which the Trojans are now encouraged by the gods to dominate; the third is the area behind the new Greek earth wall and ditch, the camp and the Greek ships in the harbour – the Trojan goal. Zeus' will (forged when, at Thetis' request, he nodded his ambrosial head in Book 1, but only now activated) is vindicated by the golden scales which turn against the Greeks; the thunderclaps are perceived by the two sides as deterring or encouraging. Now Zeus' will is in operation, the still-continuing Greek successes are marked as a tragic flouting of the gods. This marking out of the territory into permitted and forbidden areas also applies to the Trojans, because Zeus' will operates in partnership with the Fates. Since they have decreed that Troy will fall, the new-found Trojan confidence is also ironized as heedless of the eventual tragedy ahead. Hektor's words ring rashly; his derision of the Greeks' dyke is ironized (as often, with Hektor) by the audience's knowledge that Troy, not the Greek ships, will finally be destroyed. So the Trojans, despite their god-assisted advance, have a no-go area, a zone which it is now overweening or hubristic to occupy: the camp and ships beyond the dyke.

This tragic 'charging' of the geography of Troy with danger zones changes the perspective in which fights are seen: from now on, individuals seem not so much to go out to fight as to meet their fate.

There are memorable incidents in Book 8. Teuker has a time of pre-eminence, his victims mostly just names apart from

peerless Gorgythion, Priam's mighty son, born of lovely Castianeira, goddess-like in form, whom Priam once married. His head, weighed down by the helmet, fell to one side, like a garden poppy heavy with seed and spring rain.

The poppy, fragile, beautiful, is a symbol of the pathos of the death of young men in war that resonates through the ages. Virgil translated this in Book 9 of his *Aeneid*:

> Euryalus fell, the blood flowing down his lovely limbs, and his neck drooped down on his shoulder like a bright flower scythed by the plough, bowing as it dies, or a poppy weighed down by a chance shower, bending its weary head.

Poppy

But this book's action is placed within many frames: that of the rival gods with their own interests and allegiances; that of the frame of destiny, of Troy's destined fall; that of the leaders on both sides, who sense that the tide has turned in favour of the Trojans and they have to deal not just with the vicissitudes of battle but with the tide of history.

The book starts on Olympus, with Zeus threatening the very individualistic gods with awful physical punishment if they interfere with his 'plan': a mixture of personal will and understanding and of care to implement the destined end.

As always with stories of the gods, the account is delightful. Zeus speaks like a powerful but blustering CEO or head teacher, with constant threats to his authority from his quasi autonomous staff: if I catch any one of you interfering with my plan I will do such things … and don't think I can't; I will throw any dissenters into the deepest pit, through the iron gates and bronze threshold of Hades:

> If you tied a chain of gold to the sky and all of you gods and goddesses took hold, you could not drag Zeus the Mighty down to earth however hard you try.

Zeus' daughter, Athene, placates him:

> Father, son of Kronos, Lord over all, we
> all know your power but nevertheless we
> pity the Greek fighters, doomed to die
> and fulfil their sad destiny. We will obey
> your order and keep back from battle but
> we will still give them good advice, so
> they are not all doomed because of your
> angry opposition.

The scene ends with the image of Zeus,
clothed in gold in his shining chariot,
flicking his fine golden whip over his
bronze-hoofed horses with flowing manes
of gold.

Then the camera moves to the Greeks
and Trojans, streaming out for battle under
the watchful eye of Zeus, holding his golden
scales over both sides until the 'fates of the
Greeks tipped down towards the bountiful
earth: their death day was heavier'.

Athene

Next we have Nestor, valiant and aged, whose horse was struck with an arrow
from Paris' bow, leaving him exposed. Diomedes shouts to Odysseus to help,
but he, intent on retreat, ignores him. Diomedes drives up to the exposed elder
fighter, telling him to leave his chariot and retreat in his own, drawn by the fine
horses he had taken from the Trojan Aeneas.

Chariot Fighting

The two of them carry all before them, including killing Hektor's charioteer:

Hektor's mind was darkened by bitter sorrow, yet he left his dear companion to lie there, despite his grief, pressing on in his need for another charioteer.

They 'would have driven the Trojans up against Troy's wall, penning them in for slaughter', until they come up against Zeus and destiny. Nestor realizes the interdict and tells Diomedes to retreat; he, however, straightforward hero that he is (remember how he fought all, including goddesses!), cannot face Hektor's taunt if he retreated. Nestor reminds him that his status and reputation are such that any such taunt would not hold. One can almost hear Nestor calming down a Diomedes who, like his horses, is champing at the bit. But despite Hektor's predicted taunts against his courage and manhood, he does acknowledge that this is not his day, that Zeus is against him, and he retreats.

Hektor, triumphant, vaunts:

Hear that! Zeus wills me victory: death to the Greeks and great glory to me. Look how flimsy and useless is their wall which we can easily surmount and their protecting ditch our horses can easily leap. Once I reach the hollow ships, be sure to bring fire so I can burn their fleet and in the smoke and confusion kill the panicking Greeks.

He speaks lovingly to his horses, asking them to repay the honey-sweet wheat lavished on them by his dear wife Andromache before aiming them at a glorious victory – Nestor's famous shield and Diomedes' Hephaistos-forged breastplate – before running the Greeks into the sea.

On the one hand this is standard battle rhetoric, encouraging his troops and taunting his enemies with their deficiencies. On the other, it is vaunting, claiming Zeus and victory for himself. He calls the Greeks *nēpioi* (fools), out of their depth, uncomprehending of the bigger picture: it is a narrator's term. As often, Hektor, so clearly in the right in terms of defending his city and family, is shown to be in the wrong in going against the sweep of history. Here, *he* is the *nēpios*.

Hektor's triumphant advance to the Greeks' boundary ditch is halted by Agamemnon standing in the middle of the Greek ships by that of Odysseus:

Agamemnon, gripping his purple cloak with one great hand shouted aloud: 'Greeks, for shame, wretched creatures only fit for parade! What now of our boasts that we are the best, the empty boasts you shouted loud, gorging yourself on the beef from straight-horned cattle, downing the brimming bowls of wine?'

This call, from the lord of the feasting hall for those he has hosted to live up to their alcohol-fuelled boasts, resounds through epic poetry: the elegies of *Y Gododdin*, of those heroes who go to the great seventh century CE battle of Catraeth, are framed by the refrain – mead was their delight; mead was their poison:

> Men went to Catraeth at morn
> Their high spirits lessened their life-span
> They drank mead, gold and sweet, ensnaring;
> For a year the minstrels were merry.

But the *Iliad* is not a simple elegy for the death of heroes: here as often, the response to the commander's spurring is to put new heart into the forces. Agamemnon turns to an archer, Teuker, calling on him to be a glory to his father who raised him though he was a bastard, and promising rich reward when Troy falls. Teuker replies, as is proper to the provocation, that there is 'no need to urge one who is already willing. I have worked with might and main, never resting.' We then have a vivid account of the trade of the archer, generally considered *un*heroic:

> Teuker, flexing his curved bow, would take his place behind the shield of Ajax. Peeping out, he would spy his chance and let fly his arrows before dodging back, like a child to its mother, behind Ajax' protecting shield.

Teuker is given a properly heroic entry: he has his time of pre-eminence in this book, with those he killed 'accruing glory to his account' until he comes up against Hektor in close combat and is carried back wounded to the camp. But elsewhere archers are seen as less than proper warriors in 'glory-giving battle', which is always imagined as hand-to-hand, spear-to-spear, man-to-man combat. (One of the charges against Paris – who after all is the cause of this war! – is that he rarely faces the Greeks in individual combat, but 'scuttles' at the back, shooting his arrows from safety.)

With Teuker wounded, Hektor drives the Greeks back beyond the protecting ditch, to the consternation of the two pro-Greek gods: Hera and Athene. Despite the histrionic threats by Zeus at the start of the book, they decide to help; Athene, like the rebellious daughter she often is, complains of Zeus' unfairness and ingratitude, given that he has forgotten all she did to rescue Herakles, his son, from the underworld. Zeus, rather, is blinded by Thetis' blandishments and is only concerned to promote the Trojans to mark the size of the hole that Achilles' absence makes in the Greeks' fighting strength.

Zeus sees the two goddesses arming and sends Iris to turn them back. He threatens dreadful violence against daughter Athene, but comically shrugs his mighty shoulders at the behaviour of his wife: 'what is she like!' ('I am less cross with Hera; she always sets herself against anything I decree.') Hera, however, immediately caves in; these goddesses, who a few lines ago were so concerned with the dreadful plight of the Greeks, now say, let us leave them to it. Saying, 'let this one live and this one die as chance decides', Hera wheels her team round, and the Hours unyoke the flowing-maned horses and tether them at their ambrosia-filled mangers, while the goddesses take their places by the other gods on golden couches. Athene and Hera mutter rebelliously while Zeus, saying he is unconcerned with their sulks, again threatens them with a demonstration of his might.

But into this lively interlude comes a glancing reference to the tragedy about to unfold. Zeus says that if they stay around they will shortly see the fated climax: Hektor and Achilles fighting over the body of Patroclus.

The narrative now moves back to 'Hektor, beloved of Zeus' – calling off the fighting at nightfall, setting the watch and ordering a feast in the camp in happy anticipation of the morrow's firing of the Greek ships and final victory, with the camp fires vividly described:

> As the stars about the gleaming moon shine bright in still air, and every mountain peak, headland and ravine stand out clear, the sky's bright air displaying all the stars to gladden the shepherd's heart: so the thousand Trojan fires shone. By each fire fifty men waited for Dawn to mount her golden throne.

Nevertheless, Zeus' words hang over the scene.

Book 9

Agamemnon's Embassy to Beg Achilles to Return to the Fighting

Ajax and Achilles playing dice

Book 9 is a suspenseful, shimmering tragedy, with all the Greek heroes involved in the action.

Zeus' plan has the immediate effect of depressing Agamemnon; he again proposes returning home. Diomedes and Nestor dissuade him, instead persuading him to try to undo his spurning of the Greeks' best fighter. Agamemnon acknowledges his folly and sends them with Odysseus as envoys to Achilles, to offer generous restitution and recompense. The envoys are warmly greeted by Achilles and Patroclus as Achilles' 'best-esteemed friends'. In the name of that affection, Odysseus appeals to Achilles to save the Greek ships from Hektor: out of pity for their plight even if he cannot bring himself to relent towards Agamemnon and accept the compensation offered. He tempts him with winning 'triumphant glory' for himself by killing Hektor. Achilles, however, is impervious. The whole basis on which he has been exerting and endangering himself has, he says, been destroyed; as Chapman memorably translates:

> *With equal honour cowards die, and men most valiant,*
> *The much performer, and the man that can of nothing vaunt.*

The destiny and the reward of the best and the worst have been equalized; the reciprocity in the relations between Agamemnon and those he leads has gone; none of the respect for bonds that underpinned the summoning of the army remains. There is therefore no reason left to fight the Trojans. No amount of material recompense can wipe out the outrage inflicted by Agamemnon. Material possessions cannot be weighed against a man's life; especially not against Achilles' life. For he has a uniquely definite, unchancy, choice-dependent fate – either a short life with glory but no homecoming or a long life without glory.

Achilles' speech is overpowering; only Phoenix, his old tutor, can respond. He tells a long tale of restitution refused until it was withdrawn and the work done for no reward. This elicits the blunt statement that Achilles no longer needs the honour granted by human society and that someone who loves him should therefore hate those whom he hates, sharing affections and honours alike.

Ajax sees that Achilles is not to be moved even by his friends, that he clings to his anger despite society's provision of compensation even for the killing of a brother or a child, so much worse than the abduction of a slave girl.

Achilles assents with his reason but cannot tolerate the outrage. His reply is that until he himself and his men are affected, he will not fight: a slight shift in position which shows that he feels, even while rejecting, the force of his friends' need for him (a sensitivity that Patroclus will appeal to in Book 16, with tragic results). Odysseus takes that answer back, while Phoenix stays the night. Diomedes outspokenly condemns Agamemnon for pleading with Achilles, as it has only made him more obdurate and full of pride. Achilles will fight again, he predicts, when his fighting spirit and the god drive him to it.

Book 9 follows Book 1 as an act in the tragedy that is the 'rage of Achilles, the destruction of many, many heroes, giving their bodies to the dogs'. We are given vivid insight into each of the main players' psychology: Agamemnon's reflection on his high-tempered words that started this rift, and Achilles' response to his hugely generous restorative offer. The scene goes from the Greek camp, in the grip of

panic and intolerable grief. Like the churning, teeming sea when suddenly the North Boreas and West Zephyrus winds rise, whipping up the dark waves into crests, hurling seaweed on the shore, so the passionate spirit of the Greeks was in turmoil in their breasts,

to the shelters and ships of Achilles' Myrmidons, where we have a vivid picture of Achilles spending his time away from the battlefield singing of immortal fame-giving heroic deeds. Agamemnon's embassy, bringing the offer of restitution if he comes back to fight, find him playing his finely ornamented, silver-bridged lyre, delighting in its sweet tones. (This is part of the spoils when he razed Andromache's and Chryseis' hometown.) Patroclus is seated opposite, silently listening. Achilles welcomes the embassy into his tent – 'angry I may be, but you two Greeks I love more than most'. He seats them on royal purple coverings, while Patroclus sets out a great wooden board in the firelight, laying out huge sides of lamb, goat and boar, rich with fat. When all is ready – bread in fine baskets, roasts heaped on platters – and after a sacrifice, the guests help themselves to the feast.

Agamemnon

The book starts with Agamemnon's near-panic at the state to which Achilles' absence from the fighting has reduced his men:

Agamemnon ordered the clear-voiced heralds to summon every man by name; they assembled, deeply troubled. Agamemnon rose to address them, tears running down his cheeks like a dark stream gushing over a sheer cliff.

We have such a vivid picture of Agamemnon's character! Like a modern politician in a tight corner, he tries various lines – the powers-that-be deceived me, too trusting as I am – and then proposes they accept that things are going against them and they should just give up and go home.

That straightforward hero Diomedes is the first to react. He calls Agamemnon out on his 'mad folly' and, smarting from Agamemnon's various slighting 'spurring ons', speaks out against Agamemnon's ambiguous position: he may have the honour his sceptre brings him but he doesn't have the necessary fighting spirit – 'So, there are the ships if you want to go home with the tail between your legs; we're staying here until we have taken Troy, which is the reason we have been fighting.'

The Greek assembly acclaims Diomedes, which leaves the task of negotiating a compromise between Agamemnon and Achilles to wise Nestor and wily Odysseus. Nestor recommends they take a dinner break and that Agamemnon, often accused of being greedy, lay on a feast. He takes Agamemnon back to the cause of all this, to:

the day when you enraged Achilles and took the girl Briseis from his hut, against everything we advised. I tried urgently to dissuade you then, but you would only attend to your proud, high-passioned heart, dishonouring a very great man, by taking his prize and keeping her. Even though it is late in the day, let us reflect on how we might persuade him: supplicate him to respect the bond between comrades and placate him with generous gifts.

Agamemnon breaks down, blaming an attack of madness – *atē*, spirit of destruction – but:

Since I was out of my wits, I am willing to give exemplary compensation: I will name the glory-giving gifts: seven tripods, unmarked by the flames; ten talents of gold; twenty shining cauldrons; twelve prize-winning swift horses – a man would not lack gold and riches if he had only the prizes they have won for me. And seven supremely skilled craftswomen, whom I chose as spoil for their surpassing beauty when Achilles took well-built Lesbos. And one of those will be Briseis, whom I took from him, with my solemn oath that I never slept with her, as men do with women.

All these shall immediately be his; if the gods grant that we take this great city of Priam, he may be first when we Greeks divide the spoils, load his ship with gold and bronze, and choose the twenty most beautiful women (always excluding Helen).

Finally, if we return safe home to Argos, finest of lands, he shall be a son to me, and he will be honoured equally to my son Orestes. And son-in-law – he may choose one of my three daughters without bride-price, and I will add the greatest dowry ever given. His sceptre will be recognized over seven well-populated cities, all near the sea, rich in flocks and herds, who will give honour and tribute.

All this I will do, if he lets go of his anger.

How can this not appeal to Achilles? – Achilles, who said that Agamemnon had destroyed the honour (*timē*) system, of honour-giving, public rewards for leadership, effort and risk? As Agamemnon said, this is exemplary compensation: glory-giving, more-than-compensation and very handsome recognition both now and for the future.

But, there is a rider, that as well as letting go of his anger, there is a second requirement on the 'best of the Greeks': 'Let him give way and submit to me – for Hades of all the gods is hated most by mortals for being hard and unyielding – for I claim sovereignty and seniority over him.' Then, perhaps wisely or perhaps disastrously, rather than going in person, Agamemnon sends a carefully chosen delegation to make the offer: straight-talking Ajax, Achilles' old tutor Phoenix and wily tongued Odysseus, with two heralds to record and solemnize the agreement.

After the libations, over the feast – always in the *Iliad* a bonding and re-bonding experience, here positioning Achilles as host to his long-time comrades – Odysseus seizes the moment and emphasizes how desperate is the Greeks' situation and how needed is Achilles. The situation is critical and he warns that Achilles will bear the pain of the consequences if he refuses to be the Greeks' saviour. He repeats Agamemnon's more-than-generous reparations.

Achilles says no. Neither Agamemnon nor any other Greek will change his mind, because what Agamemnon has done is literally irreparable; he repeats what he said in Book 1:

> No quarrel with Trojan spearmen brought me here to fight: they are not *aitios* [have done me no personal harm]. No horse or cow of mine have they stolen, nor have my crops been ravaged in my homeland. No, in order to do you *charis* [grace, respect] you shameless cur, we followed to try and win *timē* [honour], for you and Menelaus, from the Trojans. And you neither see nor care; and even threaten to rob me of my *geras* [prize].

Here he reminds the embassy that Agamemnon took away his prize, Briseis, even though the war was to get back Helen. Both Helen and Briseis are *geras* (prizes), though, as Achilles also says, Briseis 'fits his heart'.

But, Achilles says:

> Here, there is no gratitude for ceaseless battle with our enemies. He who fights his best and he who stays away earn the same reward, the coward and the brave man win like honour, death comes alike to the idler and to him who toils.

Even the return of Briseis untouched does not solve the problem: how can Achilles fight the Trojans without cause, to benefit someone who has literally destroyed his *raison d'être*, his reason for living/existing?

All fighters in the *Iliad* question or embrace the 'heroic equation' – death and danger for everlasting glory. But the choice is starker for Achilles. We hear for the first time that he, extraordinarily, has a choice over his fate: his mother Thetis has told him he can remain and fight at Troy, forget about all homecoming but win endless renown, or sail home to his native land, lose fame and glory but live long.

Briseis

What claim can influence him? What bond can be appealed to? Phoenix, who brought him up from a baby, tries:

> When you were a child, ignorant of the evils of war, you would refuse to eat in the hall until I set you on my knee, feeding you titbits, and holding the cup to your lips. You would spill the wine all over me! I treated you as my own son. So, subdue your proud spirit, Achilles, and don't be so obdurate. The gods themselves may be swayed, as were the heroes of old.

He also offers a lengthy exemplary tale of Meleager's long nursing of and then last-minute retraction of a grudge, and appeals to him to 'subdue his great spirit' (*thumos*). Achilles rejects all, as he rejects all external arbiters of his actions: 'I have no need of such honour.'

Ajax says to Odysseus that there is no point in staying:

Ajax

> Achilles' proud hearted spirit [*thumos*] has made him savage. In his harshness, he has turned away from the bond of comradeship, even though we have done him such honour. He shows no pity! But a man accepts blood-money even from his brother's or his son's killer; the killer is not expelled from the land if he pays the blood price to the next of kin, whose pride and angry spirit are appeased by the compensation.

Achilles recognizes and accepts the reasoning, but 'his heart swells in anger' when he remembers how he was outraged by Agamemnon – he, recognizably, cannot stomach the insult. Ajax later says that Agamemnon should not have tried appeasement as that has only pandered to and fostered Achilles' inordinate pride and sense of self-worth.

Ajax' appeal is eminently reasonable. Achilles' spirit is obdurate because of a girl: 'They are offering seven, the best there are by far, and a host of gifts besides. He should come back to his friends and allies.' What Ajax can't understand is that 'compensation' is part of an exchange mechanism, and that Achilles sees that Agamemnon has invalidated not just the honour system but the whole structure of values on which the daily small decisions are based. Ajax saying 'he lost one girl and we're offering seven' precisely misses the point!

But Achilles says something that will be significant – that he will ignore the fighting until the Trojans' fire reaches his and his men's ships. He has always said that he has no personal reason to fight the Trojans and that Agamemnon has made it impossible to fight for him: the cardinal rule of Greek identity is that one benefits friends and harms enemies. Tragedy comes when the claims clash or become divided: Achilles cannot now benefit Agamemnon by fighting Agamemnon's enemies. But he can, he now sees, fight them when they become his enemies, when they harm him and his Myrmidons, when he is personally touched by the harm.

Achilles

In Book 1, he said he would leave the Greeks and sail away. But now he is still here before Troy, still brooding over the insult that so enraged him. The tragedy that will unfold is that Achilles will now become personally involved, far more disastrously than by keeping fire away from his ships.

Achilles and Patroclus

Book 10

A Night Raid

Book 10 is a night interlude with a different atmosphere to other books: it is darker and more antiquarian in its interest in ancient arms. (Because of this, and because its events are not referred to in other books, it has been thought an addition.)

Agamemnon, Menelaus and Nestor all wake in the middle of the night and rouse the Greek leaders. Nestor senses that the Greek position is at a critical point and proposes a reconnaissance of the Trojan intentions; those who undertake it are to be richly rewarded with 'fame of all men canopied with heaven' and a choice gift. Diomedes chooses Odysseus as the best companion once Agamemnon, almost comically protective of his brother in this dangerous exploit, has hastily stipulated that Diomedes should not take rank into account. Odysseus puts on his Mycenaean boar's tusk helmet and with a prayer to Athene they set out.

Meanwhile, Hektor also calls for a scout to win honour and Achilles' horses by establishing the Greeks' position and morale. Dolon volunteers, but runs straight into Odysseus and Diomedes. He offers a ransom for his release; Odysseus reassures him and asks him for information. Dolon gives it; when they have what they need, despite a ritual plea for mercy, they kill him out of hand. They capture the wonderful horses of Rhesus while indulging in a bloodbath. They return in triumph with the horses, which, strangely, are never again mentioned.

The book starts with Agamemnon and Menelaus awake with their nightmares while everyone else was 'overcome with gentle sleep':

Just as when Zeus, fair Hera's lord, thunders when he brews a storm of heavy rain or hail, or a blizzard to cloak the fields with snow, or opens the jaws of rabid war, so Agamemnon groaned from the depths of his being, and his heart quaked within him. When he looked towards the Trojan plain, he was dazzled by the host of fires

Horses

burning before Ilium, by the din of flutes and pipes, and human voices. Then disturbed in his mind and grieved at heart, gazing towards the ships and his own army, he tore his hair out by the roots so that Zeus above might see.

He and Menelaus simultaneously decide that something needs to be done, dress in their best (Agamemnon in tunic, a fine pair of sandals on his gleaming feet, a tawny lion skin over his shoulders, a large and glossy pelt that reached his feet, and broad purple double-cloak of thick wool; Menelaus in a spotted leopard skin and bronze helmet) and go to the shrewd Nestor, who appeals to Odysseus and the ever-reliable, ever-up-for-it Diomedes to devise a plan at this time of crisis: 'We are in dire need: our fate is balanced on a razor's edge, the survival or utter ruin of the army.'

The leaders decide on Diomedes setting out on an expedition to the Trojan lines under cover of darkness. Agamemnon, anxiously protective of his brother, is urgent that Diomedes should not choose the best – *aristos* – in rank: 'don't let undue respect for birth, or royalty influence you'. Diomedes freely chooses Odysseus, 'whose eager heart and brave spirit is eager for every adventure and Athene loves him. Together we might go through blazing fire and return: his is the most knowing mind of all.'

There is then a fascinating and important arming scene: Diomedes has an ox-hide skullcap, smooth and uncrested, 'such as young bloods wear nowadays', and Odysseus, with spear and bow, wears an example of the fabulous 'boar's tusk helmet': 'cleverly made in leather. On the inside there was a strong lining on interwoven straps, onto which a felt cap had been sewn in. The outside was cleverly adorned all around with rows of white tusks from a shiny-toothed boar, the tusks running in alternate directions in each row.' There seems a different way of painting the heroes in this book: Diomedes' leather cap is a fashionable 'vintage' item, and we have the history of Odysseus' helmet:

Boar's Tusk Helmet

Odysseus' grandfather Autolycus stole it when he robbed the Thessalian chief Amyntor's house, and gave it to Amphidamas of Cythera to take to the port. He in turn gifted it to his guest, who passed it then to his son Meriones to wear, and now it was Odysseus' head it guarded.

So armed, they set out like a pair of lions through the dark, through the remnants of slaughter, the corpses and the weapons darkly stained with blood.

Meanwhile, Hektor is also holding a night-time strategy meeting and decides to offer a reward – in standard 'heroic' terms – for information from a spy:

> Who will volunteer to do a deed, and win a rich reward? I guarantee a chariot and a pair of stallions with high arched necks, the best the Greeks have tethered by the ships, to whoever makes a foray towards their camp and finds if their swift fleet is guarded as before, or whether defeat has them preparing flight, and a fatal weariness leads them to slacken watch.

Swiftly, this episode turns very dark indeed. When spying, Dolon is spotted and chased down by Diomedes and Odysseus 'like two sharp-fanged hunting dogs pursuing a doe or a screaming hare through the woods'. Terrified, Dolon, offers both a ransom and also to reveal the Trojans' dispositions and defences. As well as this invaluable information, he reveals the whereabouts of a golden prize:

> On the edge, Rhesus is camped; he has the tallest, finest horses I ever saw, whiter than snow and fast as the wind. His chariot is finely worked in gold and silver, and he brought his gold armour with him, huge and wondrous to look on. It is armour fit for a deathless god, not a mere mortal.

Diomedes responds brutally:

Prize horses and chariot

You can forget all thought of escape, now you've told us what we needed to know. If we release you now you will live to return to our ships and fight, or spy on us once more. You will die now and never again be a danger to the Greeks.

Despite an attempt at supplication, 'Diomedes sprang at him with his sword striking him square on the neck. The blade sheared through the sinews, and Dolon's head fell in the dust even as he tried to speak.'

The book finishes abruptly and darkly. The horses of Rhesus are greeted with wonder, and Odysseus reports: 'Diomedes killed their master and twelve of the best men in his camp as well. And we caught and killed a man near the ships, and that makes fourteen, whom Hektor and the rest of the proud Trojans sent to spy on our camp.'

Book 11

The Greek Leaders in Last-ditch Fighting

Battle joined

Books 11 to 18 cover the grim and bloody fighting on a single day, a day when Zeus' promise to Thetis to show the Greeks how much they need her son is dreadfully fulfilled.

The battle starts with the sides facing each other like two lines of reapers who move down facing furrows, grain-stalks falling towards each other.

Agamemnon has his aristeia, *his time of pre-eminence, killing two sons of Priam whom Achilles had previously captured and ransomed, like a lion upon twin fawns. Other victims include two sons of an opponent of Menelaus, despite their ritual pleas for mercy, and Iphidamas, who left his bride on his wedding night to win glory at Troy.*

Hektor, on the watch, waits until Agamemnon is wounded: as Zeus told him, it is now his turn to be pre-eminent. Odysseus and Diomedes perceive that the tide is with the Trojans, but fight hard until they too are wounded. Ajax fights valiantly until he has to retreat like a donkey which has got into the wheat-field, slowly driven back by children guarding the crop. In this simile, as in others, the point of similarity – stubborness, strength, imperturbability when threatened by lesser foes, the insensibility and dignity of the movement – is embroidered into an evocative picture of real life in the non-heroic world, so that the initial comparison is only the starting point of the interest of the scene.

Achilles, who has not returned home as he threatened but is watching from the stern of his ship, sends Patroclus to establish who is wounded; it is the invaluable healer, Machaon. He goes to Nestor, who is drinking from a cup similar to one actually found ('Nestor's cup'), but Patroclus refuses to sit down because he must get back to Achilles. Nestor regales him with a long tale about his exploits when he was young, with the implication that glory is enjoyed when it is won among companions and celebrated in public, not privately dwelt on. Nestor reminds Patroclus, presumably still standing, of their fathers' advice – Achilles' that he be always pre-eminent in battle; Patroclus' that as the elder he should counsel Achilles. Nestor suggests that he reason with him or, fatally, that he at least stand in for Achilles to help the losing Greeks. Patroclus, moved by Nestor's words, then sees for himself the crisis among the Greeks. He is appealed to by the wounded Eurypylus, whom he tends; he does not get back to Achilles until Book 16.

After the dark and sometimes Dark Age world of Book 10, we move back to the Greek heroes. Agamemnon, roused by the Spirit of Discord (*Eris*), puts on his glorious shining bronze armour, beautiful greaves with silver lacing and his corselet, a precious guest-gift, with ten circles of dark blue cobalt, twelve of gold and twelve of tin, decorated with cobalt snakes. Then he slings round his shoulders his gold-studded sword and silver-chased scabbard and gold fastenings. Finally, he takes up his large Mycenaean-type 'man-enclosing' shield: ten circles of bronze with twenty bosses of shining tin and a central boss of cobalt, all decorated with a Gorgon with Terror and Fear, and a silver-chased strap with a three-headed serpent. To complete the awe- and terror-inspiring outfit, he puts on a two-horned, horsehair-crested helmet with nodding plumes. As if to salute him, the narrator records that Hera and Athene make the heavens thunder.

Similarly, Hektor, 'glittering in his armour like Zeus' thunder-flash', heads up the Trojans who face the Greeks 'like opposing lines of reapers cutting swathes through some rich man's field' – although it is not swathes of corn but men that will fall thick and fast.

Battle is joined, with the gods 'each remote in their palace, quietly watching'. All morning, as the sun rises higher, the weapons find their mark and warriors fall, but 'at the hour when a forester, weary of felling tall trees, longing for food and sweet wine, sits down in some mountain glade', the Greeks – rallying their comrades through the ranks – show their *aretē*, their excellence, and the enemy bands break.

Most of the action is heroic: Agamemnon's, Hektor's, Diomedes' and Odysseus' fights are made memorable by similes. Agamemnon kills two sons of Priam previously ransomed by Achilles, 'like a lion springing on two young fawns, crunching them and ripping their heart out, with the doe standing helplessly by'. He falls on the Trojans 'like a forest fire driven everywhere by the wind'. Hektor rouses the Trojans' spirit, 'as when a huntsman siccs on the shining toothed hounds'; he kills the Greeks 'as when the west wind whirls and batters the south wind's clouds, so the huge waves crash and foam and scatter'. Diomedes and Odysseus wreak havoc, 'as when two wild boars hurl themselves on the pursuing hounds', while Ajax spreads havoc on the Trojans ranked against him on the plain, 'as when a swollen river cascades its water down the mountain and inundates the plain, sweeping fallen trees as driftwood into the salt sea'.

Some of the similes frame heroic difficulties. Ajax's pre-eminence is halted 'by Father Zeus':

> He drew back, stunned, and gave ground like a wild creature, swinging his seven-layered ox hide shield across his back, and withdrew step by step.
> As a tawny lion driven from the cattle-yard by dogs and farmhands, who have watched all night long to prevent him seizing the best of the herd and, when he charges, keep him at bay with javelins and flaming torches which he shrinks from despite his furious hunger, turns tail at dawn baulked of his meal; so Ajax retreated before the Trojans, unwillingly and discontented, fearful for the Greek ships. And as an obstinate donkey that gets into a cornfield and is beaten with boys' sticks, ignores their cries and, used to blows, turns in to crop the standing corn until despite their lack of strength they drive him off with difficulty, having eaten his fill; so the proud Trojans harried Ajax, their spears thudding against his shield, while he at times in fury would bravely turn on them, holding the knot of horse-taming Trojans at bay then retreating again.
> So he blocked their path to the swift ships.

Here Ajax is both driven back like a lion and only retreats like a donkey forced back by a gang of boys, but still manages to obtain his object: blocking the Trojans' route to the ships, which would be 'game over', as would the Greeks' capturing Troy's citadel.

Similarly illuminating is the way the suddenly isolated Odysseus deals with his fear, consulting his 'passionate heart', his *thumos*:

Perturbed yet proud, he asked himself: 'What shall I do? Shame if I flee in fear of enemy numbers but worse to be cut off, since Zeus has routed the rest of the Greeks. But why does my own passionate *thumos* within me debate these things, if I am to be always pre-eminent, [*aristeuein*]? Only cowards run from battle, a true warrior stands his ground, to kill or die.'

The battlefield encounters are watched over by the Muse, whose job it is to record the heroes and their victims. The first in this book is one of the most memorable in the *Iliad*:

Tell me now, Muses, that dwell on Olympus, who of the Trojans or their noble allies first faced Agamemnon. Iphidamas it was, tall and powerful, who was reared in fertile Thrace, the mother of flocks. His maternal grandfather reared him from an infant in his palace and when he reached glorious youth, offered him his daughter in marriage to hold Iphidamas there. But newly-wed, he abandoned his bride looking for glory at Troy. He sailed with twelve beaked ships, left those fine vessels and reached Ilium on foot. And now he faced Agamemnon, Atreus' son.

When they clashed, Agamemnon's first spear-thrust was turned aside, while Iphidamas in turn struck Agamemnon's belt below the breastplate. Yet though he put his full weight behind it, trusting in his strength, it failed to pierce the silver belt, and the spear-point bent like lead. Agamemnon tore it from Iphidamas' grasp and, furious as a lion, struck him on the neck with his sword, and loosened his limbs. He fell, and slept the sleep of bronze. Pitiful youth, he died for the land of his birth, far from his bride of whom he had little joy, though he had given much to win her, a hundred oxen, with a thousand sheep and goats promised from his countless flocks.

This heroic episode finishes with Agamemnon stripping the body and carrying off the fine armour through the Greek ranks. Then the brutality of war hits – Iphidamas' brother tries to drag the corpse back by the foot, but Agamemnon hacks his head off, which falls onto his brother's despoiled body.

Earlier in the book, Hektor has been warned that it is Agamemnon's day, but to watch out for his wounding. Now 'sharp pains began to break Agamemnon's strength, as the sharp pains of labour come on a woman in childbirth', and Hektor sees his time has come and proceeds to wreak havoc in the Greek ranks.

The ever-vigilant Odysseus teams up with Diomedes to stop the Trojans' advance, 'as when two wild boars hurl themselves slavering on the dogs who are hunting them'. Among the victims are two sons of a seer, who foresaw their death but couldn't persuade them not to go to Troy. They do come up against the sharp-shooting Paris Alexander, who pins Diomedes through the skin of his foot, but Diomedes is sarcastic about his 'pretty curls, eye for the young girls' and challenges him to face him man-to-man with real weapons. He likens Paris' arrow to the scratch inflicted by a woman or a careless child, whereas Diomedes' spear is an instant widow-maker: his victim's wife lacerating her cheeks in lamentation, his children are fatherless, while he, soaking the earth with blood, has vultures not young girls hovering over him. However, when he pulled the arrow out, he has to go back in his chariot in agony.

Odysseus is also wounded – a spear-thrust glancing down his ribs – and isolated as he earlier feared, set on by Trojans 'as a stag with branching horns still strong though wounded and starting to weaken is attacked by scavengers who in turn are scared off by a prowling lion'. Ajax beats off the Trojans and Menelaus helps him retreat.

In the midst of the scrimmage, the chariots of both Greeks and Trojans 'trampling down shields and corpses, till the axles were sprinkled with blood splashed up by the flying wheels and hooves', the healer Machaon is wounded. The watching Achilles sees Nestor bringing him back and sends Patroclus to check; a seemingly small action which the narrator marks as 'the start of evil to him'. (It is notable that here the narrator foreshadows the outcome of events. The death of Achilles is nowhere described, but the narrator, and we, know the end of his story.)

Patroclus goes to the tent of the aged Nestor, served by the 'lovely Hekamede', awarded to Nestor 'because he was the best of them all in counsel', who mixes the very best Pramnian wine with barley and grated goat's cheese for them. We get a lovely glimpse of the shelter, as befits Nestor's Mycenaean palace as excavated at Pylos: a cobalt-footed table, bronze basket and beautiful cup, which can be compared to that found at Mycenae, made of beaten gold. The narrator is conscious that Nestor belongs to an earlier generation than his and his audience: 'this cup another man could with a huge effort lift but Nestor, old though he was, lifted it without strain'.

Patroclus arrives and sees that the wounded man is indeed the invaluable healer Machaon. Perhaps with experience of Nestor's habit of narrating long stories about past deeds, he says, 'I can't stop, I have to get back to Achilles.' But Nestor does indeed detain him; you can almost hear Patroclus edging back as Nestor starts with, 'if only I had the strength now I had when I...'.

This is the longest of Nestor's stories, perhaps part of a traditional 'Lay of Nestor' epic cycle, brought in for archaizing effect? The others are Nestor going to help the Lapiths against the centaurs in Book 1, in Book 7 where he kills a giant in single combat, and in Book 23 when he reminisces about his past athletic achievements. It is intriguing that here, in the description of a young Nestor taking part in a border raid, Herakles is mentioned. The incoming Dorian peoples are often referred to as the 'Herakleidae', the children of Herakles, so what seems to be a border skirmish between Mycenaeans and a band of northerners could perhaps be a folk memory of the Dorians taking over Mycenaean lands after the fall of Mycenae.

The 100-line story is framed as exemplary: it is preceded by Nestor's description of the present situation as critical and is perhaps meant to culminate in the take-home lesson that 'this is what heroic behaviour is' or 'this is what glory feels like, glorious deeds celebrated by all' – in contrast to Achilles, who is 'enjoying his *aretē* [valour] alone': almost a contradiction in terms! This is to spur Patroclus into winning Achilles back to the fight, by telling him of the Greeks who are wounded. (Patroclus has described Achilles' present mood as dangerous, and indeed he has been sent to find out who is wounded not out of compassion but to gauge whether the Greeks' need of him has been fully demonstrated.)

But Nestor reminds Patroclus of when, before the war, he and Odysseus visited Achilles' home, and found both of their fathers. Peleus urged his son Achilles to be bravest and best of all, but Patroclus' father advised him that though Achilles was the nobler-born and the better fighter, he as the elder must use his wisdom and lead him with good advice. He must now try to persuade Achilles to come to the aid of his comrades – an appeal to Achilles based on the claim of a common bond between fighters which he has steadily refused to acknowledge – and if he won't, makes the ultimately fatal suggestion that Patroclus take his place, in Achilles' armour.

Patroclus, readily fired up with compassion and his mission, speeds back to Achilles but is held up again, this time by running into the wounded Eurypylus, who reinforces Nestor's message of crisis – all the bravest and best of the Greeks are now injured. But here is one at least whom Patroclus can help: brought up with knowledge of herbs and medicine, he can act as a paramedic and cut the arrow out, cleansing the wound and bandaging it with a bitter root.

Book 12

Hektor and Sarpedon Pre-eminent

The wall around the Greek camp that offended the gods is attacked by the Trojans, although the poet reveals that it will not fall until after the taking of Troy, when Apollo and Poseidon will turn the rivers on it. Hektor, his triumphs ironized as always by the sense that he is actually bringing his doom down on himself, follows the advice of the cautious Polydamas to attack on foot but quarrels recklessly with him over whether to follow an omen. The two Ajaxes meanwhile encourage all the different ranks of Greek fighters, drawn together in this emergency.

Sarpedon encourages his friend Glaukos to join him in making a full assault on the wall. He reminds him that the pre-eminent position they enjoy at home comes from their being pre-eminent in battle. (Sarpedon has several times reminded Hektor that he has no common cause with him: he

Warrior

has left his wife and child to be an ally to take part in the 'glory-giving battle'.) He continues, surprisingly to modern ears, to say that if they were immortal the last thing he would ask of his friend would be to undergo the pain and risk of battle; but as death will come, the only option is to stake and risk their mortality to gain immortal glory. This speech has long been quoted and translated as a central statement of heroic values, of what drives the hero; it is remarkably free of aggression or delight in battle for its own sake.

Sarpedon and Glaukos on the Trojan side and Ajax and Teuker on the Greek side of the wall all do valiant deeds; the contest is evenly matched, like neighbours disputing a field boundary. Zeus' scales, likened to those of a poor spinster weighing her day's work of weaving, are evenly balanced until gradually they turn in favour of Hektor, who breaks through the wall.

B ook 12 starts the build-up to the epic's tragic conclusion, with the gods' anger at the Greeks building a defensive wall to protect their ships – because they did not offer sufficient sacrifices and perhaps because they were taking the initiative. The gods can always take the long view. The poet relates that:

> While Hektor lived, and Achilles nursed his anger, and Priam's city remained intact, the Greeks' mighty wall remained. But when the best of the Trojans were dead, and many Greeks too though some survived, and Troy had fallen in the tenth year, and the Greeks in their ships had sailed for their native land, Poseidon and Apollo agreed to destroy it, for nine long days turning against it the might of all the rivers flowing from Mount Ida to the sea. And Zeus rained incessantly and Poseidon Earthshaker with his trident directed the waves' force against the bastion's reinforcing logs and stones.

The poet and the gods can foresee the smoothed-out post-war landscape, with the rivers back in their courses.

But for the moment the narrative is back in the turmoil of the battle around the Greek wall, where without Achilles, Hektor is still winning the day, fighting like a whirlwind:

> like a lion or a wild boar, exulting in its strength, whirling this way and that among the hounds and huntsmen, till the men close in, flinging a shower of spears. Despite this, fearless, again and again it turns on them, as it wheels about charging the ring of men again and again, forcing the huntsmen to back off. But its very courage condemns it.

With this warning framing, the narration describes Hektor's assault on the Greek wall, setting his men against the barricaded ditch in front. Not just the narrator but the ever-admonitory Polydamas warns of the danger: the difficulty of the horses negotiating sharpened stakes in the ditch, the killing space beyond too narrow to fight in, even on foot. Hektor accepts the safety-first advice, draws up five battalions and attacks dismounted, with great success. Only one Trojan leader ignores Polydamas' advice: Asios 'in the pride of his swift running steeds drove on – Fool! [*nēpios*] – for he would not evade dark spirits of death, or return again in glory with chariot and horses to windy Troy, for black destiny waited for him at the hands of sharp-speared Idomeneus. 'He

Hektor

set his horses at the side gate of the Greek camp, manned but unbarred and standing ajar for fighters fleeing back, his men following confident they had found a weak spot and they would get through to the Greek ships – 'Fools! [*nēpioi*]' says the narrator again, as two invincible Greeks *were* defending the gates, 'like two oaks, rearing upwards and so stably planted that they are able to withstand storm and tempest; they fought like two wild mountain boars facing a pack of men and dogs, charging on both sides, tusks ripping up the trees around them, till the huntsmen strike with clashing bright bronze and they die, screaming'. Such is the noise of the battle for the gate, as the defenders fling stones which 'fell to the ground like snowflakes dropped by the winds' blast'. Asios complains to Zeus that the Greeks are defending 'like fleet flying wasps or bees defending their home hollowed in the rock'. Zeus did not listen. The narrator allows himself a very rare comment:

> It would be hard for me, even if I were a god, to narrate all, for everywhere about the wall of stone rose the wondrous-blazing fire as the hard pressed Greeks defended their ships.

The Trojans press on, but there is an omen: an eagle flies over with a blood-red snake alive and writhing in its claws. It still has fight in it, arching back to strike the eagle on its breast, and the bird in pain lets it fall among the Trojans and flies off down the wind. Polydamas again intervenes, interpreting the omen as a warning that as the eagle let the snake fall before reaching its nest to feed its young, so although Trojans may break the wall and push back the Greeks, they will fight for their ships and kill many Trojans, forcing the rest to retreat.

Hektor's response is difficult to gauge: he is surely right to argue that his assurance from Zeus is good enough to pursue their advantage, but the tone of his rejection of Polydamas' usually wise advice – 'I don't care if birds fly towards dawn and the sun, or west towards the dark' – and his impugning of his motives ring dangerously. Here again Hektor is framed as a *tragic* hero, refusing advice, going too far.

The action turns to Sarpedon, the wholly sympathetic character fighting for the Trojans (who has reminded Hektor that he has a wife and baby son waiting for him at home). He speaks to his second-in-command, Glaukos, in a famous speech about the necessity and cost of being a hero:

> Why boast we, Glaukos, our extended reign,
> Where Xanthus' streams enrich the Lycian plain,
> Why on those shores are we with joy surveyed,
> Admired as heroes, and as gods obeyed […]
> Unless great acts superior merit prove,

And vindicate the bounteous powers above?
'Tis ours, the dignity they give to grace;
The first in valour, as the first in place. [...]
Could all our care elude the gloomy grave,
Which claims no less the fearful than the brave,
For lust of fame I should not vainly dare
In fighting fields, nor urge thy soul to war;
But since, alas! ignoble age must come,
Disease, and death's inexorable doom;
The life which others pay, let us bestow,
And give to fame what we to nature owe.
Brave though we fall, and honoured if we live,
Or let us glory gain, or glory give!

(Alexander Pope)

Sarpedon and Glaukos take on the assault:

Holding his round shield, a lovely thing of beaten bronze, gold-edged oxhide-lined, Sarpedon advanced on the Greeks like a lean mountain lion spurred on by hunger to attack the walled sheepfold. Though the flock is guarded by armed herdsmen and their dogs, the lion undeterred keeps leaping on the flock, to seize a sheep or be swiftly struck down.

Combat

The Greeks summon the two Ajaxes. The greater Ajax kills first 'with a jagged stone such that no two men nowadays could lift'; his victim falls from the bastion like a diver. Sarpedon grasps the top of the bastion and opens up a route. The Greeks rush to defend it, and the two sides struggle 'like two parties with their measuring ropes arguing over the boundary stones in a shared field, fighting in that narrow margin'. Over the top of the battlements they hack at each other's round ox-hide shields; the pitiless bronze cutting into many a fighter's flesh, into his exposed back or clean through his shield itself:

The whole length of the bastion was spattered with Greek and Trojan blood. Still the defenders held, unable to panic the attackers, and the fight hung in the balance, like the scales in which a woman carefully weighs the wool she has spun on a balance scales, to earn a meagre wage and feed her children.

The book ends with a similarly graphic description of the bloody and glorious fighting, as Hektor verges on the ultimate victory – the firing of the Greek ships and trapping the Greeks into a killing ground behind their own defences:

Hektor urged on the attackers. 'On, on, horse-taming Trojans: break down the Greek wall, and set the blazing torches to their ships.' Meanwhile he seized a huge pointed rock, one that two of the strongest men these days could barely have levered it up, yet he lifted it easily, like a shepherd lifting a ram's fleece in one hand, and smashed it against the solid, tall, well-fitting double gates, pinned with cross bars and a single bolt. Bracing himself, feet firmly planted, he hurled it and broke both hinges and smashed the gates open. Glorious Hektor, face dark as night, body gleaming with bronze, leapt through: none but a god could have checked him. Eyes blazing fire, he called for the Trojans to scale the battlements and pour in through the broken gates, while the Greeks were driven back to the hollow ships.

Book 13

Menelaus, Odysseus, Ajax and Idomeneus: Epitaphs for their Victims

Zeus' attention elsewhere, Poseidon rallies the two Ajaxes and the Greeks, the more so after his grandson is killed by Hektor. As a contrast to the god-inspired delight in battle voiced by the Ajaxes, there is an interchange between Meriones and Idomeneus. These, catching each other unawares away from the fighting, loudly declare their valour and distance themselves from the signs and wounds of a coward; they then put their declarations into bloody practice. Idomeneus is pre-eminent until he comes up against Aeneas; the fighting is evenly matched thereafter, until Hektor and the two Ajaxes confront each other. In this long and bloody book, men who are winning their bride-price are beloved

Poseidon

sons-in law, have been hospitable, are caring or sweetly graceful, are lovers of innocent pursuits, are beloved of their parents – all die, bloodily and graphically, or like trees, felled and left.

Book 13 starts among the gods: Zeus turning his shining eyes away from Troy to northern Thrace, while Poseidon 'came down from the craggy mountain, to his gold-glittering temple in the water's depth'. He flies across the waves in his chariot, sea monsters playing around him, and drives on and heartens the besieged Greeks,

> making their limbs feel light; giving new strength to their feet and hands.
> First to the two Ajaxes, already fired up: 'You two could save the army

if you focus on your fighting spirit and not shiver in defeat. Everywhere else the bronze-greaved Greeks will stand fast, and I have no fear of those Trojans who have swarmed across the wall, but I do fear disaster where Hektor blazes, leading them on. If you stay firm and urge the others on, you might drive him from the swift ships.' Then, like a hawk in the air, poised high over the sheer rock face, that swoops down over the plain on its prey, Poseidon Earth-Shaker swiftly vanished.

He leaves the two Ajaxes literally inspired. They describe their renewed energy and eager fighting spirit, and how they are heroes precisely because when weary and dejected they can pick themselves up, regain their *charmē* – their delight in the fight – and reinvigorate their men. This is psychologically recognizable, whether or not described as inspired by an external agent.

Poseidon goes on to put heart (or in Greek, *thumos*, the site of passions, driving forces) into the discouraged Greeks, with the standard rousing formula:

Shame on you! Time to show whether you are men or boys! If you skulk away, then the Trojans' victory is certain. I never thought

Ajax

to see Greeks skulking in hiding while Trojans – who ran away from us like deer scattering before wolves and leopards – run amok among the ships. But you are the leaders, the first and best [*aristoi*].

The two sides clash, shield against shield, horse-haired helmets crest-to-crest. Hektor rages forward like a boulder rolling down from a cliff face, loosened by a river swollen with winter rain, its onward impetus unstoppable.

But the Greeks surround him and bring him to a standstill, and the Trojans coming to his aid clash with Greek heroes and fall on the body of Poseidon's grandson Amphimachus, while the two Ajaxes, full of battle passion, drag the Trojan Imbrius away, 'like two lions snatching a goat from the dogs, who carry it through thick bushes in their jaws, holding it high off the ground'. They strip off the armour and hack off the head, lobbing it into the Trojans where it lands at Hektor's feet.

Poseidon continues the more brutal tone, urging the Greeks in terms of a stark choice: either fight or stay back and be carrion for scavenging dogs. After describing the Ajaxes fighting 'like two wine-dark, horned oxen straining at the plough, sweat streaming, separated by the polished yoke as they sharply turn the furrow up to the edge of the field', there is a very realistic description of the ordinary fighters behind:

Behind Ajax the Great were his mighty men, who would hold his shield when his limbs grew weary or drenched with sweat. But behind Ajax the Lesser were his men who, lacking the bronze helmets with thick horsehair plumes, the round shields and ash spears of the heroes, had no heart for close fighting. They trusted, rather, in bows and slings of well-wound sheep's wool, the weapons they brought to Troy; they fired missiles thick and fast over the armed Greeks, playing their part in the attempt to break the Trojan lines.

The narrator then weaves into the bloody narrative various telling biographies, which shadow the death with tragedy:

Paris struck Euchenor, rich and brave, the son of a Corinthian seer, who sailed for Troy knowing his fate, since his elderly father prophesied he would either die of a fatal illness at home, or be slain by the Trojans among the ships. Now, Paris's shaft struck home; his spirit fled swiftly from his corpse, and the dread darkness overtook him.

And:

Now the hero Alcathous was son-in-law to Aeneas' father, having married Hippodameia whom her royal parents loved deeply: her matchless beauty, her skills and wisdom were unparalleled. But Poseidon cast a spell over Alcathous' bright eyes, and froze his noble limbs so he could neither turn to flee nor escape the spear. As he stood rooted to the spot, like a column or a tall leafy tree, Idomeneus the brave struck him square on the chest with a spear-thrust, splitting his bronze armour, which now rang harshly as the blade tore it. With a thud he fell, and the spear quivered, the point lodged in his beating heart.

Asios' death also is a tragic mixture of pathos and graphic presentness: he falls 'like an oak, poplar, or towering pine, felled in the mountains by the woodsman's sharp axe, to make ships' timbers' – but unlike the natural, useful repurposing of the tree felling, 'he lay outstretched before his horses, groaning and clutching at the bloodstained dust'.

Many of the telling encounters in this book, like Alcathous and Asios above, seems to come from a cycle of stories about Idomeneus' *aristeia*: his day of preeminence:

> Idomeneus killed Othryoneus, a newly arrived Trojan ally. He had asked for Priam's loveliest daughter, Cassandra, offering no bride-price but instead to drive out the Greeks by force. Priam agreed and trusting in the king's promise Othryoneus fought. But now, striding forward proudly, he came up against Idomeneus who aimed and cast his shining spear; the bronze breastplate failed to save him, and the blade pierced him square beneath. He fell with a thud to the ground, and Idomeneus vaunted over him, mocking him sarcastically: 'Othryoneus, if you could have done all you promised Priam, you would have had his daughter as promised, and be the happiest of mortals. Yet we could promise the same, and give you the loveliest of Agamemnon's daughters. So, all you have to do is sack the great citadel of Ilium and we will bring her from Argos to marry you. So come with me so we can agree this marriage by the sea-going ships. You will find us reasonable [...]' With this, Idomeneus took the corpse by the foot and dragged it through the melee.

Idomeneus' *aristeia* is introduced by a darkly comic incident, when he finds his second-in-command Meriones supposedly searching for equipment back in the Greek camp. Meriones defensively says he's looking for a spear, and both assert vigorously – protesting too much? – that they would much rather be fighting, 'ever mindful of glory, preferring to stand in the front line for glory-giving battle':

> Then the Trojans saw both clad in ornate armour, attacking as one. The strife of battle swirled about the ships' sterns, and in a storm of dust, like the dense cloud stirred from the roads by shrill gusts on a windy day, the battalions clashed together, eager to put one another to the sword. The killing field bristled with long flesh-cutting spears, and eyes were dazzled by the flash of bronze from glittering helms, burnished breastplates, and gleaming shields, as the armies met.

The narrator comments that a man would need a heart of steel to rejoice at the sight of such conflict and not be saddened:

> Meriones pursued Adamas and hurled his spear, catching the man midway between crotch and navel, where Ares gives greatest pain to wretched mortals. He doubled over the deeply embedded spear, writhing like a lassooed bullock that mountain herdsmen drag along struggling. Meriones reached him and dragged out the spear from the wound, and darkness filled his eyes.

Aeneas supported by his mother Aphrodite (Venus)

Idomeneus' *aristeia* brings him up against the Trojan Aeneas, who will become the hero of Virgil's Augustan epic, the *Aeneid*:

> Aeneas' passionate *thumos* was stirred in his breast, and full of battle fury he made for Idomeneus, who was not to be frightened off like a child but waited like a wild boar in a mountain fastness disturbed by the clamour of huntsmen, who trusting in its own strength turns to face them, back bristling, eyes blazing, tusks ready to take on dogs and men. So, Idomeneus the famous spearman waited for Aeneas. [...] The army followed, as the flock follows the ram from the pasture to the stream, making the shepherd's heart leap, so Aeneas' heart leaped seeing the warriors massed behind him.

The narrative follows Aeneas and Idomeneus, who 'strove eagerly to pierce each other's flesh with the merciless bronze', but both, as it happens, are brought up against lesser fighters

Menelaus

whose wounds and deaths are professionally described.

The battle narrative moves to Menelaus' deeds and his encounter with Paris, which should be the central duel between Helen's two partners, but once again goes awry:

Paris hit Menelaus in the chest with his arrow, but the deadly missile glanced from his breastplate. As swiftly as black bean or chickpea leaps from the broad winnowing fan when the winnower tosses it up in a gust of wind on the wide threshing floor, so did the deadly arrow rebound from the breastplate.

But the narrator now seems suddenly to remember the bigger picture. When Menelaus triumphs over his next victim, Peisander, he cries out:

'This is how we'll drive you far from our ships, rash Trojans, you horse-tamers drunk on the sound of battle. Treacherous cowards, never at a loss for shameful and base deeds, like the outrage you committed on me without respect for Zeus the Thunderer, who made the guest-laws and will topple your mighty city. You stole my wife, crossed the sea with her and a weight of treasure, though you were guests of mine, bound by the laws of guest-friendship. But you'll get your comeuppance!'

With this, glorious Menelaus stripped the corpse of its blood-stained armour and handed it to his friends.

Idomeneus, Menelaus and the two Ajaxes' heroic deeds push back at the dominant, god-supported Trojans. The final section of the book reverts to Hektor, once again checked in his personal heroic pursuit by temperate brother Polydamas' counsel and, then, the need to keep other brother Paris up to the mark. He exchanges taunts with Ajax, but as always his are tinged with tragedy; the narrator and we know that his taunts point forward to his own fate:

If you have the courage to stand against my long spear that will tear your lily-white skin, you too will die among them, and your flesh and sinew will glut the dogs of Troy and birds of prey where you lie by the Greek ships.

The book ends with these challenges. 'Then the noise of the two armies rose to high heaven, towards Zeus's splendour.'

Book 14

Among the Gods: Hera Tricks Zeus

Zeus

Nestor and the Greek leaders not on the field discuss the situation, showing their usual characteristics: Agamemnon for the third time proposes withdrawing, Odysseus roundly condemns the suggestion, Diomedes single-mindedly proposes that they return to the battlefield even though he is himself wounded.

Hera, who has been watching Poseidon's championing of the Greeks while Zeus' back was turned, comes up with a more radical plan of deception and disobedience. She goes to the pro-Trojan Aphrodite. She persuades Aphrodite to give her the sash of desirability, the 'cestus', ostensibly to reunite the two gods Oceanos and Tethys. She then bribes the reluctant god of sleep to keep Zeus comatose after she has seduced him, to give her time to affect the battle before Troy, and for Poseidon to encourage the Greeks. Fully equipped, she visits Zeus, who is overwhelmed with desire for her greater than he had felt for any goddess or woman, even his seven greatest conquests, all of which he details for her. Underneath their embrace spring soft flowers; the consequences of their union will be Trojan dead.

Book 14 opens in old Nestor's tent, over 'shining wine' and the steam rising from a bath at the end of a fighting day. But Nestor cannot rest. Going out, he is confronted by a scene of devastation: the Greek wall flattened and the Trojans triumphant. He goes to find the kings – there's a vivid image of the old man arriving like a prophet of doom. Full of dread, Agamemnon orders the ships to be made ready for an urgent getaway – yet again. And yet again, Odysseus accuses him of an unkingly, unleaderly attitude, countering his 'there is no shame to retreat in the face of disaster' with outrage at the thought of leaving the site of so much hard and prolonged fighting, shamefully abandoning the quest that has cost so much. Diomedes steps in, saying truthfully that no-one can doubt his heroic credentials: they have no option but to fight on despite their wounds.

This vivid scene from the killing field is followed by one from Olympus: the site not so much of a dignified pantheon as of a squabbling family. Hera, the powerful Mother Goddess, looks down from her golden throne at the battlefield and delights in the sight of her pro-Greek brother Poseidon shiningly active. When she turns to look at Zeus, she is filled with hate and resolves to flout him and intervene.

What follows is a gem, a glorious flight of fantasy of life in the clouds. We can imagine the oral performers, the 'Sons of Homer', polishing the story, and the audience waiting for the unrolling of the well-known but always freshly delightful tale of Hera borrowing the sash of the goddess of love.

It begins with, 'the Lady Hera pondered how she could beguile Zeus and thought the best way was to make herself irresistible, to go to Zeus in her loveliness and seal his watchfulness with post-coital slumber'. We get details of her beauty preparations – anointing herself with balm, massaging her skin with scented oil, combing her shining hair – and of her embroidered robe fastened with a gold brooch, her waist circled with a hundred-tasselled belt, and her triple droplet earrings, completing her outfit with shining sandals and luminous veil.

But she decides she has to make sure. She goes to golden Aphrodite and asks for help: to borrow her sash, which, like Othello's handkerchief, has 'magic in the web'. But she knows that Aphrodite is pro-Trojan, so she employs all her cunning to get it, inventing a plausible story that she wants to effect a reconciliation between Tethys and Oceanos, survivors of the previous regime but no longer lovers. Aphrodite, laughing as ever, unwraps her elaborately embroidered scarf on which is worked 'ravishing endearments, passionate whispers, irresistibly seductive to mortals and immortals alike'.

Then she goes to Lemnos, to the god Sleep: the journey over mountain ranges and heaving seas described in loving, vivid details. But this is a more difficult task to accomplish – despite inducements like a bespoke golden throne and footstool made by Hephaistos, the smith god, Sleep is reluctant to act against Zeus, remembering all too clearly the last time Hera asked him to overcome Zeus to help Herakles escape Zeus' anger. That anger was then turned against Sleep himself, who only escaped when hidden by Night.

Hera, however, persuades him that Zeus will be much less vengeful after a minor infringement (?!) – Hera helping the Trojans – than over Herakles. He agrees, induced by the offer of his long longed-for bride, the Grace Pasithea, though he makes Hera swear by all the spirits and rivers of the Underworld that she will keep her promise.

Hera then returns with Sleep to Zeus: 'Together they made their way to Mount Ida

Aphrodite

with her springs, the mother of wild beasts; mantled in mist, they went on over the forest, the top of the trees shaken by their passing. There Sleep stayed before Zeus could catch sight of him, hiding in the guise of a singing bird, in the topmost branches of a sky-scraping pine tree.'

Meanwhile, Hera goes light-footed and irresistibly lovely to Cloud Gatherer Zeus, who is lit up with desire when he sees her, as desire-filled as the first time they made love in secret. Suspicious, Zeus hears out her deceitful tale of reconciling Oceanus and Tethys, but then he, surely sharing too much, demands that she stay:

> 'For never before have I been so overwhelmed by desire for any woman or goddess, no, not for the wife of Ixion who bore me Perithoos, nor sweet-moving Danae, who bore me Perseus [both Danae and Perseus have a cycle of stories of their own, but Zeus goes rapidly on], nor Europa who bore me Minos and Rhadamanthus [and in her flight named Europe, and whose children were the famous rulers of Minoan Crete], nor Semele who bore me Dionysus [and whose terrible fate as a result of Hera's jealousy is referred to at the start of Euripides' *Bacchae*: Hera in disguise had persuaded Semele to make Zeus prove himself by appearing in all his glory; being mortal, she burned up at the sight] nor Demeter nor Leto nor yourself.'

Hera, acting shocked, proposes they repair to her beautifully constructed bedchamber. Zeus, however, covers them with a golden cloud, hiding their love-making even from the sun god Helios: 'So Zeus, the son of Kronos, drew

his wife into his arms and underneath them sprang up a grassy carpet of dewy crocus, clover and hyacinth for their cloud-covered lovemaking.'

While Zeus sleeps, Sleep goes to urge Poseidon to seize the opportunity and rouse the Greeks to urgent action. And so the battle on the earth below starts up again: the two sides clashing together, the narrator describing the roar of battle as like the huge crash of waves against the shore, the terrifying sound of an all-consuming forest fire or the high wind blasting through oaks.

Before the heroic account of combat, there is a streak of realism that marks out the Dark Age warfare that runs inside the epic: the Greek commanders, Agamemnon and Menelaus, first assemble their troops and reassign armour, so that 'the best fighters have the best war-gear and the worst the worst'. These are only three lines, but they give a strikingly realistic detail of ordinary warfare before we go back to the story of Achilles the epic hero; his care for his reputation and its material correlates and, soon now, we will the story of what happens when Patroclus asks to borrow Achilles' warrior identity – his armour.

The following battle is again a mixture of the heroic and the realistic. Hektor's spear-cast strikes Ajax full on, but where the two straps cross, the one for his silver studded sword and the other his great shield. Unhurt, Ajax catches up a large rock lying to hand on the beach as one of the anchor stones for the Greek ships: such a telling detail! He hits Hektor full on the chest, felling him like a great oak uprooted after a lightning strike. All the Trojan heroes circle Hektor – Aeneas, Polydamas, Agenor, Sarpedon and Glaukos – protecting him with their shields until he can be carried out of the battle.

There is then another very realistic detail – this narrator has seen men injured in battle – as Hektor comes round when they splash water over him, sits up to vomit a clot of blood, then falls back in a faint.

Seeing Hektor out of action puts new heart into the Greeks. Telemonian Ajax takes personally a random taunt from Polydamas, but his spear-cast, as so often given the vicissitudes of battle, takes the life of Polydamas' companion instead. Yet another abrogation of the exchange mechanism: here as this relates not to Achilles' heroic demand of honour and fame in exchange for dangerous effort, but to killing in exchange. The battleground chain of vaunt and challenge, a life for a life, meets the shifting, chaotic arena of a battlefield, where nobody can actually hold to the code of due revenge, voiced by the brother of the 'accidental' victim: 'Think how you have already lost one who now sleeps among the dead, beaten by my spear in revenge for my brother. That is why a man has sons to avenge his downfall in battle.' The horror of the battlefield is that sometimes it is a place of random death or random survival.

'Tell me now, you Muse, who was the first of the Greeks who won bloody spoil': the spoil in question seems to be the horrid, squalid, bloody head of

Ilioneus, blessed and loved by the god Hermes, having a spear thrust through the eye socket, pushing the eyeball out, then the helmeted head hacked clean off. His killer lifts the spear with the eyeball still on it 'like a poppy-head', and displays it to the Trojans, saying, 'Go tell his father and mother to weep now, as neither they nor his wife will ever take any delight in him.' This gruesome incident is narrated as making the Trojans newly conscious of the horror of the deaths on offer; the rich braiding together of glory, glorious death and bloody horror perhaps reflecting the weaving together of heroic stories with realities of everyday fighting that the audience knew well.

The book ends on a more 'epic' answer than this last to the narrator's question above, about bloody spoil: Ajax, Oileus' son, catches and kills most since he is the fastest to reach the Trojans as they, terror-stricken, run away. Again a realistic detail: once the battle-line breaks up, the area in front of the Greek ships becomes a killing ground.

Book 15

Hektor Takes the Fight to the Greek Ships: Patroclus' Distress

When Zeus awakes to see Hektor wounded and the Trojans in flight with Poseidon in pursuit, he threatens to repeat his former violence to Hera. Hera escapes the charge on a technicality. Zeus, pleased at her submission, prophesies what is to happen: the deaths of Patroclus, Hektor and his own son Sarpedon, all as the consequences of the supplication of Thetis. Ares angrily demurs, pleading the need to avenge his son regardless of the consequences. But Athene talks to him rationally: by now, some other mortal, better or stronger than his son, will have been or will soon be killed. It is a hard thing to rescue all the generations of mortals.

Iris is sent to make Poseidon toe the line, with the reminder that Zeus is more powerful and older than Poseidon and that the Furies side with the elder-born. Poseidon denies him the precedence if not the power, but is persuaded of the rightness of her case. He yields, provided Zeus does not in the end spare Troy.

Apollo is sent down to hearten and inspire Hektor. The Trojans dispatch many Greeks, and with Apollo's help, they wreck the Greek bastions like a child playing on a beach. As sandcastles to wanton boys are the bastions of men to the gods.

The terrified Greeks pray to Zeus; he thunders, which omen the Trojans take as favourable to them.

Patroclus, meanwhile, has been attending to Eurypylus, but on spotting the Trojans swarming over the ramparts and threatening the Greek ships, he sees that the time has come to put Nestor's suggestion to Achilles. The shape of the battle becomes more taut, and Hektor makes straight for Ajax. Teuker, Ajax's brother, goes to his aid but as he fires his arrow, his newly-twisted string breaks. All see this as a mark of divine interference – Teuker and Ajax attribute this to some pro-Trojan god; the poet and Hektor to Zeus.

Both Hektor and Ajax speak rousingly to their forces: Hektor of Zeus' plan and the honour of defending their families, Ajax of the imminence of the crisis and the respect that serves both glory and self-preservation. Hektor, in his Zeus-granted hour of glory, rages like a murderous lion. Respect, fear and Nestor's exhortations to think of their fathers are the only things that keep the Greeks from scattering.

Ajax, like a display rider, leaps agilely from ship to ship to fight and encourage the Greeks, while Hektor, like an eagle, darts for one ship to fight at close quarters. The book ends with Ajax being forced slowly back and calling for a last-ditch effort, while Hektor calls, in Zeus' name, for fire to burn the Greek ships.

Whereas Book 14 ended with the terrible consequences of Poseidon putting new heart into the besieged Greeks, Book 15 starts with Zeus awakening from his post-coital bliss on Mount Ida. But this is a different Zeus from that describing his many conquests to Hera; he threatens terrible physical punishments on any god who deceived him, reminiscent of the pre-classical Zeus – who, according to Hesiod, inflicted eternal torment on Prometheus for helping mankind – rather than the Zeus of the tragedies, who has some kind

Zeus

of 'watching brief' of cosmic balance. Zeus exclaims: 'Have you forgotten the time I hung you up with a golden chain with two anvils weighing you down?' Not surprisingly, Hera is economical with the truth; she swears by the waters of the underworld that Poseidon acted without her direction, motivated only by pity for the Greeks' plight.

In some Greek tragedies, Zeus has a 'plan' for the future, but in this book that plan seems rather to be foreknowledge. He foresees and, importantly, acts as the narrator of the unfolding events, including the deaths of Patroclus, Sarpedon and Hektor – the three deaths that form the tragic narrative from now on.

Hera flies from Zeus' Mount Ida to the gods on Mount Olympus; a striking image likens her passage to 'a thought which flashes through the mind, imagining in quick succession many places to be'. She is greeted by a minor goddess, Themis, who seems to be charged with commissions from Zeus. There is wonderfully human exchange between them, Themis asking if she is alright as she looks terrified: has her husband been threatening her again? Hera replies: you know what he's like.

Both Zeus and Hera go from terrifying natural powers – Zeus who murdered his father in a regime change, Hera his sister-wife and a mother goddess, both with cosmic powers – to being just two of the larger-than-life characters of Mount Olympus, about whom there is a wealth of stories and anecdotes. Hera explains she is the messenger of Zeus, 'laying down the law from a separate mountain', and calls them *nēpioi* (infants, fools), a tragic word denoting those who fatally misunderstand the position. For Zeus is all-powerful, right or wrong. Ares, god of war, naturally refuses to remain inactive: his son has been killed and he wants vengeance. But Athene accuses him of being out of his mind. If he interferes with the war, Zeus will turn his might on the gods, battering guilty and innocent alike.

Then we get the view of the human condition as seen from Mount Olympus: Ares should give up his anger at the death of his son, for 'by now some other, greater and better than your son, has been killed, and we cannot rescue everybody'.

Sending Apollo and the rainbow messenger-goddess Iris to receive Zeus' commands, Hera takes her place on her

Athene

throne. Poseidon, however, incensed at Zeus' instruction to stop interfering in the battle, hotly disputes his supremacy. We have here a brief but important Homeric account of the dividing up of the realms after the war with the Titans, the older gods including the parents of Zeus, Hades and Poseidon: Rhea and Kronos (the subject of a major eighth-century BCE poem, Hesiod's *Theogony* – the Birth of the Gods): 'Hades drew the lot of the land of misty darkness; Zeus the wide sky, clouds and bright aether, upper air; Poseidon the grey sea. But earth and Olympus is common to all three, so I, his equal, refuse absolutely his mind and bluster.'

The inter-domain diplomacy continues – we remember that the fifth-century BCE listeners had all, to a man, experience of town council business, as the Athenian political system was to choose monthly councillors by lot – but

Poseidon

Iris effects a sweet compromise and Poseidon agrees to submit, just this once, provided Zeus does not interfere with the destined Greek victory over Troy. He sinks reluctantly back into the sea, leaving the Greeks to rely on their own resources, while Zeus sends Apollo to restore the wounded Hektor.

The resulting change of fortune is narrated from a double perspective: Apollo's heartening of Hektor from the gods' point of (over)view is paralleled by the disheartening of the Greeks who presumed that he was dead. Relief and despair accordingly make sense in purely human terms, though the narrator attributes all to Apollo's terror-inducing presence. The Trojans stream back to the Greek defensive ditch and overthrow it, 'like a boy kicking over sandcastles'. The to and fro of battle is described: one side feeling that fortune is with them and the other defiant in the face of seemingly divine intervention. Teuker, for example, is dismayed that his arrows go astray, as if a god were personally diverting them from their target.

The leaders call on their men for a literal last-ditch effort, in the name of those who have already died or been wounded in the attempt. There is a sense that this is a crucial day and there are glimpses of the imminent tragedy – of Patroclus' and Hektor's doomed ends.

The book closes with Hektor having laid hands on a Greek ship: 'Bring fire, unite in raising the battle cry, for Zeus has given us the victory day, after the gods and my over-cautious advisers were against us.' But waiting on the high deck is Ajax, with spear poised to pick up any Trojan firebrand.

Just before this final scene, there is a narratorial side-scene, looking at Patroclus, detained while on his way back to Achilles with news and an appeal from Nestor. His story is about to recommence.

Book 16

Patroclus Fights in Achilles' Armour:
Tragic Deaths of Sarpedon and Patroclus

Book 16, like Book 1, is a complete act in the tragedy of the 'wrath of Achilles'. With Hektor on the point of defeating the Greeks, going against the fate-ordained end by firing their ships and trapping them without the means to escape, this book picks up Patroclus' story from Book 9. He returns in tears, 'weeping like a girl' to the waiting Achilles, reporting the plight of the Greeks and – tragically, fatally – begs for Achilles' arms and armour, 'to be a light to light up the Greeks' and terrify the Trojans. The poet marks the significance of this, the request that brings tragedy on Patroclus, Hektor, numerous Trojans and Achilles himself.

Achilles consents, but only if Patroclus goes no further than warding off the immediate danger from the Greek, and his own, ships. This will enhance Achilles' glory; to go beyond would diminish it and bring him up against the gods.

Meanwhile, Ajax is being battered by the Trojans, by the will of Zeus and by Hektor. With fire approaching his own ships, Achilles helps to muster the Myrmidons, who pour out like a pack of ravening, blood-slavering wolves, with Patroclus at their head. Achilles, after careful ritual, prays to Zeus that his dear friend might win glory and come back safe. However, 'Zeus granted one prayer and denied the other.' The Myrmidons, like angry wasps stirred up by idle children, fall on the stunned Trojans and force them back. Patroclus is pre-eminent in the fighting; 'blood-red death and strong destiny' close over many from both sides. Sarpedon resolves to stem the retreat by standing against Patroclus, and they face each other like vultures. Zeus, watching, sees that Sarpedon, his son, is destined to die, as he had outlined in Book 15. Much moved at the reality, he considers intervening, but Hera points out that to go against a mortal's marked fate would disrupt the boundary between mortal and immortal. Rather, Zeus must accept that the proper end, the reward, for a mortal is to have due burial and a physical memorial, a focus for the commemoration that dead heroes receive. Zeus weeps bloody tears for his son.

Sarpedon dies, like a tree felled or a bull savaged, clawing in the dust. He adjures Glaukos, already wounded, to fight over his body. Glaukos, overwhelmed with grief and pain, prays to Apollo; he calls on the Trojan leaders to avenge him,

Patroclus' *aristeia*

their mainstay. Against the raging Trojans line up Patroclus and the Ajaxes, eager to strip Sarpedon's body, which soon becomes buried under weapons and fighting, like flies over a milk pail.

Hektor sees that the scales are turning against him and loses heart, leaving the Myrmidons to despoil the corpse, which is spirited away by Sleep and Death. But the scales are also turning against Patroclus, killer of Zeus' son. In the grip of passion, Patroclus forgets Achilles' injunction, 'which if had he kept, would have kept a black death from him', and chases the Trojans not only away from the ships but right across the battlefield up to the walls of Troy. The poet asks him, as though he could be the narrator of his doom, who else he took with him to his death. Patroclus is like 'one of heaven' as he attacks the walls of Troy; on his fourth assault, Apollo tells him to cease what exceeds his fate. Patroclus gives way. Apollo tempts Hektor to triumph over him.

Patroclus, 'so near his own grave death', mocks the dying fall of Hektor's charioteer and fights Hektor over the body, while Trojans and Greeks contest for dominance like 'winds striving to make a lofty wood bow to their greatness'. Bodies fall like trees; the Greeks come out on top, 'past measure'. Three times Patroclus charges and wins superhuman victories; then the end of his life appears as, unseen, dreadful Apollo strikes him. Achilles' helmet is taken up by Hektor, 'whose death was near', and 'in confusion, thus dismayed', Patroclus is wounded by a passing Trojan. Hektor sees his advantage and delivers the final blow; he vaunts that the vultures will prey on him, that the mighty Achilles will not come to his aid, even though Hektor is sure the mighty Achilles told him not to come back without defeating him. The dying Patroclus answers that he has been beaten not by Hektor but by the gods, together with destiny, which will shortly wait on Hektor in the shape of Achilles. Patroclus' soul flies away, 'sorrowing for his sad fate, to leave him young'. Yet Hektor refuses to accept the words as prophetic and takes Achilles' armour.

Book 16 is dramatic in all senses, building to the crisis that brings in Achilles and brings on his fate: Patroclus' death. Achilles has been obdurate when asked to come back into the fighting, saying that Agamemnon has broken the contract between summoner and heroes answering the call, that they are fighting for 'imperishable fame' rather than in response to a threat to 'their own' – *philoi* (friends, comrades, allies – those a hero is bound to by bonds of obligation and kinship as well as emotion). Although the appeal of the embassy in Book 9 failed, even strengthening Achilles' isolation and intransigence, his closest *philos* – Patroclus – now makes a triple appeal to Achilles to those bonds of *philia*. Patroclus reports that their closest friends are wounded and suffering, and that Achilles' own ships are in danger: the ships that are the Greeks' last line of defence and chance of escape are now exposed

Achilles and Patroclus

to Hektor's attack. Thirdly, and disastrously as the poet highlights, Patroclus says that he – his closest companion – is distressed, and he begs Achilles to act (a supplication, the calling on a superior or more powerful person to heed a request, is a formal act that must be acceded to).

The poet finely crafts the tragic narrative of this crisis book: with moving speeches, action made vivid and affecting by similes, unusually addressing Patroclus directly and commenting on the disastrous consequences of his and Hektor's actions.

It starts with Patroclus having returned to Achilles with news:

Patroclus, warm tears pouring down his face like a dark running stream flowing down the face of a sheer cliff, returned to Achilles, leader of men. He pitied him, and spoke winged words: 'Why are you crying like a little girl, Patroclus, running to her mother's side, clutching at her skirt, begging to be picked up? Why do your soft teardrops fall, Patroclus? Have you had bad news of me or mine?'

The narrator then addresses Patroclus directly:

Then you answered, Patroclus: 'Achilles, greatest by far of the Greeks, don't be cross with me: there is such grief on the Greeks! All the best warriors are laid up wounded with spear or arrow, the healers are working day and night, while you are obdurate, nursing your anger, totally without pity. Surely you were born of the grey sea rather than living parents: you have a cruel mind. But have you been given some warning from the gods? If so, at least let me go and lead the Myrmidons out, to be a light for the Greeks and a terror for the Trojans.'

Thus far, this is a reasonable response to the situation, and one suggested to Patroclus back in Book 11. But the offer includes a tragic as well as an heroic error: Patroclus proposes to lead out the Myrmidons not just like Achilles, but as Achilles: in Achilles' armour. Armour is both the skin and the identity of a hero. Chivalry had rules for establishing the nobility while preserving the anonymity of 'the unknown knight', and both Greek and medieval societies had stories of the sacrificial substitute who offered himself to die in the likeness of the king. Admetus, in the story dramatized by Euripides, is given the favour by the gods of electing a substitute when fated to die. (Intriguingly, anthropologists have suggested that the origin of Greek tragedy lies in the rituals around the transfer from the killing of the year king to ensure fertility to the killing of the king's substitute – the *therapōn*, the word used here for Patroclus. Many fertility rituals survive as the sacrifice rather of a substitute 'king barleycorn' or a corn dolly.) However, even if there are ritual associations here of the *therapōn* dying in the place of the king, of Patroclus in some way acting out and prefiguring the death of Achilles, this crucial moment is dramatized as a double tragic error.

For no hero should assume the armour and identity of another – that would be an attempt to fool the Muses who have in their keeping the individual heroes' immortal fame. The frequently advanced idea of tragedy as coming from a fatal error followed by a sense of overweening confidence that leads to disaster – which does not work well in surviving Greek tragedies – is fully played out here. Achilles formally requires Patroclus to lead out his Myrmidons and to show himself, but not to fight: that will add to, not compromise, Achilles' own honour and glory. He warns him not to, 'in the exultation of slaughter', press on to Troy, and after pouring an offering from a beautifully wrought cup he prays:

> Though I stay here by the beached ships, I am sending my friend with a host of Myrmidons to war. Grant him glory, far-echoing Zeus, and strengthen his heart and mind, so that Hektor may discover my companion's (*therapōn*) skill in war, and that his hands rage invincible whether or not I am with him. And when he has beaten back the enemy from the ships, let him return to the ships complete with armour and his men unscathed.

It is notable that he says he dreams of a time when, Patroclus now validated as an equal, they two together take the ultimate prize. Dream on: 'Zeus granted one prayer – Patroclus' warcraft – and denied the second, his safe return.' The narrator is clear that there will be no such happy ending: he calls Patroclus a great childlike fool (*nēpios*), 'for it was his own doom and death he was begging for'.

There is a vivid picture of the mighty Myrmidons, an elite force cooped up in shelters by the ships, being let off the leash:

> Like a pack of ravening wolves filled with unspeakable fury, mountain wolves who have brought down a branching antlered stag and tear it with blood-stained jaws, then go in a mass to drink, lapping the dark water with slender tongues, dripping blood and gore, their spirit untroubled and their bellies gorged.

The narrative immediately darkens with the pathos of other paths, other hopes, for the Myrmidon leaders who are about to face death:

> The first company was led by Menesthius of the gleaming breastplate, son of a river-god. Lovely Polydora bore him, a mortal woman who lay with the ever-running stream, but he was named as the son of Borus, who married her freely and gave a handsome dowry. The second company of Myrmidons warlike Eudorus commanded. His mother Polymele, a fine dancer, bore him when a maiden: great Hermes fell for her when she caught

his eye, among the chorus of girls dancing for Artemis, goddess of golden arrows and the hunt. He took her swiftly to her chamber and lay with her secretly. She bore him this glorious son, Eudorus, finest of runners and fighters, and Echecles, powerful and steadfast, paid a vast bride-price to make her his wife. There his old father Phylas cherished and nurtured the child tenderly, loving him dearly as if he were his son.

Patroclus

But they stream out in full confidence, 'like a horde of wasps that little boys poking at their nest have stirred up to stinging anger'. Their entrance into the fray has the desired result – the Trojans are shocked and terrified at seeing Patroclus, 'thinking that Achilles had renounced his great rage and turned to the way of *philia* [obligations to comrades]'.

What follows is an account of Patroclus' *aristeia*, his time of absolute pre-eminence, as talked of by fighters, duellists and sports-stars: a time when nothing can miss. First, he drives the now panic-stricken Trojans from the ships, then puts out the ship-threatening fire and fights superhumanly – or at least the narrator describes his effect, 'as when Zeus stirs the mountain cloud cap and bright air spills from the heavens down the deep ravines',

'as when Zeus brings on the hurricane and the cloud deepens from Olympus' and 'as when Zeus sends down the most violent waters underneath the hurricane in deep rage against mortals who have roused him to anger'.

But Patroclus, despite his borrowed feathers, will prove to be neither immortal nor invulnerable.

In Achilles' shining armour, he kills Trojans 'one after another, leaving them on the black earth'. There is a shocking image of how (channelling rageful Achilles?) he spears a victim, 'on the right of his jaw, driving it past the teeth, and pulling its shaft back dragged him over the chariot's rim, like a man astride a jutting rock landing a mighty fish hooked on the end of his line. He hauled him from the chariot, gaping on the end of his spear, then dropped him on his face as his life fled.'

The narrator's attention and sympathy moves to the Trojans, and in particular the most sympathetic character, Sarpedon, leader of the Lycians. In Book 5, there is a telling speech, pointing out the cost to him of fighting the Greeks 'though there is nothing of his in Troy to fight for':

> Sarpedon sternly rebuked noble Hektor: 'What has happened to your courage, Hektor? Did you think to hold Troy relying only on your brothers and brothers-in-law? And where are they? I don't see one! They cower like dogs before a lion, while we who are simply allies do the fighting. And a long journey it was here: I left far away in Lycia my darling wife and baby son, and great possessions too that any man would envy. Yet I urge on my Lycians, ready to fight myself, though there is nothing here of mine for the Greeks to carry off or drive away; while you just stand there.'

And in Book 12, we have the achingly down-to-earth speech of Sarpedon to his second-in-command, Glaukos, which finishes with the thought that if they could be immortal, the last thing he would ask of him would be to face the pain and danger of battle. But since death was all around anyway, as heroes they had no choice but to go out to be the victor or victim of a glorious encounter.

So we are very much with Zeus here in Book 16, when he sees that Sarpedon, his son, is destined to die. Much moved at the reality of mortality, he considers intervening:

> 'I am filled with pity that Sarpedon, so very dear to me, is fated to die at the hands of Patroclus! Even now I am in two minds, whether to gather him up from the fighting and set him down alive in his rich land of Lycia, far from this grievous war, or allow him to fall to Patroclus.'

Zeus

'Dread son of Kronos,' Queen Hera replied, 'what do you mean? Are you planning to save a mortal from the pains of death, one long since doomed by fate? Do so, but don't expect the rest of us to approve! No, if he is so dear to you, and it pains your heart, let him go down to Patroclus but, after his spirit has departed, send Death and sweet Sleep to carry him away to his broad land of Lycia, where all his kin may mark his resting place with a mound and memorial stone, the proper mark of honour of the dead.'

Hera points out that to go against a human's marked fate would disrupt the boundary between mortal and immortal. Rather, Zeus must accept that the proper end and reward for a mortal is to have due burial and a physical memorial,

a focus for the commemoration that the dead receive: the *geras*, the proper mark of honour, the sufficient and only material correlate of a dead hero. The father of men and gods accepts her advice, but sends a blood-red shower of rain to the earth, to honour his beloved son whom Patroclus would slay in the fertile land of Troy, far from his native land. Zeus bows to the proper and inevitable, accepting that he could but may not interfere.

The rest of the book is the very human, grippingly and vividly dramatized tragic story of the death of Sarpedon and fight over his body, and the eventual, doomed death of Patroclus at the hands of Hektor.

The spotlight stays on Patroclus, as he kills Sarpedon's body squire (another *therapōn* – by shielding Sarpedon, dying in his stead). The return strike hits Patroclus' horse, making the rest of his team rear up and tangle until Automedon, Achilles' and Patroclus' charioteer, cuts free the trace horse. Now Sarpedon and Patroclus finally face each other. Sarpedon again throws wide, but Patroclus' spear finds its mark and he dies, crashing down like an oak or a white poplar, a natural image, or more tragically, like a towering pine tree felled by the sharp axes of shipwrights: the living wood, unlike the living body, transformed into something useful, planks for a ship. This evocative craft image comes back later, continuing to contrast the 'dead meat' of this sympathetic character's corpse with an image from husbandry; both sides fight over his body like flies over the milk splashing into the bucket.

Sarpedon is given one last moving speech. Dying like a bull clawed by a lion in the middle of his herd, he calls on Glaukos to protect his body from being despoiled (a charge that Glaukos, already badly wounded, tries to obey; summoning up all his strength and praying for help now that 'the best of men, Sarpedon, son of a Zeus who would not stand by his children' had died). The Trojans, hearing the news, rally to defend his corpse because, 'though he was an outsider, he and the men he brought with him were Troy's bulwark'. Sarpedon leaves a huge gap – in the defence of Troy and in the narrative. We, like his faithful second, Glaukos, and Zeus, will miss his generous and 'grounded' presence, as the narrative turns to psychology and the actions of the three actors now bound fatefully together: Patroclus, Hektor and Achilles.

The spotlight is on two of those for the rest of the book, with Achilles as a brooding 'felt absence', a waiting non-combatant at the far side of the line of Greek ships. Hektor kills one of the leaders of Achilles' Myrmidons and the narrator addresses the grieved and angered Patroclus: 'Like a flying hawk that scatters the crows, you Patroclus made straight for the Trojans and Hektor.'

(There is a lovely aside in the melee over Sarpedon's body. The Trojan Aeneas, whom Virgil was to celebrate as the ancestor of the line of the Julii and the first Roman emperor, Augustus, sneers at Patroclus' companion, Meriones, for athletically dodging a spear: 'What a dancer! But if I had hit you, I would have stopped you for all time!' Meriones answers, in effect, 'that's war: you can't stop everyone who comes against you, for you are only human; if I hit you with my spear, it would be you going down to Hades.' Patroclus responds with a call for fewer words and more action – a braiding together of heroic convention and realistic depiction of what goes on in the front line.)

Not only Achilles but also Zeus is represented as intimately concerned with the fight over Sarpedon's body and Patroclus' impending death at the hands of Hektor. When the Greeks manage to strip off Sarpedon's shining armour, Zeus, as Hera advised, orders his body to be rescued from under the bodies killed in the fight over it, washed clean, anointed and carried by Sleep and Death to his homeland for due burial and a grave marker.

The narrator turns to Patroclus, whom he calls *nēpios*, fool! (literally, 'infant' – used always for someone who doesn't understand the situation, the human condition, the cosmic structure); if only he had heeded Achilles' instructions, he might have evaded the spirits of death: 'Whom first and whom last did you kill, Patroclus, with heart full of battle fury, as the gods called you to your death?'

The battle has moved beyond the geography of the central zone: the Greeks are now trying to take Troy and the Trojans to fire the Greek ships to prevent escape. From now on, the narrative charges such zones with tragedy: 'So the Greeks following Patroclus might have taken towering Troy, had not Apollo beaten him back.' Patroclus' advance is a quintessentially tragical 'going too far':

> Three times Patroclus tried to mount the bastion, like more than a mortal, three times he was beaten back, and at the fourth Apollo warned him to give way: 'It is not destined for you to take the proud city of Troy.'

Hektor now considers the best course of action at this crucial time. An advisor – or was it a god in the guise of a counsellor; who can ever be sure? – asks him why he has stopped and, deviously (?), tells him to seek out Patroclus because 'Apollo [the double-tongued!] might grant you such a glorious victory'. Patroclus first hurls a jagged stone at Hektor, which hits his charioteer between the eyes. He 'fell out of the chariot like a diver, and Patroclus mocked him: "See what a gymnast this man is – if only he were an oyster diver, he could feed an army

Patroclus

with them!" So, Patroclus, in your battle fury you pounced on the charioteer and fought Hektor over him, like two mountain lions over a deer.'

The view widens until the battle over the body becomes a microcosm of the whole war:

> Like the east and south winds, fighting it out, shaking the depths of some mountain valley, smashing together the forest trees: shaking the branches of oak, ash and smooth-barked cornel together with a roaring crack of breaking branches, so the Greeks and Trojans battered each other over the body with spears, stones and feathered arrows.
>
> Then beyond their destiny the Greeks were stronger and stripped the armour and despoiled the corpse; three times Patroclus charged like Ares, the God of War; three times he cut down nine men but the fourth as he rushed forward like something more than human, that, Patroclus, saw your end.

Hektor

The first blow against Patroclus is attributed to Apollo, wrenching off the great horse-crested helmet that served to guard Achilles, once untouchable on his head but now, fatally, passed to Hektor, 'whose own death was close at hand'. The second strike follows when, standing stunned, Patroclus is hit by a Trojan spearman who melts back into the crowd when he sees whom he has hit. The third and final attacker is Hektor, who, when he sees how wounded Patroclus is, stabs him right through the belly. He falls, to the horror of all the Greeks:

> As a lion overpowers a tireless wild boar high in the mountains, fighting over a little spring they both want to drink from, with neither ceding ground, but the lion eventually forces the boar down, so Hektor finished off Patroclus, vaunting over him. 'Patroclus, you thought of devastating our city and enslaving our Trojan women. Fool! [*nēpios*] when you came up against me! Now you're meat for vultures. Achilles must have said "Don't come back until you have stained man-slaying Hektor's tunic with his life-blood." Such folly!'

Patroclus answers:

> 'The victory shout goes to you, Hektor, but you are only the third attacker: you would never had beaten me if I hadn't already been vulnerable and

Death of Patroclus

denuded of arms. Think on this: you now have brought powerful destiny down on yourself: standing beside you are Death and your fate at the hands of the mighty Achilles.' He spoke, and death closed upon him; his soul fluttering free of his body went down to the House of Death, grieving to leave glorious youth and manhood behind.

Hektor, meanwhile, not content with killing Achilles' beloved companion, chases after Achilles' immortal horses.

Book 17

The Fight over Patroclus' Body

The Fight over the body

Menelaus bestrides Patroclus' body, and there kills Euphorbos, Patroclus' first wounder. His death, however, is described in a long pathetic simile, as like an olive tree with spreading branches curled with snowy flowers, watered with delicious springs, which is uprooted by a sudden gale.

Apollo recalls Hektor from chasing Achilles' divine horses. Menelaus debates whether to withdraw from facing Hektor and the god: it would be prudent, but the hasty abandonment of Patroclus' corpse and arms would offend the Greeks. He makes a 'lion-like retreat' and eventually returns with Ajax to the now despoiled body of Patroclus.

Glaukos meanwhile upbraids Hektor for abandoning Sarpedon's corpse and showing ingratitude to his allies. He demands they get Patroclus' body inside Troy to use as barter for Sarpedon's armour. Hektor rebuts the charge and assumes Achilles' divine armour. Zeus, addressing him as the poet addressed Patroclus, strengthens him for what will be his final battle, granting him glory.

Hektor calls on all the allies and offers half the spoils and equal glory to whoever gets Patroclus' body inside the walls. They rush to obey, the fighting very fierce until the ground runs with blood. The bloody struggle over the body continues, and is compared to the struggle to stretch and cure a fat-drenched ox-hide; the body, like the whole expedition, has become something that cannot be given up without loss of honour, even when the cost is high.

Achilles' mother, Thetis, conceals Patroclus' death from him, while Achilles' horses stand like statues on a tomb in grief for him. Zeus pities them, as deathless creatures involved with mortals and subject, like Thetis, to a grief that too is deathless.

The bitter fighting continues, the Trojans having the advantage. Finally, however, the Ajaxes start to clear a path for the body of Patroclus, as, the myth goes, Odysseus would later clear a path for that of Achilles. Patroclus' death foreshadows and in some ways brings about that of Achilles – there is a strong sense that in borrowing and dying in Achilles' armour, his warrior's skin and identity, he has ensured the death of the man he was impersonating.

Book 17 starts with the after-fate of the first man to wound Patroclus, Euphorbos, who wants to complete his victory by stripping the corpse of Achilles' armour. He challenges Menelaus, who is standing guard over Patroclus' body, to combat. Menelaus wonders at his surely overweening pride, fury greater than a leopard, a lion or a wild boar. He warns Euphorbos to get back among the ordinary fighters, where he belongs. But Euphorbos has a personal score to settle as well, for Menelaus killed his brother and he wants revenge, not just for the killing but also for Menelaus' gloating over the fate of his young wife and his parents. Their grief will be assuaged, he hopes, by his bringing back to them Menelaus' head and armour. But Menelaus proves too strong an opponent for the young man,

who fell with a dull thud, his armour clanging round him. His hair that was as lovely as the Graces', the locks braided with gold and silver thread, was drenched in blood. Like a mighty gust of wind in some lonely place that uproots a fine olive sapling – a tall upstanding one that its planter set in a hollow, drenching the new sapling with generous water, so that quivering in every breeze, it burst into white blossom – and lays it low on the ground, so did Menelaus kill Euphorbos, he of the strong ash spear, and stripped him of his armour.

The pathos of this simile lies in the different tendings or drenchings – the woodsman spraying the quivering blossoms with 'generous water', Menelaus spraying the braided hair with blood.

Menelaus

The pathos is more direct in the next simile – Menelaus is likened to a mountain lion snatching the finest cow of a herd, first breaking her neck, then savagely (or naturally) feasting on the innards, while dogs and herdsmen dare not approach. Similarly, the Trojans dare not take on Menelaus, who continues pre-eminent until Hektor realizes that he is needed in the front line. Menelaus has a difficult ethical decision: isolated as he now is, should he fight for Patroclus' armour or retreat before the oncoming charge of Hektor? Troubled, he consults his 'great hearted *thumos*':

How can I abandon Patroclus and this noble armour, who died fighting in a war to recompense me? Every Greek who sees it will condemn me. But if, out of shame, alone, I stand up to fight Hektor of the glittering helmet and all his host of Trojans, they may well surround and overpower me. Yet why this debate with myself? None of the Greeks will fault me for giving ground to Hektor who has a god on his side.

Sound reasoning? The narrator dignifies his not-very-heroic retreat, abandoning Patroclus' body and armour 'like a bearded lion driven from a sheepfold by the dogs, and by men shouting and brandishing their spears, so his mighty courage congeals'. So the Trojans are reduced to dogs and farmhands, though they are made brave by the task of defending their homestead.

The setting for the rest of the book widens from dialogues – whether internal or between challengers on the field – to something broader, with the two dead bodies of Sarpedon and Patroclus centre stage. Their corpses, the bodies' and armour's use as bargaining chips in the ongoing struggle, and their significance as dead leaders to those who survive and cared and care for them, are all woven into the drama.

Menelaus finds Ajax and together they attempt to stop Hektor, who has already stripped off the precious armour and sent it back to Troy, from wreaking his threatened vengeance on Patroclus' corpse, hacking off his head and throwing it to the dogs. Ajax, 'carrying like a wall his shield [a Mycenaean shield], bestrides the body like a lion over his young who turns to protect them from hunters, standing in the pride of his strength'.

Meanwhile, Sarpedon's second-in-command Glaukos raises starkly the question of the responsibility of the leaders on both sides to those who freely fight for them:

> Hektor, splendid to look on, time to look to the defence of you and yours now you won't have the Lycians to defend them! Day after day we have gone out to fight for the sake of your city, a desperately hard struggle, but no more, because you do us no grace, you treat us with no respect. You have abandoned Sarpedon, your ally and close friend: left him as prey to be despoiled, he who was your bulwark when he lived.

The argument is that if Hektor had any sense of responsibility for those who come to his aid, any acknowledgment of the deep and reciprocal bond between fighting men or leaders to allies, he would do the body 'grace' (*charis*). It is significant that he says that if that's the way they are treated, Hektor can find out how the Trojans get on with only themselves – those that are directly implicated – defending their own. We remember Sarpedon in Book 5 accusing Hektor of ingratitude, on the grounds that Hektor had asked for help for essentially a family matter, and yet where is the family now? And reminding him that he himself has left his beloved home and baby son far away and drives his men on though 'there is nothing of my own here'. So fragile is the bond between summoner and summoned! Glaukos continues:

> If the Trojans have any guts, any sense of fighting for their own land and city, we could together make quick work of getting Patroclus' corpse inside the citadel and use it in exchange for Sarpedon's body and his glorious armour.

Hektor, as so often through the epic, fires up aggressively at the suggestion, latching on to the accusation of cowardice. Seemingly unheeding, he goes to array himself in Achilles' divine armour: the armour that has already led Patroclus to his death and that Zeus, and we, know will bring on that of Hektor. In no heroic culture is it wise or proper to wear another warrior's armour – his skin, his identity. Hektor, like Patroclus, is filled with extraordinary energy and strength: the divine armour is tragically empowering.

Hektor

Then he responds to the allies, reminding them of and reinforcing the contract between them and the Trojans:

> Listen, all you host of allies. I summoned you from your cities, not because I lacked numbers, or needed them, but because you were keen to defend the women and children of Troy from the fierce Greeks. So I spend my people's wealth in gifts and sustenance for you, to maintain your strength and courage. So now is the time for every man to engage: to attack the enemy, to live or die. I will share half the spoils with whichever of you drives Ajax off, and drags Patroclus' body into our ranks of us horse-taming Trojans. I will also share the glory.

Inspired, they make straight for Ajax. The narrator, with perhaps later, non-heroic values, says tersely: 'Fools! Since many lives were torn out over a corpse!'

Ajax also reflects on the situation, confessing to Menelaus that his consciousness is occupied less by the fate of Patroclus' dead body – which is now no more and no less than a feast for carrion – than by their living ones. Hektor looms over their future.

Just like Hektor moments earlier, Menelaus has to address those who have long ago responded to his call, refreshing and renewing the contract:

> Friends, leaders of those from the land of Argos, you who drink freely at Agamemnon's table, and command the Greek army, honoured by Zeus with glory, I am addressing you together, for in the heat of battle I cannot discriminate between leaders and men. So now, charge together to rescue Patroclus' corpse, your hearts filled with fury and shame that it should be left to delight the dogs of Troy.

Hektor leads the charge against the now resolute Greeks – 'as when the pounding surf of the sea meets the outflow of a rain-swollen river, the sea-strand resounding with the roar of wave against wave' – over Patroclus' body, helped by Zeus, who had not cared about Patroclus but now – like the audience – cannot bear to see his body as carrion for dogs.

The rest of this pivotal book pans in and out of the defence of Patroclus' body, with gruesome close-ups – a Trojan managing to hook his shield strap round the body's ankle but being prevented from dragging it out from under, then speared 'through his helmet's cheek-piece so that his brains spilled out through the eyepiece. He let fall the foot, dying over the body, far away from his home and unable ever to repay his parents' care.'

The bitter, bloody fighting over the body, making the ground run red, is horridly likened to 'men straining at a great bull's hide with under-skin fat still on, that a tanner gives them to stretch. They stand in a circle close packed together and all pull with all their might, so its moisture is expelled while the fat sinks in.' Then the poem pans out to the overview of the significance of this body on this day of the war, Aeneas seeing that if they pull back to Troy at this time of strength (and the gods' approval), the whole balance of power will shift. The narrative is shot through with 'what ifs' and double determinations, where actions are shown as simultaneously external – coming from a sense of gods' encouragement – and internal – explicable as the warriors' strategic sensibility.

The heroic perspective is put into the mouths of the Greeks: there is no glory for them if they retreat; it would be better that they died with Patroclus than give up his body to the Trojans to take back to Troy as a trophy. Likewise for the Trojans, the body becomes an objective in itself: like Troy itself, once enough blood has been spilt in the endeavour, it becomes a trophy worth dying for.

There is a felt absence: Achilles, brooding, back by his ships, waiting for news of what we know has happened. But there is a simpler pathos already present: his immortal horses stand grieving for their charioteer Patroclus and for what is to come. Achilles' death is foreshadowed in the *Iliad* only in passages like this:

> Harnessed to their beautifully ornamented chariot, they stood as still as the grave steles, their heads bowed. The hot tears poured down to the dust,

Horses

as they wept in love and loss for their charioteer, dirtying their flowing manes. Zeus saw their grief and pitied them, and said sadly: 'Unfortunate pair, why, oh why did we give you, who are ageless and deathless, to that mortal king, Achilles' father. Did we mean to yoke you to sorrow with these humans? For what is there of all the things that move and breathe on earth that is more wretched than men?'

Achilles' foreshadowed death runs through these last few books; its tragedy only hinted at in the grief of those immortals 'yoked to him', like these horses and his mother Thetis, herself tragically married to a mortal.

Zeus has taken the horses under his protection, but Hektor, proud possessor of Achilles' armour, now goes after them. He fails; as on several other occasions in the narrative, Hektor is going against the grain, against wise advice, against Zeus' plan.

The book ends with Menelaus and the two Ajaxes making a last effort to repatriate Patroclus' body, straining to get it back to the ships, while the Trojans give a great cry and charge towards them with swords and leaf shaped spears, 'as hounds in the hunt running before a pack of youths rush at a wild boar, eager to drag him down to destruction, but giving ground and scattering widely in flight, while the boar wheels among them trusting in his strength'. The fierce conflict rages like a fire that sweeps suddenly through a city, setting the houses on fire so they crumble in the intense glow, while a strong wind drives it on. They struggle forward with the corpse, like mules on a rough mountain track exerting all their strength to drag a log, to be used for a beam perhaps or a ship's timber, hearts pounding as they heave wearily, soaked in sweat. And behind them the two Ajaxes hold their ground, as a wooded ridge holds back the overflow of rivers, turning the powerful streams back over the flood plain, preventing the fierce flood breaking through.

However, the Trojans – led by Aeneas and glorious Hektor – are relentless. Like a flock of jackdaws or starlings fly, screaming in alarm, when they see a death-dealing falcon swoop towards them, so the Greek youths give up the fight, and flee with frantic cries before the pair. Many a fine weapon is lost on both sides of the Greek ditch.

Book 18

Hephaistos Forges Achilles' New Armour

Achilles, waiting in fearful anticipation, guesses even before news is brought that Patroclus is dead. Patroclus is his beloved; is his responsibility (he had assured Patroclus' father that they would both come home victorious). But he has died

Hephaistos

because Achilles refused to help their friends; he has died in Achilles' armour and in Achilles' stead. Achilles cannot cope with the loss and is overborne by rage and grief.

His grief reaches Thetis, who comes to him as she did, tragically as it has turned out, in Book 1. The favour showed him by Zeus at her request has had a terrible outcome: he is doomed if he kills Hektor, yet must wreak vengeance for his friend. He regrets, but lays aside, the wrath that caused his inaction and Patroclus' death; she laments for the best of sons, now doomed to an early death. He too is aware of the everlasting grief brought on her by his death, but he does not now seek to evade it. She offers the only comfort she can – new armour, so he can go back into battle to find the vengeance and renown that is all that his short life can now offer him.

The struggle over the body is suddenly resolved when Achilles shows himself; a sight that brings panic to the Trojans even though he is unarmed. The Greeks bring the body back, a warrior's cortège; the sun sets in a mark of the disjointedness and extremity of the death. On the Trojan side, Polydamas, as always, counsels caution and retrenchment. Hektor, antipathetic to him and his advice, is unwilling to give up the day's advances or to 'retreat to Troy's old prison' even if it means a trial of strength with Achilles. The Trojans, 'fools', applaud this worse counsel: 'Athene robbed them of their brains, to take the ill advice' (as often, a god is shown as externally influencing a course of action which is equally pictured as determined by the psychology of the individuals).

Achilles spends the night in grief-stricken reminiscence, in tending the corpse and in vowing vengeance and offerings: Hektor and twelve Trojan princes as human sacrifice.

Hephaistos the smith god agrees to forge for him divine armour to replace that which was despoiled from Patroclus, to do him honour for the rest of his short life and so that other men wonder at it when he comes to meet his fate. On the wonderful shield is depicted the cosmos, two cities and a wedding feast. Also depicted is an arbitration over a blood price – such things can be mediated in the non-military world – and the second city at war, with gods helping the defenders. Elsewhere, a pastoral scene is disturbed by an ambush, and there are agricultural scenes of ploughing and harvest and herding of cattle and sheep, with a bull the prey of lions. The last scenes, like the first, are of festivities, a dance floor with finely dressed young people, revolving in song and dance, and the Ocean encircling everything.

Thetis takes the shield with the rest of the shining armour, when it is finished,
to Achilles, who will never again see everyday, human scenes such as those depicted.

Book 18 shifts away from the battle, poised between the Zeus-endorsed Trojan dominance – Achilles' absence measured by Hektor's advance over the Greeks' defensive ditch – and the destined fall of Troy.

Achilles is brooding, turning over and bringing into the light his dark fears: to his *thumos* he asks why the Greeks are being pushed back. What has happened to Nestor's and Patroclus' plan to show Patroclus in Achilles' armour? Has he despite Achilles' warning lost his head and pursued the fighting in his own right? Has he assumed more than just the appearance of Achilles?

Nestor's son, in tears, brings him the terrible news. Achilles is overwhelmed, disintegrating in horror and grief. He rolls on the ground in paroxysms, pouring black dust over his head and tunic, tearing his hair and cheeks (like the female mourners on Greek ceramics). We get a side-glance at how loved Patroclus was by a reference to the effect on Briseis and the other war-slaves, a grief later beautifully articulated in Book 19. Achilles' companions fear for his sanity, while his cries reach his nymph mother, whose sea cave resounds with the Nereids' grief. Thetis laments, timelessly,

> 'the bitterness in this best of child-bearing, a son faultless, strong and powerful, a hero among heroes. He grew straight and tall, like a beautiful young tree and I nurtured him like the pride of the garden. I sent him to Troy but I know now he will never come home. But now he still sees the sunlight and I must go to him to try to comfort him, useless though that will be.' So saying, she left the cave with the weeping nymphs. They parted the waves till they came to the fertile land of Troy.

Thetis grieves like all mothers. But like Achilles' immortal horses in Book 17, she is not like all mothers; as Achilles says, she is immortal and must live forever with the grief, since he now has no option but to avenge Patroclus' death and bring on his own.

Achilles is racked with horror at the outcome of the request made to his mother at the start of this story of the 'wrath of Achilles'. In this book he has to redirect that anger – that passionate investment in defending a heroic identity – into a complex of emotions at the death of Patroclus. Achilles reflects on the irony of how Zeus' plan, to help the Trojans so that the Greeks recognized how much they needed Achilles, has worked out. He has lost Patroclus, to whom he was bound by ties of responsibility as well as affection:

I have lost Patroclus, whom I loved more than any of my companions; more than my life. And now you must bear the grief of losing your son, as my *thumos* does not drive me to carry on living, once I have taken vengeance on Hektor for killing Patroclus and stripping him of the immortal armour. […] I bear responsibility for his death, since I did not stand by him and take care of him, so he died far from home.

Oh, would that *eris* [discord] were ruled out of the cosmos – *eris* between men, between gods, between natural forces – along with the anger that swarms like smoke inside men's breasts, sweeter than honey-drops.

So I will go now and find Hektor and accept death whenever Zeus and the other gods decree it. Not even great Herakles escaped his doom, dear

Achilles

as he was to Zeus. I too, if a similar fate has been spun for me, will lie quiet when I am dead. But for now, let me win great glory too, and make many a Trojan woman ceaselessly lament. Do not try to stop me, though you love me; I will never be persuaded.

Thetis does the only thing she can; as a goddess, she can provide god-made armour … in which to die.

There are three scenes that come before the making of the armour, a famous passage that has inspired artists, poets and translators from Virgil to W.H. Auden and beyond. The first is the final battle over and the bringing back of Patroclus' body on the bier, accompanied by Achilles and his other companions, mourning.

The second is a Trojan assembly, panicked into meeting by the reappearance of Achilles. Polydamas, Hektor's cautious but wise brother, advocates retreat to Troy and the defence of the citadel, but Hektor, as so often, rejects this advice. He does so for two reasons. One is that expected of Hektor, that he is not to be cowed into hiding from Achilles. But the other is more double-edged: in contradistinction to Troy as the glorious citadel, a prize beyond price, Hektor talks of a real city, like Odysseus' Ithacan palace, denuded of much of its worth which has gone in rewarding and feeding Trojan allies.

Reading the *Iliad*, it is difficult to imagine the Trojan War as already in its ninth year. All the action is concentrated into the few fateful days that saw the start and consequences of the 'anger of Achilles' – signalled as the theme of this episode in the cycle of narrations about Troy, otherwise known as 'Ilium'. But the narrator can imagine and narrate a Dark Age city that has been besieged for a long time. It is that sort of city, as Ithaca is that sort of palace, that the narrator is visualizing when he puts into Hektor's mouth the argument that Troy is no longer that fabulous treasure store: 'There was a time when men spoke in wonder of Priam's city for its wealth of gold and bronze, but our fine treasures have gone and many dear possessions have been traded far and wide. If anyone is concerned with their possessions, gather them together and pool them: much better for us to use them than for the Greeks to take them.' Hektor carries the day – and the narrator condemns the Trojans as *nēpioi*, fools, for following Hektor's rather than Polydamas' advice.

In the third of these scenes, we see Achilles with his terrible 'man-killing hands' on Patroclus' chest, lamenting 'like a bearded lion whose cubs a hunter has snatched from some dense thicket. The lion returns, and grieves at their loss, then filled with ferocious anger, tracks the hunter through many a glade to find them.' He bemoans:

> How idle the promise I gave to Patroclus' father, that when I'd sacked Troy I'd bring back his glorious son, with all the spoils. But now we are both fated to stain this same earth here at Troy with our blood, both fated not to return home, but rather this soil shall cover me after you. Great-hearted Patroclus, I shall not hold your funeral rites until I return with the head of your killer and his armour, and at your pyre I will slit the throats of twelve fine sons of Troy, in rage at your killing. Till then lie here, tended by the women we enslaved when we took their rich cities; they will grieve for you, weeping night and day.

Those women, among them Briseis – Achilles' companion, of whom we hear so little – we hear later did indeed grieve for Patroclus, 'who was always kind to them'. In a moving passage, Patroclus' body is then prepared for the burial that will come when Achilles has extorted sufficient – but can there be sufficient? – vengeance: 'A large cauldron was set on blazing coals; the flames played about its bronze belly till the water boiled. Then they laid him in the bath to wash away the clotted blood and anointed him with rich oil, filling the wounds with nine-year-old ointment. Then they laid his body on the bier, shrouding it in soft linen and a white robe.'

Shield of Achilles

Thetis goes to the lame smith god Hephaistos, god of technology, to have him forge Achilles' new armour. (They have a history: when Hephaistos was thrown out of Olympus, Thetis and another daughter of Ocean caught him and hid him from Hera's anger.) Thetis is greeted by his wife, who charmingly, domestically, calls to her busy husband out in his workshop that he has a visitor, and leads Thetis inside, sitting her down on a splendid chair, elaborately adorned with silver studs, with a footstool beneath. Hephaistos stops the bellows – he has been working on twenty tripods with 'automatic' golden wheels – and wipes his forehead and massive, hirsute torso. Automata in the shape of young women, with artificial intelligence and language, support the lame god as he goes to greet his visitor and ask what she needs from him?

Thetis explains all that has happened since Agamemnon slighted Achilles and asks for new armour for her now short-lived son. Hephaistos agrees immediately, only wishing he could do more. He starts the twenty bellows and sets up crucibles to work bronze and tin, gold and silver.

The Shield of Achilles

Hephaistos forges an elaborately worked round shield: the outer band with the cosmos: sun, moon, stars, ocean. There are two cities: one at festival time where a marriage is being celebrated, with the bride being led from home in a torch-lit procession, with wedding hymns and youths circling, dancing to lyres and flutes.

Elsewhere, a market assembly has been called to settle a dispute over blood-price. Arbitrators have been appointed to settle the amount due to the victim's family; the arbitration is in full force before the elders on benches of polished stone, with the people kept in order by heralds.

Around the other city are two attacking forces, disputing among themselves whether to attack and reduce the city or, as Hektor had half-suggested as a possibility when the Greeks were gaining the upper hand, to strike a bargain with the attackers. But the citizens are determined to resist; the women, the children and the old stand on the ramparts, while the men march out. Surveying the scene are two glorious gods in full armour, double the size of the warriors. The scene unfolds – an ambush prepared by a ford, where the sheep and cattle are watered, the herdsmen watching, innocently playing on pipes. Chaos ensues as rival groups clash when the trap is sprung; there is fighting and corpses, with the figures of Discord (*Eris*), Confusion and Fate worked into the scene.

On another part of the shield, Hephaistos works a beautifully tilled field, the plough-teams turning on the headlands where refreshments are provided before the return, chasing the metal skilfully to show the lines of furrows and upcast. Elsewhere, labourers are shown reaping and binding the golden sheaves, gathered up by children. Meanwhile, in another area, a harvest festival is being prepared under an oak tree: the barbeque of a huge ox.

One season depicted is that of getting in the grapes: the wine harvest, with black grapes worked on silver stems around which 'the smith worked a field ditch of dark metal and round it a fence of tin', and a path along which young men and women come and go carrying baskets of ripe grapes, dancing along in time to a lyre song.

This is a highly wrought account, in all senses. It is full of metal-working craft details: cyanus metal for the field ditch, poles of silver, fence of tin; the way that the alternating furrows have been 'wonderfully' worked is commented on. All the arts are here, of war and also of peace – dancing, flute playing, entertainers; the song that the grape pickers dance to is not an ordinary country song but is attributed to Linus, Orpheus' fellow musician, famous for his laments. Worked on the shield are allegorical figures, and two gods look on, represented as twice human size.

Like an early classical pediment such as that at Olympia, the shield represents both discord and order: discord represented by an ambush and a town being besieged; order by the stars in the sailors' and farmers' skies by which they set their courses. Both are recognizably from the ordinary non-heroic world, the world that Achilles will now not see again: unlike the scene depicted in the 'city of peace', Achilles cannot negotiate a 'blood-price' for the death of Patroclus. The scenes on the shield represent the cosmos, the world that Achilles will never see, never be part of, again.

The lame master-smith also works in gold and tin a herd of straight-horned cattle, trotting to graze by a murmuring stream beside the swaying rushes. In the next scene, two savage lions are gripping a bellowing bull, lapping the dark blood of its wounded flank. There is a fine valley landscape with sheepfolds, huts and pens, with a flock of white sheep. Then he inlays an intricate dancing floor, like that which the master craftsman Daedalus once made in the glorious palace of Knossos. Young men, and girls worth a large dowry, are dancing: the girls wearing white linen with pretty garlands on their heads; the young men fine-woven, softly glimmering tunics, daggers of gold hanging from their silver belts. Hand-in-hand they dance, skilfully, circling a potter's wheel. A crowd enjoys the lovely scene, while two acrobats whirl in time to the dance.

Last of all, round the rim he lays out the mighty all-encircling Ocean.

This extraordinarily worked shield has challenged later poets to produce something that rivals it for beauty and significance. Alexander Pope's translation is as beautifully wrought as Homer's:

> Next ripe, in yellow gold, a vineyard shines,
> Bent with the ponderous harvest of its vines;
> A deeper dye the dangling clusters shew,
> And, curled on silver props, in order glow:
> A darker metal mixed, intrenched the place;
> And pales of glittering tin the enclosure grace.

Here is a passage by George Chapman, Shakespeare's contemporary:

> Black grew the plough with mould
> Which looked like blackish earth, though forged of gold.
> And this he did with miracle adorne.
> A mighty ox was slain, and women dressed
> Store of white cakes, and mixed the labourers' feast.
> In it besides a vine ye might behold
> Loaded with grapes, the leaves were all of gold,
> The bunches black and thick did through it grow,
> And silver props sustained them from below:
> About the vine an azure dike was wrought,
> And about it a hedge of tin he brought.

In Book 8 of the *Aeneid*, here in Dryden's translation, Virgil reworked the shield decorations to very different effect: to show *his* protagonist something he will not himself live to see, the foundation of Rome and the triumphs of Virgil's emperor Augustus' ancestors. Aeneas is delighted by the armour made for him by Vulcan, the Roman smith god:

> But most admires the shield's mysterious mould,
> And Roman triumphs rising on the gold:
> For these, embossed, the heavenly smith had wrought
> (Not in the rolls of future fate untaught)
> The wars in order, and the race divine
> Of warriors issuing from the Julian line. [...]
> These figures, on the shield divinely wrought,
> By Vulcan laboured, and by Venus brought,
> With joy and wonder fill the hero's thought.
> Unknown the names, he yet admires the grace,
> And bears aloft the fame and fortune of his race.

When the large heavy shield was done, Hephaistos makes a shining, flaming breastplate, a fine helmet richly decorated with a crest of gold and greaves of flexible tin. The lame god takes the finished armour to Thetis, who flies off with Hephaistos' flashing gift.

Book 19

This Time it's Personal: Achilles Re-enters the Battle

Achilles, terrifying and radiant with passion, takes and delights in the armour. He gives Patroclus' body treatment suited to a hero and gathers his forces; he publicly remits his anger against Agamemnon and sorrows for all the dead who have fallen because of their strife. Agamemnon publicly acknowledges that he was in the wrong but he sees his actions as forced on him by fate. However, he acknowledges that it is for him to make amends, as proposed before by the envoys in Book 9. This time Achilles does not spurn them; they are for Agamemnon to give or not, as he thinks fit, but the important task now is to get back to the fighting.

Achilles vows not to eat or drink until he has avenged Patroclus; he cannot attend to such things until he has discharged the fury in his heart. Pragmatic Odysseus advises that Achilles' mind should be set at rest by an oath sworn by Agamemnon that he has not touched Briseis, and that the troops should eat first.

Achilles

After all, many men die; the best thing is to bury them, mourn them and then eat and drink to have strength to carry on fighting. Achilles is subverting the wise order of things. After a sacrifice, the council ends with Achilles musing on the delusions that led to his anger and conflict with Agamemnon, and whether it was Zeus' plan to bring destruction on many Greeks.

Briseis, brought back by the Myrmidons, is overcome with weeping to see the body of Patroclus. She remembers his unfailing kindness, from the day when Achilles captured her, having killed her husband and three brothers, and his promise that Achilles would heal the wound he had made by marrying her and that he, Patroclus, would preside over their wedding feast. The women around share her laments; overtly for Patroclus but each also for herself. Achilles' mind turns to his own griefs, thinking of the past and of his father and his son, Neoptolemus, who will not see him again. Athene takes pity on him and instils nectar to keep him from fainting.

Armed with his new armour, he goes out to his horses and exhorts them to look after him better than they did Patroclus – to bring him safely from the battlefield. One horse answers, in human speech, to absolve themselves from blame for his death which is now shortly to come.

Thetis arrives to find Achilles lying weeping on Patroclus' chest. She offers him the new armour, which fires up his anger as well as his grief. Thetis advises him to unsay his rage against Agamemnon, which he does easily – he no longer cares about some insult, just vengeance. As for Briseis, precious though she seems to him in other parts of the epic, here he clings to the thought that it would have been better for all of them if she had been killed in the assault on her town, rather than be enslaved to be the cause of all this dissension. Nevertheless, that's now all past; he accepts that he must, however difficult, conquer his rage.

Achilles having formally 'unsaid his anger', Agamemnon unsays not so much his actions but his responsibility for them. It was *Atē* – attacking madness – and Zeus, Fate and the spirits of vengeance, the Furies, whom he blames instead.

In a wonderful-terrible digression, he tells the story of the duping of Zeus by Hera: how on the day Herakles was due to be born, she made Zeus swear that the child of his blood to be born that day would be lord of all he surveyed. Then she flashed to bring forward the labour of seven-month-pregnant Eurystheus' mother while halting the labour of Herakles' mother. When she tells Zeus that the great man that day born is Eurystheus rather than Herakles, Zeus, incensed, swung the goddess *Atē* by the hair and cast her out of Olympus, which is why she roams the earth to deceive mortals – like Agamemnon. 'It's not my fault, honest…'

Agamemnon now offers the same full compensation as before. Achilles accepts this in a few words but says it is time for fighting. Odysseus, ever practical, says no matter how much joy in fighting the troops have, they need food and water to sustain them. Achilles, equally typically, says he has too much passionate aggression to eat.

The compensation is delivered: tripods, cauldrons, horses, huge amounts of gold and ... women: seven skilled house-slaves and Briseis herself, whom Agamemnon has sworn is untouched.

We then get an illuminating and rare insight into one of those women: Briseis, at the centre of the story that started in Book 1 and will not end until Book 24. Briseis, as lovely as the goddess of love, Aphrodite, beats her breast and tears her hair, her soft throat and beautiful face when she sees Patroclus' grievous wounds. This peerless woman laments over the body:

Briseis

> Patroclus, dearest to my poor heart, when I left this hut you were alive, and now when I return, I find you, prince of men, a corpse. So, how I am dogged by evil. I saw the husband to whom I was married by my royal parents hacked to death by our city wall; my three beloved brothers met a like fate. But when Achilles killed my husband and sacked my city, you dried my tears. You would not let me grieve; you said you would see me properly married to Achilles in a great wedding feast back home with his Myrmidons. You were always gentle with me, now I will mourn you forever.

Then comes an important sentence; the other women lament with her, grieving together for Patroclus but also each for her own situation. That is what lament can do: express deeply felt common grief but also allow expression of particular sorrows.

Meanwhile, Achilles continues to refuse food, thinking of Patroclus and imagining a different future:

> How often, my beloved friend, you would swiftly and deftly lay out a tasty meal for us in our hut before we went out to fight. Now you lie here mangled, while I am too full of grief to eat. What worse could I suffer? News of my father's death? But he is alive and no doubt sheds tears for his son away in a strange land, battling for the cursed Helen. Or news of the

death of my dear son Neoptolemos, growing up far away? I liked to think that I alone would die here and you would be the one to return with my son to Phthia, and show him all his inheritance: my goods, my slaves, my great high-roofed halls. For I imagined that my father would by then be either dead or too weak to rule, weighed down by enfeebling old age, and the pain of waiting for news of my death.

Around him the older men lament, again grieving for Patroclus but each remembering those they had left behind them.

Filled with new energy – the narrator says that Athene instilled nectar into his nostrils – Achilles dresses in his new armour: the greaves with silver fastenings, the corselet, the bronze sword and finally the great shield, which shines like a homestead fire acting like a beacon to sailors blown off course – a light of safety. Finally, he mounts the chariot drawn by his immortal horses; one of whom speaks to him, predicting his death, not on this day but in the near future.

Book 20

Achilles Rages

The return of Achilles compels the attention of even the gods – Zeus calls an assembly to revoke his decree of non-interference, a formal mirroring of the assembly of the Greeks in Book 19. He fears that Achilles will go beyond fate and storm Troy, and so allows the gods free rein to favour whichever side they wish: Hera, Athene, Poseidon, Hermes and Hephaistos support the Greeks, and Ares, Apollo, Artemis and Aphrodite the Trojans. His plan seems now to have been fulfilled.

Achilles' first major encounter is with Aeneas, whom he taunts with being marginalized by king Priam and with the reminder of a previous encounter when the gods saved him. Aeneas replies that he is well

Achilles

able to exchange insults, like a child or a fishwife, but now is the time for action, not taunts. Achilles' five-fold shield protects him from a deadly thrust. Poseidon intervenes, perceiving that Aeneas, given false confidence by Apollo's words, will lose the encounter, and saves Aeneas for his destined end: to be the progenitor of a mighty (Roman) race who will dominate Troy in generations to come. Achilles is disgusted to find his foe evaporate.

Apollo warns Hektor not to confront Achilles, but when Achilles cuts down his latest victim, Polydorus – an 'exquisite runner', Hektor's youngest brother and Priam's favourite – he can bear it no longer and goes for him. Hektor, like Aeneas, replies shortly to Achilles' taunts and throws his spear. Three times Athene blows it away from Achilles and turns it back to Hektor's feet. Three times Achilles' deadly charge is lost in the mist with which Apollo surrounds Hektor; after the fourth, Achilles turns to slaughter lesser men.

Like inhuman fire, Achilles sweeps everywhere with his spear, refusing pleas for mercy: as oxen crush corn on the threshing floor, so Achilles tramples dead men.

Achilles' return to the battlefield brings fateful encounters with Trojans old and young alike, as might be expected from the return to battle of the 'best of the Greeks'. But everything is different now: rather than a scene of Greeks v Trojans for possession of Helen, the battlefield is the set of 'the Tragedy of Achilles'.

It starts with a meeting of the gods. Poseidon asks the question and Zeus gives the answer that everyone wants to hear: what happens now, when all bets are off, all issues off the table apart from Achilles. Zeus presides and speaks with the close engagement but external viewpoint of a theatre director giving notes:

> You know, Earth-Shaker, that I am closely concerned with both Greeks and Trojans and keep them in my mind while I see them as they fight and die. I will stay here on Olympus, satisfying my mind as I watch events unfold, while you may all without restriction go and aid any warrior as you wish, though if the Trojans have to face Achilles alone they will not last long! Even before, no-one could stand up to him, and now that his warrior heart is filled with rage at the death of his friend, I am concerned that he may evade his fate and take Troy citadel.

The gods, who for much of the epic have been under the constraint of Zeus' plan – or perhaps better, his understanding of what must come – now scatter, 'divided in their passionate hearts' (*thumos*). Hera heads for the Greek ships with Pallas Athene, Poseidon the circler of the earth, Hermes with the mind of quicksilver and the lame god Hephaistos with his powerful torso, moving nimbly despite his withered legs. Meanwhile, Ares, the god of war with gleaming helmet, takes the Trojan side, with Apollo of the flowing locks, Artemis the archer and Leto, their mother, the Trojan River Xanthus and laughter-loving Aphrodite.

This detailed description is followed by a second jewelled scene.

Zeus, the Father of gods and men, thundered ominously from on high, while down below Poseidon, lord of storm and earthquake, caused the wide earth and the tallest mountain peaks to quake. Mount Ida the sacred was shaken from foot to peak and both the city of Troy and the Greek camp shook. As battle was joined, so great was the din that even Hades rose in terror from his underworld, in fear that Poseidon

Zeus

might split the earth and open up his dark halls to gods and men.

It is god against god, but Achilles' only focus is on finding Patroclus' killer, Hektor. Yet when battle is joined, even Achilles cannot choose this single epic duel: he comes up against the other pre-eminent Trojan fighter, Aeneas, son of Aphrodite. Though up to now Aeneas has made only a minor entry in the epic, fighting Diomedes and being rescued by his goddess mother in Book 5 (a parallel but very different rescue from

Poseidon

that contemplated by Zeus for his son Sarpedon in Book 16, which elicited a moving and rare appreciation of the human condition by the immortals). The incident is somewhat comic; Aphrodite, after rescuing her son, dropped him when Diomedes scratched her hand, and she went running to her mother to be bathed better, while Apollo caught Aeneas up, setting a phantom in his place while he restored his full fighting strength. But here the contact is deadly serious: in some ways, Aeneas is a precursor and almost stand-in for Hektor, whom Achilles is making for, full of rage, 'like a lion, one that the whole village comes together to kill, which at first passes by but when struck by a spear rouses up roaring and attacks with foaming mouth, glaring eyes and lashing tail'.

This is Achilles in his fury, his fighting strength roused to attack brave Aeneas. He challenges him, asking why he has put himself forward against the 'best of the Greeks'; does he hope to put himself up as heir to Priam's throne? He is frankly sceptical about Aeneas' courage, recalling sneeringly a previous meeting when he ran away down the slopes of Mount Ida.

'I don't remember you once looking back! You fled to Lyrnessus, which I then sacked: I led away the women to slavery, though you were saved by Zeus and the other gods. Yet I don't think they'll save you today: go back to your men! Even a fool can learn from the past.'

Aeneas retorted, 'I am no child to be scared off by words. We know each other's lineage and parents and their fame. You are the son of Peleus and long-haired Thetis, the sea nymph, while I boast brave Anchises for my father and Aphrodite as my mother. One or other shall mourn a dear son this day, for before we leave the field we will exchange more than childish taunts.'

But there is more to be said by this minor Trojan figure – on whom an imperial legend is to be built in Virgil's *Aeneid*:

> My lineage: Zeus the cloud-gatherer's son Dardanus founded the ancient kingdom of Dardania, long before sacred Troy was built on the plain. Dardanus' son was Erichthonius, the wealthiest king on earth, with three thousand brood mares and their foals grazing his meadows. The North Wind took on the form of a black-maned stallion to cover them, and twelve foals were born that could race over ears of corn or over the breaking sea waves without touching their tops. The next king had three peerless sons including Ganymede, so beautiful he became Zeus' cupbearer. And in due course, Anchises begat me as Priam begat Hektor. But, that is enough – we could stand here exchanging insults all day, like fishwives. But we are here for deeds not words, the battlefield not the playground. Time to try our bronze-tipped spears.

The initial exchanges are epic: Aeneas lifts a stone such as two men nowadays would not be able to raise; Achilles raises his spear and Poseidon intervenes. This whole encounter is framed as fateful, a matter that looks back to the founding of the kingdom and forward to the future of the race, 'for Aeneas is destined to live on, so that Dardanus' race might survive, Dardanus whom Zeus

Aeneas supported by his mother Aphrodite

loved above all his children by mortal women: great Aeneas will replace Priam as the Trojan lord, as his descendants will lord it over them in time to come'.

Given that this line, linking Augustus with the goddess Aphrodite (Venus) and the Julian-Claudian dynasty with the ancient Dardanian line, is the project of Virgil's *Aeneid*, there has been speculation that this section, with perhaps others, is part of a different cycle that survived in a longer form to inspire Virgil.

The seriousness of the situation is somewhat lightened by a final view of Aeneas, wafted away to the edge of the battle, and Achilles shaking his head looking at nothing when an instant before he was in deadly combat: 'A wonder indeed! Here is my spear lying on the ground, but where is the man I launched it at? I thought his claims were empty boasts, but the gods must love this Aeneas.'

The encounter between Hektor and Achilles is deferred while both strain towards each other like dogs on a leash. Achilles is full of battle fury and kills those who come in his way. One is Priam's beloved youngest son, Polydoros:

> His father had forbidden him to fight, being his youngest and dearest son. He was a champion athlete but like a fool [*nēpios*] showed off his running along the front line, where swift-footed Achilles caught him with a cast of his spear as he shot past. He slumped to his knees with a groan, clutching his stomach as darkness overwhelmed him.

When Hektor sees his youngest brother die he can contain himself no longer and makes for Achilles, who is delighted at the oncoming encounter. But again the gods, or the chances of battle, defer the fateful meeting as the book ends:

> Achilles raged everywhere like a forest fire racing through the deeply-wooded gullies on a dry mountain-side, its swirling flames fanned by the wind through the dense wood. With the force of a god he beat down those he killed, till the black earth ran with blood. His horses trampled corpses and shields alike, as grain is swiftly trampled on a stone threshing floor under the hooves of the bellowing oxen. The axle and the wheel-rim of his chariot were black with gore as Achilles pressed on, his invincible arms splattered with gore.

Book 21

Achilles is Remorseless: Suppliants and Victims

Achilles the Slayer

Achilles chases the Trojans up to the River Scamander and pollutes the water
with blood. He captures twelve young princes for later sacrifice, gathers them up
like startled fawns, bound, and resumes his killing.

*   A young man – Priam's young son, Lykaon – is unable to escape Achilles. His*
recent history is recounted in the same way as many previous young victims,

serving both to give a sense of reality and potential to the life that is going to be cut short, and as a memorial of that life. But the biography this time is relevant: he had been captured before by Achilles, who accepted ransom for him, and he is therefore protected from harm at Achilles' hands by the sacred obligation of host to protect the guest from harm. Achilles is bemused to see in the river the youth he had consigned either to the sea or to a land far away; Lykaon is terrified. He runs under Achilles' spear thrust to grab his knees in supplication: the ritual gesture of submission that should be respected. He pleads for respect for his position and for the bond conferred by the ransom, for pity for his mother whose other son Achilles has just slain, and for mercy.

But Achilles is without mercy. No longer is he prepared to ransom or spare Trojans, especially not a son of Priam's: 'Time to die, my friend. Why do you grieve? Patroclus died, a far better man. Even I will come to my fate.' Lykaon stops trying to ward off the inevitable, and Achilles kills him and tosses him into the river with a dreadful taunt: 'Go, feed fat the fish; your mother will grieve but will have no body to lament.'

This butchery offends the divine river, choked with corpses. Achilles will move the site of his killing, but it will not stop until he or Hektor have the mastery .

Like something more than mortal, Achilles sweeps down on more Trojans, while the river calls to Apollo and his fellow river to bury him and his arms, his renown lost forever in their depths. Achilles fights on, carried along by the billowing, debris-filled flood. Hera intervenes by sending Hephaistos to burn up the river. Scamander, his waters seething, gives up his supernatural battle with Achilles. Hephaistos is called off by Hera.

Athene and Ares, still feeling quarrelsome, fight childishly among themselves. Ares (god of war!) is worsted and has to be comforted by Aphrodite. Hera now sets Athene on and smiles to see how Athene pushes the goddess of love in the chest, sending her flying on top of Ares. Poseidon exhorts Apollo to join in the rough and tumble, but Apollo refuses to fight over 'wretched men that flourish for a time like leaves'. The reader, stopped short in the middle of laughing at the gods, is reminded of the human condition and of why Achilles, like Glaukos in Book 6, risks everything for his renown.

Artemis calls her brother, Apollo, a coward, while Hera calls her a shameless hussy and boxes her ears, which sends her crying and telling tales to her father, Zeus.

Away from this playground scrapping, the not-so-wretched Achilles, 'glory being the goad that pricked his fury', carries on killing Trojans as they flee to Troy. Priam orders the gates to be opened for them and Apollo goes to their aid.

Agenor is sent to hold up Achilles, and when he sees him, he debates whether there is any escape route. He concludes that there is none, and that his only chance is to fight, as Achilles is, after all, mortal. He challenges him, calling Achilles a 'fool' to hope to take Troy before it is destined. Agenor succeeds in hitting him, but is spirited away before a return blow. Apollo, in Agenor's form, distracts Achilles, leading him up hill and down dale, while the Trojans get safely into the city.

Book 21 continues setting the scene for the imminent, fateful meeting of Achilles and Hektor in a tragic landscape involving gods of the air, sea and underworld, as well as the river-god of the Trojan river, Scamander, that runs between the citadel and the Greek camp.

It starts as Achilles drives the Trojans to a ford in the Scamander, half of them fleeing towards the city, confused by a Hera-generated thick fog, and the rest forced into the silvery currents of the river, splashing and floundering through the whirling water.

Leaving his spear in the tamarisk bushes, Achilles wades in. Just like a swarm of locusts fleeing before a raging fire fly to a river and swarm in the shallows, so the resounding pools of the swirling Scamander are filled with a horrid confusion of men and horses attacked by a demonic, sword-wielding Achilles. Hideous groans rise from the dying men, the river water red with their blood, as they hide under the banks like swarms of fish fleeing the gaping jaws of a huge dolphin.

The next scene is brief and horrid, Achilles dragging twelve youths alive from the water as a blood-price for Patroclus. He drives them like dazed fawns to the bank, ties their hands behind them with strips of their own fine tunics and has his men take them to the ships. Their quasi ritual killings will come later.

In the previous book, a young Trojan called Tros supplicated Achilles – kneeling in a way that made him vulnerable to a downward stab through his vital organs. A suppliant is protected and has a claim on the aggressor's mercy, but Tros should have known better than to beg to be spared; while he was trying to perform the supplication, Achilles stabbed down with the sword, the dark blood drenching his body and darkness covering him. Now, Achilles comes across another young Trojan prince, Lykaon. This is a second meeting: Achilles had taken him in a night raid some time before, 'where he had been trimming the young shoots from a wild fig tree with his keen knife to make chariot rails', and had ransomed him. Like Tros, Lykaon makes a formal supplication, stooping beneath the spear shaft and clasping the warrior's knees:

You remember me, I have eaten your bread after you captured and ransomed me, to sell me in sacred Lemnos for the price of a hundred oxen. Then I was ransomed, for three times as much, and now only a few days ago I return, only to find myself in your hands.

He boyishly and tactlessly – given the vengeful killing machine he is facing – adds that not only has he a claim on Achilles as a former guest, therefore protected by bonds of *xenia*, but that his mother was different from Hektor's and therefore he is only half-brother to the man who killed his friend.

Achilles responds mockingly: 'Wonder of wonders! Trojans I've killed come back to haunt me! Maybe I'll kill this one just to see if the underworld can hold onto him!'

Many times the narrator calls someone *nēpios*, fool – as indeed Tros was called. It means literally 'infant', and in the *Iliad* is used to shout out not at stupidity but at naivety. Achilles addresses Lykaon with the same word: 'Fool, do not talk to me of ransom, make me no speeches!' But this is more detailed, more reflective, perhaps more tragic:

> Before the day of destiny came on Patroclus, I had a mind to spare you Trojans. Many I took alive, selling them far away. But now not one shall keep his life, least of all Priam's sons. So, you too, my friend, must die: why so sad? Patroclus, a far better man than you, has died. And look at me, how big and fine I am; my father is a great man, my mother is a goddess. Yet death and remorseless fate hang over me too: at sunrise, evening or high noon, some man in battle will strike me with his spear, or pierce me with an arrow.

Lykaon gives up hope. Achilles kills him and lobs his body into the river, all his venom now surging out:

> Lie with the fish: they will suck the blood from your wounds. Your mother will have no body to lay out, but swirling Scamander will wash you down to the deep sea. The fish will dart among the waves, eating the white flesh. Death to all Trojans, whom I will chase up to the city. You will all die, till you have paid the full price for Patroclus and all the Greeks killed by the swift ships, while I was away from the fight.

Achilles carries on the killing until the river rises up in anger, complaining that his lovely waters are being choked with corpses. Bellowing like a bull, the river sweeps up the host of dead that are choking his river-bed and hurls them on the bank, but the living he protects with his dark waters, hiding them among the wide deep pools. He rouses a raging current against Achilles, beating him back so he could hardly stand. Achilles grabs at a fine tall elm, but it tears away at the roots, pulling down the bank and collapsing into the flood, sinking deep and damming the whole river.

He runs with the speed of a black eagle, but the river in spate chases him, determined to reduce him 'with all his strength and beauty to bones covered by sand and rubble, deprived of a Greek funeral mound'. Achilles cries out to the gods to preserve him for his destined end, near Troy – like a hero with a destiny – not to drown in the river's waters 'like a swineherd swept away when crossing a swollen river'. Poseidon responds that with Zeus' consent, he and Athene will intervene 'as it is not your destiny to be killed by a river'.

The gods raise the winds to help and Hephaistos finally dominates the waters with divine fire, burning first the corpses 'as when the autumn gale suddenly dries a newly prepared orchard, delighting the man who tends it', and then devastating with 'more than human fire' the riverbank trees and bushes, distressing the eels and fish who leap out of the water. The river boils 'like a cauldron over a great fire, built up of layered sticks, melting down the pig fat'. The river god gives up the fight against Hephaistos and allows 'brilliant Achilles' to resume his destined way.

The stage on which the final scene is to be played out has been set up and cleared for action as one involving gods and the land's natural forces.

But things on Olympus are different, where, bathetically, squabbles break out between helmeted Athene and the god of war, Ares, who has to be led away groaning by the goddess of love! Not to be beaten, Athene 'caught up with them and landed such a blow beneath Aphrodite's breasts that both sprawled on the ground', delighting Hera. Meanwhile, Poseidon decides to get involved, bringing up an ancient grudge against Priam's father, a story from a different age, and is incensed that Apollo is now helping the Trojans.

Apollo answers him in the lofty, distanced and disinterested tone of an immortal: 'You would call me bird witted if I fought with you for the sake of these wretched mortals, now full of life, eating the earth's fruit, now fading away and falling like the leaves. Let us cease arguing now, let them fight their own battles.' Or, in Pope's fine translation:

> To combat for mankind
> Ill suits the wisdom of celestial mind;
> For what is man? Calamitous by birth,
> They owe their life and nourishment to earth;
> Like yearly leaves, that now, with beauty crowned,
> Smile on the sun; now, wither on the ground.
> To their own hands commit the frantic scene,
> Nor mix immortals in a cause so mean.

This is a dark version of Puck's observation in *A Midsummer's Night Dream*, 'Lord, what fools these mortals be.'

The rest of the book similarly hovers between the mortals caught in the tragedy of the human condition and immortals in a comedy. Apollo may be disinterested, but Artemis is incensed: 'Are you just going off, letting Poseidon win without a battle? What is the point of carrying a bow if it is as about as useful as the wind? Do not dare to boast again that you would fight Poseidon hand to hand.' Then Hera wades in, calling Artemis a shameless baggage and recommending she go off and play at being a hunter in the wild rather than fight her superior; she then boxes her ears! Artemis runs to Daddy (Zeus), who hugs her, asking who had been nasty to her. With the ineffable simplicity of immortals for whom issues are ephemeral – flaring up and dying down within the day – the gods reassemble on Olympus.

After this interlude, the scene shifts back to Achilles, and to Priam's view of his onslaught looming large in his vision. The elderly king orders that the gates be opened to allow the Trojans to flee back to safety.

Achilles' advance is halted by a brave Trojan, Agenor, who faces, and voices, the same doubt that Hektor will express when he opposes Achilles:

Alas, if I fled before him like a coward, along with all the rest, he would simply overtake me and kill me. I could leave these men to be chased before him, and run until I reach the foothills and gullies of the mountain. I could, then, hide there in the woods. Then I could wash the sweat off in the river and return calmly to Troy after the day's fighting. But why even dream of that? He would see me turn to run and he is faster than me; he would certainly kill me. There's nothing for it then but to face him here. After all, he is mortal – made of flesh that can be pierced – and only has one life, even if Zeus grants him brief glory.

But this ends differently: Agenor turns to challenge him, a standard challenge but now freighted with the tragic meaning of what is to come:

No doubt you hoped to sack the proud city of Troy this very day: little fool! There are many ills still to come for you Greeks from trying to take it. There are many strong and brave fighters to guard her, to safeguard our elders, wives and children. It is you who will meet your doom here, bold and impressive as you are.

His spear rebounds from Achilles' divine armour, but Apollo prevents further action by sweeping Agenor off the battlefield. The Trojans then stream into the city.

Book 22

The Final Battle: Achilles v Hektor

Achilles v Hektor

Book 22 brings the combat-to-the-death between the pre-eminent fighters on either side, a resolution set up yet frustrated by the aborted duels in Book 3 and 7. The combat is between Achilles – the most single-minded and best fighter, caring only for his honour – for the Greeks, and Hektor, the bulwark of Troy. The events of the Iliad have, however, complicated and undermined the two heroes' standing – Hektor, by his rash, ill-tempered decision, has endangered many Trojans; Achilles, by standing on his honour and refusing Agamemnon's reparation, has allowed many friends and Patroclus to go to their deaths. A sense of personal tragedy pervades the confrontation. Hektor, who cares only for his honour as a hero and protector of his family and Troy, has made a fatal misjudgment, has exposed himself to their censure, while Achilles, who cares only for his own personal honour and his own men, has compromised both by his intransigence. Hektor, previously spurred on by the consciousness of those watching from the walls of Troy, is now shackled by it. Achilles, who declared that he cared nothing for the aims of the war but only for his integrity and heroic name, has become an inhuman, vengeful force.

Gods and Hektor's dependants look down on him, as he decides to stand his ground rather than retreat through the closing gates: he waits like a venom-filled snake guarding her lair. But when Achilles attacks him, his courage fails and he runs.

There can only be one end.

Zeus debates whether to intervene, as when he saw Sarpedon going to his death. Athene's reply is the same as Hera's was then: 'Alter Fate? Do it then, but all the rest of us gods will not approve.' Zeus retracts, and Athene flies down. Hektor runs as if in a nightmare, not able to outpace his pursuer, Achilles, keeping between him and the gates. Three times they circuit the walls, while Achilles prevents Greeks from interfering, lest they detract from his full glory. On the fourth lap, Zeus sets their 'two fates of bitter death' into his golden scales, and Hektor's is the heavier. Apollo forsakes Hektor; Athene goes to him, disguised as his brother come to help, and they turn to face Achilles.

Hektor tries to reach an agreement that the winner will not defile the loser's body, but will return it respectfully. Achilles rejects these normal terms, saying that no conditions can be laid down between them, any more than between predator and prey. Hektor should look to his hunger for slaughter: Athene will ensure that he pays with his life for the friends he killed.

Achilles casts his spear and misses. Hektor seizes on this sign that Achilles is not after all an instrument of the gods, and taunts him. He throws his spear, which also misses, and turns to his brother, the so-called 'Deiphobus', for a replacement. But he sees that he is alone, and knows that the gods have cheated him and condemned him. There is no way out. But he can at least die nobly. He draws his sword and swoops like an eagle.

Hektor is protected by the armour he stripped from Patroclus; only the neck is vulnerable; Achilles strikes and Hektor drops to the dust.

Achilles, implacable, refuses to countenance the humane request of returning his body for burial. Rather, he talks of eating him raw. He repeats his refusal to ransom his body to his parents so that they can lament properly; instead, he will deface his corpse. Hektor's dying words prophesy Achilles' imminent death; Achilles replies that he will bear his fate.

He strips the armour, and the Greeks, rushing to see the naked body of their main enemy, comment on its softness as they repeatedly spear it.

Achilles remembers Patroclus. He sends the young men back to sing of their triumph and the imminent downfall of Troy. He devises a terrible, undignified treatment for the corpse: dragging it by pierced ankles behind his chariot round the walls, to the distress of Hektor's mother and father. In anguish, they lament;

Priam desperate to beg the body from Achilles, Hecuba foreseeing her life of suffering. But Andromache, who mourned him while he was still alive, does not know of his death. She is preparing a bath for his return when she hears the cries. Seeing how he is being treated, she faints and her wedding crown falls from her head. When she recovers, she laments for herself and bewails the harsh treatment her fatherless son will experience (a harshness that the Greeks will ensure that Astyanax will not live long enough to feel).

The book starts where we left the Trojans running back into the city like startled fawns, though 'Hektor stood shackled by his fate'.

Apollo, who had disguised himself as Agenor, now reveals himself, to Achilles' rage at being baulked of his prey and what he sees to be his imminent victory over the Trojans. Apollo has interfered in his glorious victory; as a god, he does not fear reprisals. As always, the immortals are free of responsibility and the consequences of their actions.

Priam sees Achilles approach like a shooting star, light streaming from his bronze armour, and begs Hektor not to go to meet Achilles and his doom:

> If he were not protected by the gods, he would already be dead, and my heart would be a little lighter, freed, a little, of my grief for the fine sons he has robbed me of, including perhaps Polydorus and Lykaon who have gone missing today. But great though the grief for them would be, it is as nothing compared to what losing you would mean. Come inside, save the Trojans and don't let yourself be Achilles' prize, by dying giving him his triumph.
>
> And think about me, have pity on me, wretched that I am, for whom it seems Father Zeus reserves a dreadful fate. After so many sorrows, on the threshold of old age, am I to see my sons slaughtered, my daughters dishonoured, their children hurled aside in anger, my son's wives dragged away, my treasures fallen into savage Greek hands? I can foresee a terrible, shameful end, killed by some sharp spear; the flesh-eating dogs will tear my corpse apart, those very dogs I fed from my table.
>
> It is fine for a young man, killed in battle, to lie there with his wounds on display: dead though he is, it's an honourable sight. But an old man's naked corpse, his genitals exposed, his grey hairs soiled by the dogs, is the most pitiful thing possible.

With that, the old man tears his hair and his clothes, but Hektor is unmoved. Then his mother pleads with him, baring her breasts in supplication that he not face the terrible Achilles, 'for if he kills you, I will not be able to lay out your corpse on a bier and lament, dear child of my body. Nor will your wife be there; she'll be a slave, far away.'

Neither plea is effective, but we have a clear sense of Hektor's state of mind as he goes out to face Achilles. First, the narrator shows him full of fighting courage and battle strength. He waits for Achilles 'as a snake coiled writhing in its lair in the hills, full of venom from the mountain herbs, sets a fixed stare on an approaching walker'. The scene is starting to be set: Hektor standing firm, keeping his unquenched fury within, grounding his shield against the jutting bastion.

But internally, the picture is different:

> Perturbed, he spoke to his great hearted soul: 'Alas, if I retreat through the gate to the safety of the wall, Polydamas will be quick to reproach me: after all he advised me to retreat into the city the night that Achilles re-appeared. And I refused, though it would have been better! Now, if I've brought the Trojans to the brink through my stupidity, I can't bear the shame of hearing some insignificant Trojan, or his wife, say: "Hektor has brought ruin on the Trojans, only concerned with his own fighting strength."'

Consequently, the only option is to meet Achilles face-to-face, and either kill him and return safe to the city, or die gloriously beneath its walls:

> I suppose I could ditch my shield and helmet, lean my spear on the wall, and offer terms: to return Helen, her treasure and all that Paris brought to Troy, the start of it all. I could also offer to divide all the remaining treasure in the city. [...] But what's the point of thinking like that? I'll not approach him like a suppliant only to have him show neither mercy nor respect, killing me without a second thought, stripped of my armour, defenceless as a woman. This is no boy and girl affair – meeting by oak or rock! No, better to meet him in bloody combat, and see who Zeus gives the glory!

This dialogue with the self, with the passionate *thumos*, reads like a sequence, a stream of consciousness. It is as richly reflective as a Shakespearean monologue.

Then we go back to the battlefield, the scene of the destined meeting of Hektor and Achilles. As Hektor stands there thinking, Achilles looms up, the plumes of his helmet nodding, his mighty spear poised to strike, his bronze armour blazing like fire or the rising sun. Hektor is shocked into flight, pursued by Achilles like a hawk, the swiftest of birds, swooping on a timid dove, darting towards her with fierce cries as she flees, eager to seize her. So Achilles runs and Hektor flees as fast as he can in panic. He runs past the lookout point, the wind-swept wild fig tree, along the cart-track until they come to 'two lovely springs, the source of the River Scamander. One spring is warm, steam rising like smoke from a fire; the other is icy cold, even in summer. Nearby are the fine wide stone washing troughs, where once the wives and daughters of the Trojans washed their gleaming clothes.'

As in the funeral games to honour some dead hero, fine racehorses sweep round the turning-post, competing for the prize of a fine tripod or a woman, so these two warriors run three times round the city of Troy, while the gods look on. But this is no race for the prize of a bull's hide or a sacrificial ox; they run instead for the life of horse-taming Hektor.

The scene switches to Olympus, where the gods look down on this fatal scene. As before, with Sarpedon or Aeneas, when the gods become implicated in the human lives down below ('Hektor who burned many sacrifices to me'), they ask whether to interfere; as before, the ritual answer from Athene is, 'Do you wish to bring back a man, long since doomed to die, from ill-sounding death? Do it then, but the rest of the gods will not approve.' But this time Zeus distances himself, remarkably, from any binding words: 'Take heart, dear daughter, I am well disposed to you; I did not speak with my full binding purpose. Do what your heart dictates, I will not interfere.'

This strange, fateful scene is doubly dramatized, with Achilles chasing Hektor, signalling to his men that this is his kill, heading him off whenever he gets near the safety of the citadel. Like a nightmare, they run three times round the walls, and then on the fourth, the gods involve themselves:

> Then Zeus raised his golden scales and set the deaths of Achilles and horse-taming Hektor in the balance; Hektor's lot dipped down to Hades, Phoebus Apollo left his side, while grey-eyed Athene came to Achilles and spoke winged words: 'Shining Achilles, so dear to Zeus, now you and I will kill Hektor and bring the Greeks great glory; I will go and get him to turn to face you.'

Achilles

While Athene's encouragement of Achilles serves to underline his superiority, it is difficult not to feel that the gods are behaving maliciously to Hektor, to whom Athene appears as his brother Deiphobus: 'Dear brother, fleet-footed Achilles pressed you strongly there, chasing you round the city at such speed, but let us make a stand here together.' Hektor is achingly, tragically grateful to his supposed brother, risking all coming out from the safety of the fortified city to fight and die with Hektor.

But having duped Hektor into turning to face Achilles, the tragedy is played out as a human rather than an immortal scene: Hektor halts himself as well as being halted by Athene. His panic ceases, and he turns to face Achilles, his destined opponent, the greatest of the Greeks like he is the greatest of the Trojans:

> 'I am no longer afraid, Achilles: my passionate spirit now tells me to stand and face you, to kill or be killed. But come let us swear an oath before the gods; if Zeus lets me kill you, when I have stripped you of your glorious armour, I will not mistreat your body but will return it to your people, if you will do the same for me.'
>
> Fleet-footed Achilles with piercing glare replied: 'You're mad, Hektor, to chatter about covenants and oaths. Lions and men make no compacts; wolves and lambs don't make agreements but are forever at war. You and I are beyond oaths: there will be no settlement till one or the other dies and satisfies the god of war with his blood.
>
> Now summon up all your courage, all your warrior strength: there is no escape from me, and soon Athene will bring you down with my spear. You will pay the price for all my grief, for all my friends you have slaughtered.'

Hektor, so often shown to be misguided or hasty, is made to suffer one last indignity. At this moment – having survived the first exchange of spears – when he has drawn up all his strength, his selfhood, Athene returns to Achilles the spear Hektor vaunts he had successfully avoided, while the goddess-as-Deiphobus vanishes when called on to provide Hektor with a second weapon. Hektor realizes that his end is now near: 'The gods have called me to my death; there is no escape. Zeus and Apollo decided this long ago, they who were once eager to defend me. But I will not die without a fight, without glory, without some deed that men as yet unborn may hear.' Hektor swoops with his bright blade, like a high-soaring eagle that stoops to earth from the dark clouds to seize a sick lamb or a shivering

Hektor

hare. Achilles attacks with savage power, with Hephaistos' skilfully worked shield and gleaming helmet crested with golden plumes. His sharp spear gleams, bright as the Evening Star set among the midnight stars, the loveliest jewel in the sky.

Hektor's body is covered by the armour stripped from Patroclus' body; who better than Achilles to know where the weak spot is in his own armour? He drives his heavy bronze blade clean through the tender neck, crowing in triumph:

> 'While you were despoiling Patroclus, you thought yourself quite safe and forgot all about me. You fool! Far from him, by the hollow ships, was a mightier man, who should have kept him safe but stayed behind. That was I, who now have vanquished you. The dogs and carrion birds will tear apart your flesh, but him the Greeks will bury.'
>
> Hektor whispered back 'At your feet I beg, by your parents, by your own life, do not let the dogs ravage my corpse by the hollow ships. Accept the ransom my royal father and mother will offer, stores of gold and bronze, and let them carry my body home, so the Trojans and their wives may grant me in death my proper funeral.'
>
> Swift-footed Achilles glared down at him: 'You dog; do not speak to me of parents. I only wish the fury could drive me to slice and eat you raw for what you did. But know this: no living man will keep the dogs from gnawing your skull, even if some Trojan weighed out twenty, thirty times your worth in ransom, and promised even more, not though King Priam bid them give me your weight in gold. Not even then will your royal mother lay you on a bier and lament for you, the son she bore.
>
> No, the dogs and carrion birds will devour you.'
>
> Then Hektor of the gleaming helm spoke with his dying breath: 'I know you, I see you; I see your fate and know that I was never destined to influence it. But think on: the gods, remembering me, may turn their wrath on you, that fated day when by Troy's Scaean Gate, brave as you are, Paris kills you with Apollo's help.'
>
> Death enfolded him as he uttered these words, and his spirit fled from the body down to Hades, lamenting to leave his youth and manhood behind. It was a corpse that shining Achilles addressed: 'Lie there then in death, and I will face my own, whenever Zeus and the immortal gods decide.'

The scene pans out from this final, fateful meeting. The Greeks circle the body, stabbing at the corpse, saying, 'he is a lot easier to deal with now!' Achilles starts as the commander he is, his mind turning to whether the Trojans will release

Helen now their leader is gone. But immediately, remembering Patroclus, his grief and rage overtake him and he takes his revenge on the dead body of Hektor, a revenge that is so improper and horrific that in due course the gods convene to stop it:

> Achilles pierced the tendons of both feet behind the ankle, threaded through them ox-hide thongs, tying them high up on the back of his chariot. Then lifting his glorious armour on he mounted and touched the horses with his whip, and they eagerly leapt forward. Dragged behind, Hektor's corpse raised a cloud of dust, while his fine black hair spread out on the ground behind the chariot: that head, once so fine, trailed in the dirt.

The book ends with the women of Troy lamenting for Hektor and for themselves, now that he is gone. His mother, Queen Hecuba, shrieks and tears her clothes and hair, seeing her son's hair clogged with dirt. His father, King Priam, in frenzy, can scarcely be held back from rushing to Achilles and begging for his son's body: 'I grieve for those fine sons of Troy that he has sent to Hades, but most of all for my own son. If he could but have died in my arms! Then I and his mother, who to her sorrow bore him, could have grieved and lamented our fill over his corpse.' A wave of grief spreads round them and throughout the city, as if the city were on fire. Hecuba laments as only a mother can: 'How can I carry on living now? You were the pride and saviour of Troy, greeted as a god, by every man and woman in this city. But now death and fate overtake you.'

Andromache, Hektor's wife, is still in the dark, not knowing what has happened. She is busy in the inner rooms of the palace, weaving a broad tapestry dyed with precious purple, with a multi-coloured flower pattern. Touchingly, she has asked her ladies-in-waiting to set a great cauldron on the fire, so that when Hektor comes back from the day's fighting, he will have hot water for a bath. But now she hears the cries from the walls; shaking, dropping her shuttle, she calls to her women to accompany her to find out what has happened, in sudden fear that Hektor, bold to the point of rashness, has taken on Achilles single-handed.

Andromache

She runs out like a madwoman, rushes to the battlements, sees Hektor's corpse being dragged to the hollow ships, and falls in a dead faint, her golden wedding veil slipping from her head.

When she comes round, she laments for herself and also for her baby son, at worst a slave or victim, at best an orphan:

'An orphaned child is separated from his playmates; downcast and tear-stained, he plucks the cloak of his father's friends to get attention, till one holds the wine-cup to his lips just to wet his lips. And some youth with both parents still alive hits him and pushes him away from the feast, jeering. And my son, my Astyanax – 'Lord of the City' – who sat on your father's knee eating the richest meat, and when you were sleepy, slept in your nurse's arms in a soft bed, sweetly dreaming; now the dogs and worms will feed on your corpse, by the Greek ships, far from your kin, though in your house are all the fine, finely-woven clothes that women's hands can fashion. I will burn them all in a great fire, since they will be of no use to you, to honour you.'

So Andromache spoke, in tears, while the women joined in her lament.

Book 23

Achilles Arbitrates over Patroclus' Funeral Games

Book 23 is about the proper treatment of the dead – about the splendid funeral games, the tomb, the ritual of remembrance and celebration of the dead's fame. But for Achilles these are not sufficient to come to terms with Patroclus' death. He has to find some compensation to offer him: Trojan dead, twelve princes as a human sacrifice, Hektor's death, despoliation and degradation, his own going without food, drink, washing and shaving. The Achilles who refused compensation from Agamemnon for the slight to his honour, because possessions, 'once lost, may come again, but the soul, once gone, can never be restored', now seeks to offer Patroclus recompense.

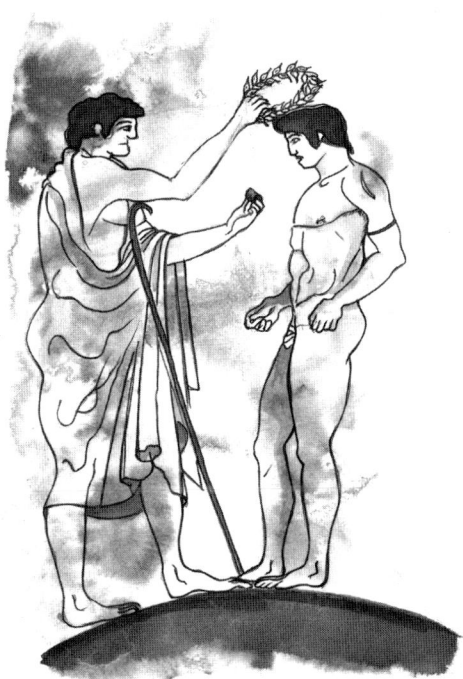

Achilles awarding prizes

His fury comes from not being able to find anything sufficient.

His sleep is disturbed by the ghost of Patroclus, complaining that he is prevented from taking up his proper place among the dead, asking not for revenge but for speedy burial, and that their ashes should in due course lie together in a single urn. Achilles tries to embrace him, but the spirit slips away and Achilles awakes in sorrow.

Preparations for the funeral are completed: there is a chariot procession and a ritual offering of locks of hair. Achilles cuts the lock which was dedicated for a safe return to the river of his home; Patroclus' death has meant he will not now return.

The chief mourners stay to build a huge pyre, and the body is wrapped in the fat of sacrificial animals and laid on it. Achilles kills the twelve young nobles, and the pyre is lit with supernatural fire. A tomb, which will also house Achilles, is made over the urn holding the cremated bones, and the funeral games begin.

Achilles provides prizes – cauldrons, tripods, horses, women and iron – from his store for the best in each of the events. In these funeral games, foreshadowing his own, he will preside over others' demonstrations of prowess rather than demonstrate his own excellence. The first is the chariot race, to be run around a mark in the ground that may be a grave marker now long forgotten (so fragile, it seems, is the hero's renown). Diomedes, popularly considered the favourite, is helped by the gods to come in first. But Nestor had given his son, Antilochus, advice on how to use his skill to excel, even though his horses are not the best – to such good effect that he comes second. This provokes Menelaus into objecting that Antilochus beat him by cunning, not by being intrinsically better: he judges that he himself deserves second prize because he is superior in power and greatness. When Antilochus submissively owns his inferiority, Menelaus graciously allows him to keep second prize. But then Achilles judges that the best man – Eumelus son of Admetus – came in last because he was fouled, and proposes to award him second place. Antilochus hotly disputes the justice of this (Achilles of all people should think before taking someone's publicly awarded prize away from him!), and Achilles smiles and diplomatically awards an extra prize of spoil he himself had taken. The unawarded fifth prize Achilles presents to Nestor, as he is no longer able to compete. Nestor remembers with relish the prizes he won when he was in his prime. So the difficult negotiation of who is best is played out and this time resolved, with prizes, not lives, at stake. Achilles has been reintegrated into society.

The next contest is boxing. Epeius claims to be the best at boxing, even though he falls short in battle. He proves to be right. Odysseus and Greater Ajax are the contestants in the next competition, wrestling (as they will for the arms of Achilles). They are locked together for so long that the onlookers get restive, and they make a final attempt to throw each other. Odysseus remembers his craftiness and trips him, and Achilles intervenes to award the prize equally.

The foot-race is next, in which, like the chariot race, Achilles would be preeminent if he had entered. Odysseus is lying second to Lesser Ajax when he prays to Athene and Ajax slips in some animal entrails. Everyone laughs, but he still comes in second. Antilochus ruefully accepts being beaten by a much older man, reminding everyone of Achilles' speed. Achilles repays the compliment with an extra prize.

The fifth contest is a gladiatorial duel over the armour of Sarpedon, with a sword to the man who gets in a vital thrust. Achilles awards the contest to Diomedes before serious injury.

The single prize for the discus is a precious five-year supply of iron. Ajax comes second for the third time. Meriones steals the archery prize from Teuker by an extraordinary shot. The spear throwing is settled without a contest by Achilles, who acknowledges Agamemnon as the best without his having to compete. This compliment completes the games and Achilles' reconciliation with the commanders.

The previous book finishes the story of the rage of Achilles that the *Iliad* started with – the rage that sent many heroes' souls to Hades. The initial insult has been wiped out in blood, compensation and restoration; Patroclus' killer has been killed in return. Achilles grieves over and laments Patroclus: lament expresses all kinds of pain and performs all kinds of emotions. But Achilles has always insisted on being pre-eminent, has expected exemption from the ordinary human condition. Book 23 is the start of Achilles having to deal with the after-effects of his rage.

Achilles first orders the drawing up of the Myrmidons' chariots and long-maned horses in formal mourning: three times they drive around Patroclus' corpse weeping terribly, for 'such is the *geras* of the dead'. The *geras* is the proper material correlate or prize; Briseis was a proper material correlate of Achilles' honour and her removal the tangible, visible marker of his loss of same.

But what can Achilles find that is proper and sufficient?

Achilles leads their lamentation, the sand and their armour wet with tears. He lays his man-killing hands on Patroclus' breast, saying: 'Be content, even in the House of Hades: I have kept my promise to you, that I would drag Hektor's corpse here and feed it to the dogs, and full of rage I will cut the throats of twelve princes of Troy at your funeral pyre.' The warriors take off their gleaming bronze armour and sit at Achilles' lavish funeral feast – roast oxen, sheep, goats and many a fine fat white-tusked hog.

Achilles himself refuses to wash or eat, until he has completed ... what? Sufficient outrage on Hektor's corpse? Sufficient expression of grief? Sufficient expiation for not looking after the lesser warrior, for not bringing him home as promised, for allowing him to go into battle in his stead?

The ghost of Patroclus appears to the distraught Achilles, demanding his funeral, lamenting their separation, predicting Achilles' forthcoming death and asking that their ashes should be mingled: 'Let them be as one, just as we were when we grew up together, when I was brought to your house, just a child, because I killed a boy accidentally in a silly argument over a game. Your horseman father welcomed me and showed me such love, and we've been together ever since.' Three times Achilles tries to embrace him, but the spirit vanishes like smoke.

Rosy-fingered Dawn finds the Myrmidons still lamenting. Agamemnon sends out men with woodman's axes and strong ropes, driving mules up on winding tracks until they come to the high slopes of Mount Ida, to fell tall oaks for a great funeral mound for Patroclus (and for Achilles). They have cut off locks of their hair and thrown them on the corpse, which gives Achilles an idea: he cuts off a lock of his own hair, uncut as sacred, and lays it on Patroclus' corpse. They build a huge funeral pyre for him, piling round it sheep and cattle carcasses, jars of honey and oil, the bodies of four proud horses and two of the nine dogs Patroclus looked after. Then Achilles completes the task he has set himself, killing twelve noble Trojan princes with his bronze blade and setting the pyre alight so the pitiless flames will consume the body of his dearest companion. Patroclus will have all the honours Achilles has promised; he pledges to him that his killer's body – Hektor's – will have none. (The gods, however, affronted by Achilles' mistreatment of a hero's body, instil his body with preserving ambrosia.)

Achilles tries to fire the pyre, but fails until he prays to the winds, which 'rose with a roar, driving the clouds before them and swelling the waves with a stormy blast until they reached the fertile land of Troy and the pyre, raising a great column of roaring fire'. The pyre burns all night long, while Achilles draws wine from a golden bowl in a two-handled cup, pouring libations and calling to the spirit of Patroclus. Circling the fire, he laments without pause, while his dear friend's bones burn, 'like a father groans as he lays on a pyre a newly married son whose death leaves his wretched parents in despair'. In the morning, they quench the pyre with red wine and collect the remains of Patroclus, separating them from the offerings, and place the ashes in a golden urn. They mark out the circle of his mound, setting a ring of stones around the pyre, then piling earth inside.

This is a memorably vivid description of a Bronze Age burial ritual. Even the most shocking act – the sacrifice of twelve young Trojans – can to some extent be matched in the archaeological evidence of human sacrifice which has been discovered on three sites, so far, in the Minoan and Mycenaean world, most notably at Knossos. What is clear is that Homer frames this ritual killing as both proper and extraordinary: as with other ordinary actions – abusing the body of an enemy, refusing food and drink – Achilles feels and acts at the boundary of the ordinary and extraordinary. The Greek word for that, for someone who pushes up against the ordinary human condition, is *deinos*, awe-ful: perhaps as good a translation as any of the quality of being a 'hero'.

Achilles tells them to make an adequate mound for the time being. When he too dies, they can join the ashes under a magnificent mound. This is the second defining quality of being a hero: Achilles has a fate, a story which will have a destined end, here outside the narrative but shaping it nevertheless.

In the *Odyssey*, in the underworld, the ghost of Agamemnon describes the funeral of Achilles: slaughter of sheep and oxen, the body anointed and swathed in finest cloths and put on a pyre. After the pyre has burned down, the bones are gathered up with wine and ointment and put in the golden amphora along with Patroclus' bones:

> Then we heaped up a great and perfect tomb on a projecting headland by the broad Hellespont. Thus it could be seen from far from the sea both by men that now are and that shall be born hereafter.

A large mound called the Tomb of Achilles was known to Homer's audiences, though seemingly built later than the Mycenaean Age of Troy. (Kum Tepe and Kesik Tepe have both been suggested.) Alexander the Great later visited it and, Plutarch records, 'sacrificed to Athena and poured a libation to the heroes. At the tomb of Achilles, after anointing himself with oil and taking part in a race naked with his companions, as is the custom, he deposited crowns and remarked how fortunate Achilles was to have had a faithful friend while he was alive and a great herald of his fame after his death.'

The rest of the book is Achilles' holding of a grand funeral games: the traditional origin of the great games, like the Olympic Games founded round about the time that the *Iliad* came together in its current form, was a hero's funeral games. One event that isn't mentioned elsewhere – e.g. in Nestor's list of his previous triumphs in the middle of the book – is the armed combat; perhaps a vestige of funerary fights to the death in order to send the dead person some companions. This is seemingly an Etruscan tradition which Romans later adopted and extended into the ever-popular gladiatorial games. But here the competitions are funeral games, not funeral death rituals. When the two armed combatants come near to a death blow, the fight is stopped and a prize awarded. Achilles brings out Sarpedon's shield, helmet and spear, captured by Patroclus: the designated 'two best fighters', Ajax and Diomedes, are to refight in a ritual sense Patroclus' greatest fight. Both are so menacing and eager for battle that the Greeks hold their breath. Three charges are graphically described before the watchers call for an end to the contest and for equal prizes, but Achilles declares Diomedes the winner.

What is compelling about the funeral games narratives – of slips and turns, rivalries and pettinesses, young challengers and old – is the arbitration of victors by Achilles, always called the first and best (*aristos*) of the Greeks. While Achilles would in any other competition come first, these are ones in which he must be arbiter, not competitor.

For the first event, the chariot race, Achilles offers splendid prizes: for the winner, 'a woman skilled in fine needlework and a large bronze tripod with ear-shaped handles'; for the runner-up, 'a six-year old mare, broken-in carrying a foal'; for the third place, 'a brand new cauldron not yet touched by fire'; for the fourth, 'two talents of gold' and for the fifth, 'a gleaming libation bowl'. Achilles and his immortal horses look on, the horses grieving for their charioteer who groomed them, while the competitors line up.

Nestor gives canny advice to his son, that although the others have better horses, he can use cunning and horsemanship to win. He gives him places on the course to aim for, including a smooth patch by a post with two white stones which he should barely graze, something perhaps 'set up as a grave marker of someone who died long ago' and whose name is forgotten: a pathetic line in this epic about the importance of one's immortal name.

The thrills and spills of the chariot race are described in loving detail, through the excited eyes of the spectators, who in a recognizable and timeless way start to invest in the race, second-guessing the outcome, disputing and disparaging others' eyesight, putting on extra bets.

Then the arbitration starts – there is an outright winner, but Achilles' first instinct is to give second prize to the best charioteer though he came in last. However, Nestor's son Antilochus objects that he came in second fair and square. Achilles finds an extra prize as compensation. But Menelaus then objects that Nestor's son cut him up on a bend and that if the course had been longer, his superior horses would have won. Nestor's son immediately and gracefully retracts all claims and hands his prize to Menelaus; Menelaus then equally graciously if somewhat condescendingly gives the prize back as he is only a lad and will know better next time.

The final prize is unclaimed and Achilles begs Nestor to accept it, as 'old age weighs on you now, and you cannot contend in boxing, wrestling, javelin-throwing or the foot-race'. This act of *charis* (grace, reciprocity) gives joy to the old man, who immediately, characteristically and somewhat comically embarks on an account of the great deeds of his youth. He finishes with his delight that he has not been forgotten, accepting the prize as a mark of the honour in which he is still held.

Then comes the boxing: a professional boxer makes mincemeat of the valiant fighter, whose friends accept the runner-up's prize on his behalf while he is unconscious. The wrestling match has all the hallmarks of a classic contest: the mighty Ajax against the immensely strong but also immensely cunning Odysseus. They are beautifully equally matched, and after a long bout Achilles declares them both winners.

The first prize for the next event, the running race – which of course fleet-footed Achilles would certainly have won – is a fine silver mixing bowl, the loveliest thing in the world, a masterpiece of Phoenician craftsmanship, which

Achilles has been given as ransom for the ill-fated Lykaon. The combatants are the other Ajax, Ajax the Lesser, and again Nestor's son and Odysseus. Ajax and Odysseus are neck and neck until, just before the finishing line, Ajax slips in a pile of entrails and ends up with a mouthful of dung! Antilochus comes in third but gives such praise to his elders – Odysseus and Achilles – that Achilles laughs and doubles his prize money.

After the armed combat come two final competitions: the throwing – the whirling and release of a lump of metal, similar to the later discus – and the archery. The throwing contains a fascinating reference to 'pig iron' as the most valuable and most useful commodity – an insight into both the composite composition of the *Iliad* and to a time between the Bronze and Iron Ages. A huge lump of pig iron that Andromache's father, the powerful King Eetion, used to hurl is offered as prize. Achilles had carried it off with other of his possessions after killing Eetion in a raid on his city. 'The winner of this will have iron enough for five years, and even if his farmland is remote, he will have no need to send a ploughman or a shepherd into town to buy it, this will supply all his needs.'

The set-up for the archery prize is fascinating. Achilles lays out ten double-headed axes and ten single-headed, of dark iron. He sets up a ship's mast a long way off and fastens a small bird to it by the foot by a cord, offering the fluttering bird as a target. 'Whoever hits the bird as it flutters wins the double-headed axes; if anyone strikes the cord that holds it but misses the bird, he shall take the second prize: the single-headed axes.'

The two contestants shake lots in a bronze helmet and the bowman Teuker takes first shot. He forgets his promise of a sacrifice to Apollo, who interferes with his sure aim so that he hits the cord but misses the bird. The other competitor, after a timely vow to Apollo, snatches up Teuker's great bow and sends an arrow through the wing of the now freed bird.

Finally comes the spear-throwing. Achilles brings a fine spear and a cauldron not yet set to the fire, embossed with flowers, worth an ox. Two competitors rise eagerly, but Achilles calls a halt to the competitions and gives the first prize to the 'first, far exceeding us' – to Agamemnon the commander-in-chief of the Greeks – without his having to demonstrate his prowess. 'Firstness' is decided by arbitration by 'the first and best of the Greeks'.

Book 24

The End of the Story of Achilles' Rage

Priam and Achilles

Alone, Achilles weeps for Patroclus, unable to sleep for memories. At dawn, he harnesses his horses and drags Hektor's corpse round Patroclus' tomb before sleeping. The gods take pity on the violated body; Apollo condemns Achilles for being excessive, for lacking both restraining shame and the capacity to endure that is part of man's lot; angering the gods and dishonouring the earth. His goddess mother, Thetis, unable to face the immortals as she sorrows for a mortal, is summoned by Zeus to hear that Hektor's body must be ransomed. She tells Achilles, while Iris goes to Priam to reassure him and offer Hermes as guide. Priam asks his wife, Hecuba, what he should do, as if the message from the gods were immaterial and his earlier intention to beg the body from Achilles had come back to him: this, as many turning points in the action, is prompted in parallel both by the gods' intervention and by the individual's nature. Hecuba scorns his proposal, saying that Achilles is savage and will neither pity nor respect him.

Priam, however, is resolute; he goes, with an omen and Hermes as his guide, into the enemy camp.

When he gets to Achillles' tent, he speaks to him as a suppliant, reminding him of his father and offering gifts beyond number. His words stir a passion of grieving for his own father in Achilles, crying now for him, now for Patroclus. A tragic sympathy binds the two bitter enemies: they grieve for their common, human lot. Achilles sets the old man on his feet; he describes the way the gods spin life for unfortunate mortals, living in unhappiness while the gods themselves have no sorrows. There are two urns at the door of Zeus, from which he dispenses evils and blessings. Achilles' father, Peleus, was given all blessings, but only one son, so now is the time to endure and grieve.

Priam's request for the return of the body provokes Achilles, though he is already minded to give Hektor back. He masters himself and thoughtfully orders that the corpse be washed, anointed and dressed, himself lifting the body onto the litter. He weeps, then begs Patroclus not to be angry at this agreement.

He provides food for them both: even Niobe ate when she was worn out with grieving for the loss of her children, so must they. They gaze at each other in wonder, Priam at Achilles' beauty and grace, Achilles at Priam's dignity and power of speech. Priam asks for a bed, worn out as he is with lack of food and sleep. Achilles orders two to be made, asking Priam how long a truce he would like for the proper celebration of Hektor's funeral. Eleven days is agreed.

Priam returns to Troy with Hektor's body, which is lamented over by Cassandra, Andromache, Hecuba and finally Helen, who remembers that he was always kind to her. During the truce they mourn for Hektor, until on the eleventh day they build a grave barrow over the bones.

And so horse-taming Hektor's rites were complete.

This is a book with a series of riveting scenes: in Troy, on Olympus and in Achilles' tent. Do we, by the end, see Achilles letting go of 'the rage, the destruction of many heroes' of the epic's opening lines? That multifaceted rage – roused originally by Agamemnon's outraging of the whole 'heroic equation' and compounded by the intense emotions awoken by the death of Patroclus – is both quintessentially 'heroic' and timelessly recognizable.

Essentially heroic is Achilles' anger at Agamemnon for flouting everything that shapes the heroes' *raison d'être*, reason for living (and dying): the bond between commander-in-chief and those whom he asked for help, honoured by both; 'the heroic exchange' of danger and death for deathless glory. Equally proper in an Achilles who is deemed the *aristos* – first and best – of the Greeks, is battle fury. Many fighters go into battle in the *Iliad* '*memaōs*', but that fighting fury seems both more easily and more properly aroused and dispersed than Achilles'.

More problematic is fury that is not peculiar to and discharged on the battlefield: when Achilles goes back to the fight he goes back not with battle adrenalin but like an avenging god, as, like Zeus, a force of *mēnis*, wrath. But, driven by complex emotions of vengeance, grief and guilt, he commits the breaches of humanity that would usually arouse rather than embody Zeus' *mēnis*: the killing of suppliants, the choking and fouling of a sacred river with corpses, the killing of a priest, human sacrifice and finally, here, the daily abuse of Hektor's body.

Book 23 ends with his final gracious act at Patroclus' funeral games, awarding the first prize to Agamemnon as *aristos*, 'first, by far, of them all, in might and javelin throwing'. So there is now no trace left of the fury aroused in Book 1. Achilles is once more embedded in the Greek force with his companions in arms, his *philoi*.

So, what remains? After vengeance has been wreaked? After the funeral? After the activity and proper rituals? The question is both timeless and timely, the exploration, the focus of this book, specific to this extraordinary hero with his extraordinary story but strikingly recognizable today.

What remains, we see at the start of this book, is Achilles' passionate inability to accept – again so recognizable – that after all the proper formalities have been completed, the only thing left is the most difficult thing of all, the acceptance that there is nothing more to be done.

The gods express the common response: many a man has lost someone even closer to them than Patroclus to Achilles – a brother or son – yet comes to a proper end of his weeping and wailing. Why can't Achilles? Is it a mark of his extraordinary intensity and (god-like) inability to compromise? And/or is it the very understandable but intolerable mixture of his emotions: grief, loss and perhaps guilt; the impossibility of finding an adequate way of expressing, an adequate release of, such overwhelming passions? Except, perhaps, to shout out at the heavens that allowed this to happen, at himself for not preventing it, at the shape of things, the cosmos, that fails to exempt *this person* from the human condition?

Throughout the *Iliad*, Achilles has been insistent on equivalence: fair reward for danger and compensation for outrage. On his shield, Hephaistos worked a scene of arbitration, agreeing the compensation for a killing: the blood-money, *wergild*, the blood-price. Achilles' *mēnis* will only finally be resolved – right at the end of the epic – when Achilles can find a way of letting go, accepting that there finally can be no compensation, no restitution for Patroclus' death.

This final book contains unforgettable scene after unforgettable scene. It starts with Achilles in tears, tossing and turning, sleepless and yearning for Patroclus, remembering both his qualities and the dangers they have experienced together.

Unable to bear it, he again goes to drag Hektor's dead body in the dust around Patroclus' grave mound.

The gods are repelled by 'deadly' Achilles' abuse of a corpse of a pre-eminent and noble warrior. They object that his mind is unbending and 'not in accord with justice', that he is cruel like a lion, rampaging in pride in his strength and spirit, and that he has destroyed pity. Finally, they say he has no *aidōs* – shame/respect for propriety, for social bonds, for others' feelings. This is a significant judgment, not least that these are all terms ('deadly', 'not in accord with justice', 'pitiless', 'lacking in *aidōs*') that are levelled at the gods.

Hera seems to accentuate this by pointing to Achilles' semi-divine parenting, but this dangerous line is immediately stopped by Zeus; Hektor, like Sarpedon, Aeneas and many other heroes, are loved by gods. But here at the end, Zeus and the narrative turn to Achilles' goddess mother, Thetis (whose request to Zeus in Book 1 precipitated events). Iris is sent to ask her to persuade Achilles to give back Hektor's body for burial.

Although the main theme of this book is Achilles' anger and the fate of both the main warriors, Hektor and Achilles, there is time and space to reflect on what their deaths mean to their parents. Later in the book we have the lament of Hecuba for her son, and throughout the epic we have biographies of victims whose parents, when they hear the news, will be intolerably bereft.

Here we have the goddess Thetis facing her only son, who is taking out his passionate anger on Hektor's body, and on himself. She has come to tell him that there must be an end, that in modern terms he is 'stuck', no longer in the process of grieving and coming to terms with Patroclus' death and all it means. She reminds him of what is healthy – eating, drinking, attending to his body, sex – and that he should accept a ransom (*apoina*). Achilles – he who has insisted that for the death of Patroclus there can be no compensation, no 'equivalent', no death price – immediately agrees; perhaps with relief.

The scene moves to the equally distraught family in Troy: the palace filled with women's lamentation, the old King Priam huddled, the dirt on his face and neck bearing witness to the mourning dust he has poured over his head. At the news that he must ransom his son's body, Hecuba lets fly her anger and hatred:

Where is the wisdom you used to be famous for? How can you go to the Greek ships and face the man who has slaughtered so many of your fine sons? You must be made of iron. From the moment he sets eyes on you, and you are in his grasp, that savage brute will show you neither mercy nor respect. No! Let us grieve for our son here for the evil thread Fate spun for my child: to be food for dogs, his corpse held captive by that man of violence. How I wish I could tear into Achilles' heart with my teeth and devour it. That would pay him back for what he has done to my son, a hero, killed fighting to defend the men and women of Troy.

Hecuba is here echoing, perhaps inhabiting, the very last words of that savage brute to her son, when Hektor asked for the loser's body to be treated properly, humanely, with dignity:

> 'Accept the ransom my royal father and mother will offer, stores of gold and bronze, and let them carry my body home, so the Trojans and their wives may grant me in death my portion of fire.'
>
> Achilles glared at him in answer: 'I wish the fury and the pain in me could drive me to carve and eat you raw for what you did, as surely as this is true: no living man will keep the dogs from gnawing at your skull, not if men weighed out twenty, thirty times your worth in ransom even your weight in gold. Your royal mother will not lay you on a bier to grieve for you, the son she bore, but rather dogs and vultures shall devour you utterly.'

But Priam is clear. If it is his destiny to die at Achilles' hand, then so be it: he will have clasped his son one last time. He puts together a fine ransom of robes, cloaks, tunics, talents of gold, tripods and cauldrons: the exchange currency of times of war. He also adds a precious, prestigious gift, a Thracian cup he was given as a guest gift. Harshly but understandably, perhaps, he shouts at his remaining sons, upbraiding them for the uselessness of their being alive when Hektor was dead.

Hecuba then hands to her only remaining defence, Priam, a jewelled cup to make the libation. Priam mounts a carefully described chariot and, with the laments of his family in his ears, drives fast through the echoing portico and out through the palace gate.

Guided by Hermes, he arrives at Achilles' tent and slips inside, unobserved, and bending in supplication, kisses 'the terrible, man-slaying hands that had slain his many sons'. Achilles looks at him in wonder, the aura around him like that of a refugee who has seen and committed terrible things.

Priam supplicates him, calls on his pity: he had fifty sons, now all lost, and the greatest of them all lies outside Achilles' tent. Reminding Achilles of his own father, he asks for compassion. Priam has done what no other man has ever brought himself to do – he has kissed the hands of the man who has slaughtered his sons.

His words move Achilles almost unbearably; the father facing the man who killed his son and the man looking at the father so like his own, whom he will now never see again. They cry together; Priam for Hektor, and Achilles for Patroclus and his old father. They cry together, heart rending, each for his own, but joined in sorrow.

When 'great Achilles had taken full satisfaction in sorrow', he rises from the chair, takes the old man by the hand and in pity and admiration at his courage in braving his son's killer, sits him down. Achilles the pitiless, who has not allowed himself sleep, food or drink, now leads Priam to them.

But Priam refuses while his son is still lying unransomed. Achilles, though reconciled, is touchy at the demand; he makes preparations, but with acute self-knowledge orders the body to be washed and anointed, and himself dresses the body with a fine cloak, lest Priam's grief at the state of the abused body turns to anger, and Achilles, responding, is angered in return … and kills him.

After this last observance, Achilles calls on his beloved Patroclus:

Do not be angry, Patroclus, when in Hades you hear that I have given back Hektor's body to his loving father: the body was ransomed for a worthy sum and I will devote a share to you.

Briseis welcoming Priam to Achilles' tent

Returning to Priam, he assures him that Hektor's body has been made ready and at dawn he may embrace him and carry him back. But now they should eat, for even the iconic Niobe, symbol of parental grief, eventually thought to eat, though her twelve children had been slain by Apollo and Artemis.

So they feast, agreeing a truce for Hektor's burial. Achilles prepares a bed for Priam, and, hand-in-hand, escorts him to it, while he sleeps beside Briseis.

Cassandra, on the lookout next morning, spots Priam returning with the body of Hektor, whereupon all the people of the city run out, shouting their grief. Priam takes the body back to be mourned according to custom, inside the palace. The lament-singers lead the women in dirges and Andromache makes the first lament, cradling the head of man-killing Hektor. As in laments from time immemorial, she accuses him of leaving her to fend for herself, and leaving his baby son and aged parents defenceless, all doomed as Troy is now doomed. She cries for their child's fate and for herself, that she wasn't by his side with a last word as a final memory.

Then Hecuba takes up the lament, and finally Helen, the cause of the war:

So many years since Paris brought me – though how I wish I had died, rather – yet in all that time I had no harsh or spiteful word from you. Though your father was always gentle, when your brothers, sisters, your brother's fine wives, your mother or any in the palace reproached me, you would turn away their anger with gentle acts and words. So I cry now for you out loud, and in my heart for my wretched self, since there is no one else in all wide Troy who will be kind or gentle to me.

(We hear nothing of Paris.)

For nine days they mourn and make preparations:

On the tenth, in tears, they laid brave Hektor's body on the pyre and set the wood ablaze. When rosy-fingered Dawn lit the sky, the people quenched the embers with red wine, and his brothers and friends, their cheeks wet with tears, collected his ashes and, wrapped in a purple robe, placed them inside a golden urn. Then they laid the urn in a hollow grave, covering it with large close-set stones, and over it they piled the barrow. Then they gathered in Zeus-beloved Priam's palace for the glorious funeral feast.

Such were the funeral rites of Hektor, tamer of horses.

So ends the *Iliad*.

But when does the wrath of Achilles end? Perhaps when Achilles cries 'in common' with the father of his great enemy: at Priam's courage, at the commonality that links them, the humanity that binds them together. Homer says that when Achilles had taken his fill of mourning and the 'desperate longing for it had left his body and deepest understanding', he raised up Priam in pity, declaring:

> The gods have spun the thread of fate for wretched mortals: that we live in sorrow, while they are free from care. There are two urns standing by the side of Zeus; one holds blessings, the other ills, and the king of gods distributes a mixture. The man who receives his life portion only from the jar of ills becomes an outcast, driven over the face of the earth by despair, a wanderer honoured neither by gods nor men. But see how the gods showered glorious gifts on my father Peleus: wealth, kingship, possessions, a goddess for a wife. Yet, here is his only son, long separated, from whom he receives no care and who is now doomed; while you were renowned for your wealth and your sons, but since the gods have brought this wretched war there is nothing but slaughter.
>
> Courage: there is nothing to be done by endless sorrow: you will not bring him back and life will bring you more to endure.

What he lets go is not just his passionate, all-consuming anger, but the longing for it, deep in his body and deepest understanding. He accepts at last that there is no compensation for spilled life blood; there is nothing to be done.

Heroic Values, Heroic Psychology

Keywords: *aretē* (male-ness; excellence), *aristeia* (time of being first, pre-eminent), *geras* (material correlate, prize), *timē* (worth, (evidence of) honour), *euchos* (victory shout), *kleos* (name on lips and so 'glory', 'renown')

'Epic' is a war genre, of heroes finding and proving themselves in battlefield encounters. The adrenalin and excitement charge of the combat is the ultimate test of a man: of *aretē* (ara = masculine, so *aretē* = the quality of being male). *Aretē* is often thought of, by later philosophers, as 'virtue', but is better understood as 'competitive excellence':

> All morning, as the sun rose higher, the weapons found their mark and warriors fell, but at the hour when a forester, weary of felling tall trees, longing for food and sweet wine, sits down in some mountain glade, at that time the Greeks rallying their comrades through the ranks, showed their *aretē* and the enemy bands broke. (11.84–90)

The archaic poets of the seventh and sixth centuries BCE sang of the *aretē* of various glorious youths. Their songs, like the epics, both create and celebrate the youth's *kleos* – his fame (literally, name on people's lips):

> I have made you wings on which to fly
> across the endless sea and all the earth
> with ease, you'll soon be at every dinner, every feast,
> and many a man will have you on his lips,
> and lovely lads accompanied by flutes
> will sing of you in voices sweet and clear
> and orderly [...]
> not even in death will your fame [*kleos*] fade, but men
> will always cherish your undying [*aphthiton*] name.
> (Theognis *Elegiac Poetry* 237–46)

They composed in celebration of victorious athletes:

And in the Isthmian Games they attempted the greatest number of contests, and adorned their homes with tripods and cauldrons and goblets of gold, as befitting victory garlands. Their *arete* shines clearly, in the naked foot-races and in the shield-clashing races for heavy armoured warriors.

That is by Pindar (in *Isthmian 2*), who wrote and sang praise-songs for the victors of the Olympic and other games, a generation after the *Iliad* and *Odyssey* were canonized into stable performance texts. The ultimate test of a man's excellence, however, is on the battlefield, and Troy is the iconic site where heroes came to prove themselves, the ultimate test-site for *arete*.

They fight – as Nestor is always reminding the Greeks – to live up to the heroes of old, whose *kleos* Achilles sang to himself in his tent (9.199), and to feature in the famous stories of the heroes at Troy, in all those other Iliads, other cycles of 'stories of Ilium', such as the bard sang to Odysseus at King Alkinous' court, whom 'the Muse inspired to sing of the heroes' glorious deeds, a tale whose fame had risen to high heaven' (*Odyssey* 8.65).

The heroes have days of pre-eminence (*aristeia*, being first and best), where they shine and carry all before them. Diomedes, for instance, relishes 'his strength and daring, eager to prove himself the finest of the Greeks and win *kleos*'. They fight within a social structure and value system which gives meaning and value to heroic actions.

Or does it?

For unlike the victor in a games such as was celebrated by Pindar and other 'praise poets', first-ness on the battlefield once awarded has to be reclaimed, re-won, fought for again. Achilles is universally acknowledged as the *aristos* of the Greek force, but his pre-eminence is stripped from him by the power play of the commander-in-chief.

For the *Iliad* is neither purely a memorializing account enshrining the *kleos* of the great heroes, nor a lament. It is the story of the *mēnis* (wrath) of Achilles and the resulting deaths of heroes, complexly reflected and reflected upon.

What makes heroes fight?

neikein (spur, reproach), **nemesein** (upbraid), *otrunein* (stir up), **menos** (strength), *memaōs* (battle fury – as distinct from Achilles' *mēnis*, his settled state of wrath), **thumos** (passion container), **phrenes** (mind), *aidōs* (respect for bonds, shame), *euchos* (victory cry, vaunt) *kleos* (fame)

Ares the war god *otrunein* the *menos* and *thumos* of each. (5.470)

They fight for the public award of prizes of honour, as we hear from Nestor:

If he learnt these answers and returned unharmed, huge and heaven-high would rise his *kleos* and well rewarded. Let every leader among the fleet grant him a black ewe with a suckling lamb, a gift as never seen before, and he will always be remembered at our feasts and banquets. (10.204–17)

Hektor asks for a similar volunteer who will 'win a rich reward; I guarantee a chariot and a pair of stallions with high arched necks, the best the Greeks have tethered by the ships'.

To this, Dolon cautiously replies:

My heart and proud spirit of adventure [*thumos*] stir [*otrunein*] me. But first swear to me you will grant me the chariot inlaid with bronze, and Achilles peerless horses. (10.303–07, 319–23).

Ajax the Lesser says:

'Now the heart of passion [*thumos*] in my breast is filled with fire for war and conflict, and my hands and feet feel new strength.' Ajax the Great replied: 'I too feel new strength [*menos*] in feet and hands, and I am eager to grasp the spear and fight, even to battle Hektor, in his fury [*memaōs*].' (13.73–80)

Agamemnon to Teuker:

'I swear to you, that if aegis-bearing Zeus and Athene let me sack the fine citadel of Troy, I will hand you, first after myself, an honourable prize, a tripod, a chariot with its team of horses, or a woman for your bed.'

'Most *kudos*-worthy Agamemnon,' Teuker replied, 'no need to urge on [*otrunein*] one who is already urgent.' (8.289–94)

The fighting spirit (*menos*) often *does* have to be aroused by the leaders. Agamemnon says to Idomeneus:

Above all the Greek horsemen, my lord, I honour you, on and off the field, as I do at the feast when the Greek leaders drink the elders' deep-red wine. Though the rest of the long-haired Greeks drink their given portion, your cup, like mine, is ever-brimming for you to drain whenever your *thumos* desires. Now rouse yourself for battle, and be the warrior of old you vaunted you were [*euchos*]. (4.257–64)

Later, Agamemnon, gripping his purple cloak with one great hand, shouted aloud:

Greeks, for shame [*aidōs*], wretched creatures only fit for parade! What now of our boast [*euchos*] that we are first [*aristoi*], the empty boasts you shouted loud, gorging yourself on the beef from straight-horned cattle, downing the brimming bowls of wine? (8.227–33)

This call from the lord of the feasting hall for those he has hosted to live up to their alcohol-fuelled boasts resounds through epic poetry. The elegies of *Y Gododdin*, of those early seventh century CE British heroes who go to the great battle of Catraeth, are framed by the refrain that mead was their delight; mead was their poison:

> Men went to Catraeth at morn
> Their high spirits lessened their life-span
> They drank mead, gold and sweet, ensnaring;
> For a year the minstrels were merry.
> Red their swords, let the blades remain
> Uncleansed, white shields and four-sided spearheads,
> Before Mynyddog Mwynfawr's men.
>
> Men went to Catraeth with a war-cry,
> Speedy steeds and dark armour and shields,
> Spear-shafts held high and spear-points sharp-edged,
> And glittering coats-of-mail and swords,
> He led the way, he thrust through armies,
> Five companies fell before his blades.
> Rhufawn His gave gold to the altar,
> And a rich reward to the minstrel.
>
> (trans. Joseph P. Clancy)

This is what we might call the epic layer – the heroes assembled, feasted and duly rewarded by Agamemnon and by Hektor. And the *Iliad*, like *Y Gododdin*, does record the heroes and their deeds – and indeed their rewards – making a celebratory song of minstrels, bards, that rise heaven-high. The keeper of the heroic records, of conquests and defeats, is the Muse:

> Tell me now, O Muses whose home is on Olympus – for you are goddesses, omniscient and omnipresent, whereas we hear the report of *kleos* – who were the leaders of the Greeks. (2.465–66)

Conquests and defeats, as Sarpedon graphically describes it, mean having the victory shout (*euchos*) over the corpse of the vanquished – or being that corpse, being vaunted over.

As in *Y Gododdin*, some of the records are elegies for the doomed deaths of those heroes.

But the *Iliad* is many-layered, as well as many-textured: Golden Age heroes' deeds and dooms, but also the tragedy of the wrath of Achilles; the randomness as well as the fatedness of deaths and escapes.

A day in the life: *aristeia*

This battlefield narrative is often recorded in terms of epic encounters, such as Diomedes' *aristeia* in Book 5: a freestanding book of Diomedes' day in the sun, a narrative which takes him up to even fighting the gods. The textured account shows us the battlefield as a place of *kleos*-granting duels, but also one of pathos, of victims recorded either in terms of their wounds or the biographies which give us a moment to go beyond this particular battleground to those waiting at home.

The battlefield encounters are watched over by the Muse, whose job it is to record the heroes and their victims. The first in this book is one of the most memorable in the *Iliad*:

> Tell me now, Muses, that dwell on Olympus, who of the Trojans or their noble allies first faced Agamemnon. Iphidamas it was, tall and powerful,

Aristeia

who was reared in fertile Thrace. [...] Pitiful youth, he died for the land of his birth, far from his bride of whom he had little joy, though he had given much to win her, a hundred oxen, with a thousand sheep and goats promised from his countless flocks.

This heroic episode finishes with Agamemnon stripping the body and carrying the fine armour off through the Greek ranks. Then the brutality of war hits – Iphidamas' brother tries to drag the corpse back by the foot, but Agamemnon hacks the brother's head off, which falls onto his brother's despoiled body.

Here we have three layers of battlefield narrative: the formal appeal to the Muse to record the *kleos*; the biography that is both formally heroic and rich in the pathos of the loser in the heroic contest; and finally the bloody business of war, the anything-but-glorious fight over the corpse, with the graphic detail that Iphidamas' brother's head is hacked off as he is trying to recover the body.

The heroic exchange – *kleos aphthiton*, undying fame

In Book 1, Achilles' implacable rage is roused by Agamemnon's abrogation of the 'heroic system' which grants *kleos*.

There is no such problem for Diomedes, whose heroic status is celebrated in Book 5, where his literally super-human pre-eminence is such that he is given special sight to see the disguised immortals: besting a god is dangerous! This *kleos*-affirming and -granting narrative is, however, multiply framed: starting with the calling out of Idomeneus to live up to his boasts in the feasting hall, it goes to the 'stirring' of Diomedes himself, challenging him to match his father's deeds – 'it seems his son is better at talking than fighting'. Diomedes accepts the reproach and goes into battle, recreated in natural – and perhaps naturalizing? – simile after simile: the Greeks advance 'as when the thundering surf crests and breaks, smashing against the rock', 'raising the dust like that from the threshing floor', with 'two young champions like two young mountain lions preying on fat cattle' against the Trojans, who are 'like sheep in the fold waiting to be milked, hearing their lambs bleat'.

Diomedes carries all before him, like a river in spate overflowing containing dykes. This simile, unlike those above, goes beyond vivid description to the cost inflicted: 'The river sweeps on over the retaining banks into a beautiful orchard, destroying the hard work of many young men.' These are young men such as Diomedes is about to slay.

Bloody and random as some of the fights are, an epic glow is everywhere cast by the manner of the telling and also, all-too-mortal though they are, by being placed in the sight of and in relationship to the immortals, who in this book mix the two worlds – Troy and Mount Olympus – by coming down to fight. The gods by turns elevate and render comic the fights: the goddess of love but also the god of war can squeal in pain and outrage when hurt by a human.

If the fighting is elevated, it is also tragically contrasted. Only for an immortal can a wound be kissed better, whereas for mortals, once the 'soul has escaped the barrier of the teeth', life blood spilled on the ground, there is no recall.

In his pre-eminence, Diomedes comes up against a Lycian ally of Hektor, Sarpedon's second-in-command, and issues the ritual challenge: 'Who are you who dare to come forward to fight me, me whose spear is all-conquering?' Glaukos replies:

> Why ask me about my lineage, since we are all mortals, like leaves on a tree which flourish and then fall to be replaced by next year's leaves. Yet, since you ask … (7.452–53)

Suddenly, the terror at the heart of heroic fighting is revealed: without *kleos*, a human will be no more than leaves on a tree, whose only purpose is to fertilize the next crop. Only *kleos* is *aphthiton*, undying, or literally that which cannot be worn away; otherwise, man is seen from the perspective of the gods, who ask why anyone should be concerned with those who grow like leaves on the trees, who flourish unindividuated for a season and then fall to nourish the next generation. When Poseidon is angered by the Greek fortification which he sees as challenging the Trojan walls he built, Apollo advises him to let it be:

> You would hardly call me wise if I fought with you for the sake of these wretched mortals, now full of life, eating the earth's fruit, now fading away and falling like the leaves. Let us cease arguing now, let them fight their own battles. (21.461–67)

Or, as Pope translated the passage:

> Apollo thus: "To combat for mankind
> Ill suits the wisdom of celestial mind;
> For what is man? Calamitous by birth,
> They owe their life and nourishment to earth;
> Like yearly leaves, that now, with beauty crowned,
> Smile on the sun; now, wither on the ground.
> To their own hands commit the frantic scene,
> Nor mix immortals in a cause so mean."

Without *kleos*, as Glaukos and the gods say, man is no more than unindividuated leaves on the tree: 'The wind blows and one year's leaves are scattered on the ground, but the trees bud and fresh leaves open when spring comes again' (6.119–22). Or in Chapman's translation:

> 'Why dost thou so explore,'
> Said Glaukos, 'of what race I am, when like the race of leaves
> The race of man is, that deserves no question; nor receives
> My being any other breath? The wind in autumn strows
> The earth with old leaves, then the spring the woods with new endows;
> And so death scatters men on earth, so life puts out again.'

Memorials

When Hektor goes out to fight a champion put forward by the Greeks, he imagines how his opponent will have

> a mound heaped up for him by the broad Hellespont, that future voyagers sailing by, in their benched ships over the wine-dark sea, shall say: 'This is the mound of a warrior long ago, whom glorious Hektor slew in his prime.' So shall they speak, and to my undying glory. (7.87–92)

The tragic irony is the poet's: the last lines of the *Iliad* are of the making of a burial mound – Hektor's.

But the *Iliad* is a complexly tragic narrative, in which the heroes' fighting is reflected on and refracted through many viewpoints, many focalizations. Hektor's end comes when, before being killed by Achilles, he trips 'on an old grave marker of someone forgotten'.

In modern children's stories, a Greek hero's death is marked by ascending into the heavens, a spear puncturing the *ouranos*, the dark cover of the sky, and creating a star. But what kind of memorializing mark can any Iliadic hero make? This is the conclusion to Alice Oswald's version of the poem, *Memorial*:

> Like leaves who could write a history of leaves
> The wind blows their ghosts to the ground
> And the spring breathes new leaf into the woods
> Thousands of names thousands of leaves
> When you remember them remember this
> Dead bodies are their lineage
> Which matters no more than the leaves
> Like when god throws a star
> And everyone looks up
> To see that whip of sparks
> And then it's gone.

Heroic Bonds: Hektor, *aidōs* and the Wrath of Achilles

Key words: *kleos* (name on lips), **geras** (material correlate, prize), **timē** (worth, [evidence of] honour), **aidōs** (respect, inhibiting shame, consciousness of others' judgments)

All the heroes in the *Iliad* fight within a system: a *timē*-enhancing summoner of forces rewarding dangerous exertion with *kleos*-granting prizes. The prize is a material correlate (*geras*) of that intangible system. In Book 1, that system is broken wide open, which breaks other bonds too – the blood bond between allies, comrades and warriors. And the respect for bonds – *aidōs*. Achilles says that the bond is fundamentally broken and withdraws both from the *kleos*-granting fighting and from his comrades.

Hektor is equally bound up in a system. He has summoned allies and is also negotiating problematic relationships with two of his brothers – Paris, the cause of this war but someone who treats claims on him lightly, and Polydamas, who has a claim on Hektor's respect as advisor and interpreter of omens, but does not always respect Hektor's position as leader and as premier fighter. We see Hektor as head of the family and clan of allies.

This plays out through the *Iliad*. Agamemnon's abrogation of the *kleos* system in Book 1 brings on the wrath of Achilles, which condemns to death so many heroes and which sees Achilles – and the epic – questioning what is the *geras* of a human life.

As for Hektor, we watch him negotiating the claims on him and the effect of those claims on the decisions he makes at the times of crisis, pitching him up against the larger forces of his and Troy's destinies.

Achilles' only concern is his imperishable *kleos*. His world is of the heroes of old, whose *kleos* Agamemnon's embassy found him singing to himself in his tent (9.199), and who feature in the famous stories of the heroes at Troy, all those other Iliads, such as the bard sang to Odysseus at King Alkinous' court, the bard whom 'the Muse inspired to sing of the heroes' glorious deeds, a tale whose fame had risen to high heaven' (*Odyssey* 8.65).

The positive mark of and permanent record of *kleos* is tangible: *geras*. Both the *Iliad* and *Odyssey* tell stories of objects with a history, whose value is more than, and differently evaluated from, a monetary one.

The story of the *Iliad* starts with Achilles being deprived of a *geras*, a prize, a token of recognition of his contribution to the fighting:

> Agamemnon has robbed me of my *geras*, given by the sons of Greece, a *geras* for which I laboured. When the Greeks sack some rich Trojan city, it's not I who win the *geras*. My hands bear the brunt of the fiercest fight, but when the spoils are shared, your *geras* is the greater. (1.158–68)

Briseis is a prize. That Achilles cares for her is secondary: it is what she represents that matters. Helen and Troy also feature as 'prizes'. The terms of the duel between the rival husbands, Paris and Menelaus, are:

> If Paris kills Menelaus, Helen and all her treasure are his to keep; and we leave. But if Menelaus kills Paris, the Trojans must yield up Helen and her riches, and pay the Greeks proper compensation [*timē*], on a scale men shall remember. And if Priam and his sons decide not to pay the *timē*, we will fight on to win our due. (3.286–90, 458–59)

In the non-heroic world which Hephaistos works on Achilles' shield, the world which Achilles will never (again) experience, there is a scene of *wergild*, of an arbitration of the 'price of a man' after a killing.

When Achilles and Hektor finally come together to fight, Achilles replies to his request that the decencies be observed, and the loser's corpse be respected, that 'Hektor will pay the price for the killing of Patroclus'.

But what is the price of a man?

The later part of the *Iliad* sees Achilles grappling with that question: not just the price but the *geras*, the proper mark or sufficient material correlate of a man?

Bonds: *aidōs*

Aidōs is a present, imagined or aroused inhibiting emotion, sometimes translatable as 'sensibility', 'self-consciousness' or 'social consciousness'. When Hektor challenges the Greeks, 'though they were gripped with *aidōs* – consciousness of their heroic identity – they were too frightened to respond' (7.93).

In Book 1, we have Achilles' withdrawal from fighting and from society. Agamemnon has broken the bonds of trust, reciprocity and value – the bonds that must be respected, *aidōs* – that have bound Achilles into 'his own' (*philoi*); he will not come back into the fighting until 'his own' are implicated.

When we meet Hektor, he is surrounded by 'his own' – his family, dependants and those he respects. In Book 6, he takes leave of his wife and son, explaining that he has to go out to fight, even though he is the main and only defence of Troy, his mother, wife and son. For, he says, 'I feel *aidōs* before the Trojans and their wives with the trailing dresses, lest someone might say...' There is a splendid stand-off between Hektor and Paris Alexander in Troy: Hektor, battle-scarred and battle-weary, finding fellow prince and brother Paris, beautiful, in his separate palace. When Hektor 'stirs him up' to fight – as all leaders must, rousing the *menos*, the fighting spirit – there is the extra edge: big brother to younger brother (who replies in effect – 'yes, you're right, but you do go on!'). But here there is much more at issue. He calls on Paris not only as fellow prince and fellow fighter, but as the cause of the war: 'Shame on you, sulking here while our allies die protecting the city!'

Paris is characterized as completely free from shame. He likens Hektor's 'upbraiding' to the ear-piercing, nails-on-blackboard, scraping sound of the saw on hard wood, shrilly, remorselessly, going backwards and forwards.

Hektor, on the contrary, is characterized as very conscious of *aidōs*, and tragedy enters his story when his sense of heroic action pulls against this. Despite his rousing of Paris, he twice ignores his wise, soothsayer brother Polydamas. When Polydamas interprets an omen as a warning, Hektor tetchily rejects both advice and omen (12.197–252). He does listen in Book 13 when Polydamas advises him in the heat of battle to regroup, and he gratefully obeys. But when Achilles comes back on the scene, raging for revenge, and the Trojans are thrown in disarray, Polydamas urges retreat to the city walls. Hektor hot-temperedly rejects that advice in favour of taking up the fight against Achilles, misguidedly trusting once more in Zeus' personal patronage and promise of success (18.247–313).

The turning point of both Hektor's and Achilles' story is the killing of Patroclus, which finally brings the two heroes up against one another.

Hektor is conscious of his fault in ignoring Polydamas' wise advice, and troubled:

> Alas, if I retreat through the gate, to the safety of the wall, Polydamas will not be slow to reproach me, since he advised me to withdraw our forces to the city, on that fatal night when Achilles re-appeared. I refused, though it might have been better! But if I hid from the fighting like a coward, I would be shamed before all the Trojans, and their wives in their trailing robes would say, 'Hektor has brought ruin on the army, trusting too much in his own prowess.' (22.96–107)

Hektor as hero, as a leader (over-)conscious of what is due to others, begged by his parents not to face the maddened Achilles, comes up against an Achilles who has broken away from all claims on him, from all bonds of *aidōs*. He turns to face him asking for respect in the sight of the gods and for himself as warrior:

> Come, let us swear an oath before the gods; if Zeus lets me kill you, when I have stripped you of your glorious armour, I will not mistreat your body but will return it to your people, if you will do the same for me.

But he hears the dreadful reply that 'there can be no oaths between such as us, any more than between wolves and lambs. *You will pay the price.*' We know how terribly that price was extorted.

The wrath of Achilles: the breaking of bonds

Key words: *menos* (strength), *memaōs* (battle fury – as distinct from Achilles' *mēnis*, his settled state of wrath), *thumos* (passion container), *phrenes* (mind)

The opening words of the *Iliad* are: 'The *mēnis* of Achilles which brought the death of many heroes.' Throughout the *Iliad*, heroes go into battle *memaōs* – adrenalized, and with their *menos* (fighting spirit) roused. But *mēnis* is something different – a settled state of rage, roused not by the leaders' encouragement but by injustice.

It is caused by, and results in, a deep rupture. By taking away Briseis, Agamemnon breaks the agreement between summoner of forces and his main fighter, as well as the bond between comrades, *philoi*. These bonds and their rupture are key to what happens in the *Iliad*.

Key words: Words related to heroic bonds include: *aitios* (responsible), *aitia* (reason, cause), *philos* (one's own), *charis* (reciprocity, grace, graciousness), *timē* (price, honour) and *aidōs* (shame, respect for others and others' claims).

The story of the wrath of Achilles starts with Agamemnon abrogating his responsibility for offering rewards and prizes to the heroes who fight in his cause. The heroes fight for *kleos* and for the summoner of forces who provides it; it is not personal, not for one's own, nor for one's own cause. Achilles firmly points out that there is no personal cause – *aitia* – for which they are fighting. Their opponents have done nothing to their loved ones *philoi*; they are not *aitios*, responsible:

> No quarrel with Trojan spearmen brought me here to fight: they are not *aitios* – have done me no wrong. No horse or cow of mine have they stolen, nor have my crops been ravaged in my homeland. No, in order to do you *charis*, you shameless [without *aidōs*] cur, we followed to try and win *timē*

[honour, price] for you and Menelaus from the Trojans. And you neither
see nor care; and even threaten to rob me of my *geras*, my prize. (1.148–161)

With reciprocity and respect for bonds gone, there is no reason left to fight the
Trojans. He is not fighting for his own, his kin, his wife, etc, those to whom
he is *philos*, so in no other sense is Troy his enemy. *Philia* is the connection one
has with one's kin and one's kind, one's own. Now Agamemnon is no longer a
philos of Achilles.

The 'heroic equation' of immortal fame, *aphthiton kleos*, for dangerous and
skilful endeavour, has, Achilles says, been destroyed. This is a rupture that
stymies Achilles because he is unique:

> For my mother told me I have a twofold fate: if I stay here and battle, then
> lost is my return home, but I will have my *kleos aphthiton*; if I return home
> lost then is my glorious *kleos*, but a long life is before me. (9.410–16)

Or as Chapman translated it:

> The one, that, if I here remain to assist our victory,
> My safe return shall never live, my fame shall never die;
> If my return obtain success, much of my fame decays,
> But death shall linger his approach, and I live many days.

But now, after Agamemnon's action:

> With equal honour cowards die and men most valiant,
> The much performer, and the man that can of nothing vaunt.

It is a destruction of the *kleos* and *timē* system, invalidating the system of *geras*,
the giving of prizes as material correlates of honour, rendering the receiver and his
deeds the subject of song at feasts, like those offered by Nestor and Hektor to the
spies in Book 10. Now, the destiny, the reward of the best and the worst have been
equalized; the reciprocity in the relations between Agamemnon and those he
leads has gone. None of the respect for bonds that underpinned the summoning
of the army remains, so there is no reason left to fight the Trojans. No amount of
material recompense can wipe out the outrage inflicted by Agamemnon. Material
possessions cannot be weighed against a man's life, especially not against Achilles'
life, with his uniquely definite, choice-dependent fate – either a short life with
glory but no homecoming, or a long life without glory.

Achilles and bonds: *aidōs*, *philoi* and betrayal of social trust

Promoting/benefitting (*philein*) your *philos* (kin, friend, ally); opposing (*echthairein*) your *echthros* (enemy, opponent)

Book 1 brings a fundamental rupture: between Achilles and Agamemnon; between the most powerful fighter and the most powerful leader. The rupture is to the exchange mechanism of heroic fighting – of glory-giving reward for death-defying feats at the extremity of skill, danger and exertion.

That rupture is to two value systems: that of *aidōs*, the respect for bonds, and *philia*, the most pervasive bond between family, friends, allies, 'our own'. For as Achilles sees, when Agamemnon destroyed that exchange mechanism he also destroyed both Achilles' proper observance of the *aidōs* due to the commander of forces and, even more fundamentally, the principle of all adult action – that you promote/benefit (*philein*) your *philos* and oppose/diminish/fight (*echthairein*) your *echthros* (enemy, opponent). For the Trojans are not Achilles' personal enemy, so for Achilles to fight is to promote Agamemnon's interest, he who has constituted himself Achilles' enemy.

In Book 9, Agamemnon calls on Achilles to accept exemplary reparation while also demanding he acknowledge Agamemnon as his leader. The argument is made by his *philoi*, those bound to him by long companionship, fellow Greeks who have been wounded and driven back by Hektor's pre-eminence. The call is also made in the name of the respect for past care, now to be reciprocated (Phoenix, his old tutor, asking that Achilles attend to him as an example of proper and wise flexibility).

Jonathan Shay, a seminal psychiatrist treating veterans with post-traumatic stress disorder (PTSD), recognizes many aspects of Achilles' psychology, including what he identifies as his final 'snapping'. He identifies in Book 1 a betrayal of trust which he likens to that felt by Vietnam veterans over the betraying behaviour of commanders in the field and politicians back home in the US. The rupture goes beyond the immediate incident and immediate power structure to a sense of a rupture in the cosmos – *kosmos* in Greek means order, but also implies something beautifully, harmoniously constructed. So there is a loss of trust in the world structures as both ordered and ordered fairly.

Such a loss of trust in 'what's right', combined with a breaking of the social bond which normally governs conduct, can, Professor Shay shows, lead to a loss of confidence in the environment (in Homer, perhaps, expressed as Zeus' plan). Furthermore, the social bond dictates and renders automatic some decisions about how to act. When that is broken, each decision has to be newly made.

In Achilles' case, the rupture is straightforward: the automatic rule of benefitting *philoi* by harming enemies that would normally keep him fighting has necessarily led to withdrawal. In the Vietnam veterans Shay reports on, the betrayal of trust and interruption to automatic, trusted, decision-making are the start of a fragmenting and unravelling of identity. He sees Agamemnon's action as starting a destructive arc that could be likened to the experiences that can lead a combat soldier to a breaking point.

Achilles' *mēnis*: does he go 'berserk'?

'A soldier who routs the enemy single-handedly is often in the grip of a special state of mind, body, and social disconnection at the time of his memorable deeds,' writes Shay in *Achilles in Vietnam*. Common throughout the *Iliad* is the description of the stirring of the blood of the warrior in combat, the adrenalin and sharpness that seem to guarantee victory if the vicissitudes of the battlefield allow. The river god in Book 21 declares that here we have Achilles fighting not with stirred *menos*, battle adrenalin, but with bloodlust.

'Vietnam narratives reveal that the events that drive soldiers berserk are betrayal, insult, or humiliation by a leader; death of a friend-in-arms,' says Shay. He recognizes as an aspect of PTSD that, after triggers such as those he recognizes in Book 1 – betrayal, loss of trust, leading to withdrawal – and Book 16 – the death of someone who is, or has become in the mind of the survivor, significant – the warrior enters a state he likens to that of Old Norse 'berserkers', which probably means 'bare skinned', without armour – feeling invulnerable and/or indifferent to death or danger.

Vietnam survivors report their berserk state: 'I was a f***ing animal'; 'I felt like a god, this power flowing through me'. Nothing matters; they are blind, sometimes literally, to anything other than the kill, though in retrospect they can reflect on the trigger: 'I felt betrayed. I lost all my mercy after that.'

This certainly fits with the river god – furious at the pollution of his waters – describing Achilles' killing as 'evil, more than human, ruthlessly'. Is he in that altered state of mind recognized by Shay and described in Norse epics, characterized as feeling like a beast, a god, disconnected from human community, without restraint, invulnerable?

Like a god; like a beast

Throughout the *Iliad*, heroes are likened to animals 'doing what comes naturally' – preying on the weaker and vulnerable – and to inhuman forces like a mountain fire, lightning or violent storm. The point of these similes is perhaps that rather than normalizing that very behaviour, they highlight the very unnaturalness of the battlefield and the heroes' necessary mentality.

One of the most coldly shocking moments in the *Iliad* is the exchange of words before the climactic battle between Achilles and Hektor, quoted above. Hektor asks for the agreement that, should he lose, his body be treated with respect and returned to his parents for burial. Achilles' chilling reply is that 'lions and men make no compacts; wolves and lambs no agreements'. What is precisely bestial is to will, to plan, to act *deliberately* as if an animal. Unlike a simile, which points up the similarity between human and animal behaviour, this points up Achilles' inhuman bestiality.

For Shay, these elements are part of a narrative of damage: of minds altered by long exposure to danger, deprivation and traumatizing events, sometimes aggravated by substance abuse or physical neglect: a build-up of pressures triggering flashbacks and disintegration. Shay's veteran case studies are broken narratives of individuals whose narrative identity has been interrupted: memory loss and partial, impaired or hallucinatory recall all prevent the construction of a coherent account of the past, hold on the present and continuity of self into the future. He points to discontinuities in Achilles' story, where he reports disorientating dreams (like that of Patroclus appearing to him, reproaching him for forgetting him).

In Book 16, everything comes to a head. Achilles has been obdurate when asked to come back into the fighting, saying that Agamemnon has broken the contract between summoner and heroes answering the call. Although the appeal of the embassy in Book 9 failed, even strengthening Achilles' isolation and obduracy, now his closest *philos*, Patroclus, makes a triple appeal to those bonds of *philia*: reporting that their closest friends are wounded and suffering; that his own ships are in danger – the ships that are the Greeks' last line of defence and chance of escape are now exposed to Hektor's attack; and, disastrously as the poet highlights, that he – his closest companion, his most *philos philos* – is himself distressed. Patroclus begs Achilles to act, in a call on Achilles' *aidōs*, his respect for a supplication – for a supplication, the calling on a superior or more powerful person to heed a request, is also a formal act that must be acceded to.

The result is of course that he agrees to send Patroclus into battle in his armour, as *therapōn* or ritual substitute. There is something deeply wrong about impersonating another, attempting to embody another persona, narrated as an attempt to deceive not just the enemy but also the Muse, the recorder of *kleos*.

Shay identifies a similarly affecting sense of 'wrongness' in some veterans' accounts of what we might too easily label as 'survivor guilt': the sense that someone died the death meant for you, that the bullet with your name on it killed your neighbour. Like the Vietnam survivors' accounts – of the person behind and the person in front being felled while they are unaffected; of the change of shift that leaves them safe when their replacement is killed seconds later – the Homeric narrative is full of tragic ironies, such as when the spear aimed at Menelaus is 'brushed away' by a god and an arrow fired at a leader instead hits the charioteer. Shay discriminates in Achilles' subsequent bloodlust components he recognizes from his treatment of Vietnam veterans. Achilles clearly expresses direct guilt: he shouts his distress that he was not there to protect Patroclus as he had promised Patroclus' father.

But Patroclus is called and goes into battle not instead of, but *as* Achilles. Patroclus has clearly died in Achilles' place, as his *therapōn*, his substitute. So, rather than survivor guilt there is something even more for Achilles to deal with: he had firmly charged Patroclus not to fight in his armour, not to *represent* him, and in a real sense he has died *as* Achilles.

The tragic narrative imagines a different future that is now denied: one where Patroclus and he take Troy and, if Patroclus survives Achilles, he goes back to Achilles' son and brings him up – both futures where Patroclus substitutes for him, and in some sense, in some imagined future, becomes him.

The end is that their ashes will be mixed in a single urn; the union that Achilles' allowing Patroclus to wear his armour brings to them both.

Before and after Lykaon

Although there are so many parallels between Jonathan Shay's veterans' stories and what is reflected in Achilles' psychological breakdown, there are significant re-layerings. Rather than the veterans' broken narratives, we have Achilles' own words, the parameters of *mēnis* outlined by Achilles himself.

After Patroclus' death, Lykaon, one of Priam's sons whom Achilles had previously ransomed after a raid, stoops under the spear-shaft and, grasping his knees, makes a supplication. This is a formal act of submission, laying himself open to the downward shaft, on the double count that first, Achilles is bound by a bond of *xenia*, as Lykaon had eaten at his table while waiting to be ransomed; and second – inadvisedly! – that he was from a different mother from that of Hektor who killed Patroclus.

Achilles, 'unhoneyed', replies:

> Fool [*nēpios*], do not talk to me of ransom, make me no speeches! Before the day of fate overtook Patroclus, I had a mind to spare you Trojans. Many I took alive, selling them far away. Now not one shall keep his life, of all that the gods send to my hands before Troy, not one solitary Trojan, and least of all the sons of Priam. You too, my friend, must die: why so sad? Patroclus, a far better man, has died. Or look at me, how big and fine I am, my father is a great man, and a goddess bore me, yet death and remorseless

fate await me too. Either at sunrise, evening or midday, some man in battle will strike me with his spear, or pierce me with an arrow from his bow. (21.99–114)

That is to say, previously he respected the common social bonds, the mechanism of exchange of captive for ransom. But now, like the Vietnam veteran above, 'he lost all his mercy'. But, unlike the Vietnam veterans, Achilles can reflect precisely on his process: he can locate his state of mind in terms of both past and future self, and he is in full possession of his narrative identity. When he goes on to treat Lykaon's body as fish meat, he does it in full possession of his human senses.

The *geras* of the dead: Zeus weeps bloody tears for his son

In Book 16, Zeus, watching, sees that his son, Sarpedon, is destined to die and considers intervening. Hera says that Zeus must rather accept that the proper end, the reward, for a mortal is to have due burial and a physical memorial, a focus for the commemoration that dead heroes receive. He should

> send Death and sweet Sleep to bear him away to Lycia, where his brothers and all his kin may mark his resting place with mound and stele, the *geras* [sufficient material correlate] of the dead.

A system where prizes are important for what they represent – honour and war objective – in the *Iliad* comes into question; finally, what is recompense for the death of Patroclus?

The end of Achilles' *mēnis*?

Once, Achilles would respect – show *aidōs* to – all kinds of bonds. Now all bets are off: supplication, proper treatment of the dead. He says to Lykaon's corpse: 'Lie with the fish: they'll suck the blood from your wounds.' He also rejects Hektor's request that the victor respect the other's corpse: 'Do not talk to me about oaths and good faith between us: full payment of bloodshed and revenge, rather.' And he cares nothing for the distinction between *philoi* and *echthroi*, friends and enemies; only for satisfaction for the bloodshed of Patroclus. He is beyond all the social conventions, niceties, celebrations, marriage feasts and blood arbitrations illustrated by Hephaistos on his shield:

> To the light of blazing torches, the brides were led out through the city to wedding songs. Young men circled in the dance, whirling round to flutes and lyres, while women stood in their doorways gazing.

The men had gathered in assembly: two contesting the blood price to be paid for another's death. One claimed to the people he had paid all that was right, but the accuser refused his offer and the both of them sought arbitration. The elders sat in judgment on the sacred bench, a semi-circle of polished stone, with two talents of gold at their feet. (18.491–509)

The quarrel in Book 1 is over a prize, a *geras*; Book 23 is about the thoughtful, respectful (showing *aidōs*) and gracious (*charis*-giving) awarding of prizes by Achilles, arbitrating between 'firstness' and 'best' at Patroclus' funeral games.

Between these two events there is the bloody narrative of Achilles' revenge, of his attempt to extort a sufficient blood price for the death of Patroclus. The narrative of breakage and rupture – intensified by the warrior conventions but universally recognizable – then follows a tragic arc of revenge, first on Patroclus' killer and then on his corpse. But the big questions remain: what is, what can possibly be the end of Achilles *mēnis*? And the universal question: what is the *geras* of the dead? What value can stand up to the human condition?

Every reader, every reading of the final books of the *Iliad*, has to answer for themselves as well as Achilles.

Part II

The *Odyssey*

Odysseus' Travels

The *Odyssey* is the story of Odysseus returning home from the great, defining Trojan War, to those he left so long ago. His story is set against those who welcome him and those waiting for him back home; the question for them, us and perhaps Odysseus himself, is what if anything they will recognize in this adventurer of the young hero who went to war?

Introduction: The Journey Home from War

The *Odyssey* starts with a triple framing: firstly, of Odysseus himself, one of the Greek leaders whose return from the Trojan War is hindered by the gods, stuck on Calypso's island; and of his son and wife, similarly stuck between their past identities – Penelope as Odysseus' wife and Telemachus as his heir – and the opening up of the potential for agency over an independent future, as desirable woman and adult man.

When Odysseus finally reveals his identity to those who are going to take him home, he starts his story by saying he is Odysseus, son of Laertes, on his way to his 'family home on rugged Ithaca, not fertile, but good for nurturing strong young men: nowhere is sweeter'.

His first adventure after Troy is near, in all senses, to the fighting he had been engaged in during that long war: an attack on a town for sustenance and spoil, the sort of raid that has been going on throughout the Trojan War and no doubt since time immemorial. The raid starts straightforwardly with a victorious attack on a nearby town of the Cicones and sharing out of the spoils. There is then the first sign of breakdown of discipline – or of a leader's authority in this initial post-war encounter? – that is eventually ruinous. Victorious, Odysseus orders his men to retreat and divides up, fairly, the spoils. Nevertheless, they refuse and stay nearby, carousing and feasting on their newly won goods, wine, women, sheep and cattle. Meanwhile, the Cicones gather their neighbours and, in the morning, surround Odysseus and his men, 'as thick as leaves or flowers spring up in their season'.

The fight continues until evening, when the Cicones finally prevail. Odysseus and his men escape to the ships, but six have been killed, left behind near those who died at Troy.

This is the start of Odysseus' companions and the ships carrying them going 'off piste': rather than them all returning in good order, there is the start of a dissolution of the bonds of men to their leader and that of the hero to the gods and cosmos:

And now all unscathed should I have reached my native land, but the wave and the current and the North Wind beat me back as I was rounding the southernmost tip of Southern Greece and drove me from my course.

From this point, the story changes; the return is no longer that of a Trojan War hero bringing his men back home, but of a warrior whose adventures gradually strip him of his previous identity, as his men and possessions are slowly lost. From now on, we have not Odysseus the commander but Odysseus the *polytropos* of the opening line – many-travelled (many ways, many turns) but also of many storied identities (many tropes, fictions):

> Tell me, Muse, of that man of many ways, who wandered far and wide after sacking Troy's holy citadel.

The *Odyssey* starts with the invocation to the Muse, to help the bard to tell the story of Odysseus *polytropos*,

> who wandered far and wide, after the fall of Troy. Many the men whose cities he saw, whose minds he got to know. Many were his sufferings on the sea, trying to win through alive to a return, a *nostos*, for himself and his men.

The first word in the *Odyssey* is *andra*: man or Man. From the time of the Athenian Tyrants – who 'canonized' the previous multi-versions performed by the 'sons of Homer' storytellers, and by poets and artists from Virgil to James Joyce, Derek Walcott and beyond – the *Odyssey* has been recognized and responded to as about not a man, but 'Man'.

For Odysseus is someone with extraordinary stories to tell – encounters with every kind of man and beast, every kind of society – and also with a story recognizable to warriors in all times and all places, including our own: of the problems of return from battle to the home and family left far and long behind, the problem of transitioning from an established identity and place in an army to having to build one in the world outside.

The central books of the *Odyssey* are set at the court of the Phaeacian King Alkinous. Odysseus arrives on the shore of Phaeacia, naked and battered, literally stripped of everything, every relationship, every mark of identity. On Phaeacia, as an anonymous stranger being cared for and restored before being carried home, he hears the bard sing about the Trojan War, which moves him to tears. What is notable is that the tears are a response to the representation not of suffering but of one of those 'glorious deeds of men, whose fame rises to the heavens' that we hear so much about in the *Iliad*. So, why does Odysseus cry? Perhaps at the immediacy of the reminder of the past when he was one of those men, did some of those deeds, had such a fame?

The second burst of weeping, behind his covering cloak, unlocks the story of his journey: from Troy to home but also from military commander to anonymous wanderer, with nothing to offer his hosts but his accounts of his many encounters.

So, as a guest must in repayment for the hospitality, he tells his story: the famous, fabulous stories of monsters, giants, a goddess and a witch; of every kind of society, every kind of hosting. Phaeacia is a place of stories – of stories told by the incomparable bard and, eventually, of those told by Odysseus himself. It is a place where others' stories come up against those of Odysseus: Nausicaa's, as prophesied, is to marry a heroic stranger; Circe's to have children like Telegonus with an epic story of their own. For the *Odyssey* is just one – though an extraordinarily crafted and reflective one – of the epics retold and performed into and beyond the Classical period. Odysseus borrows some adventures from others' stories, such as those of Jason and the Argonauts. Like the rhapsode (the stitcher-together of tales) who sang those epics, he is conscious both of the other and of others' stories that he can adapt and adopt.

The *Odyssey* starts with Odysseus' son Telemachus visiting the palace of Nestor and that of Menelaus and Helen. The narrative is sited in the Mycenaean world the Greek leaders left for the Trojan War, at its height in the thirteenth and fourteenth century BCE. Meanwhile, the identity-concealing fictions Odysseus tells back home on Ithaca incorporate stories of Phoenician, Egyptian and Cretan pirates, slavers and traders recognizable from the pre-Classical 'Dark Age' world of the ninth to seventh centuries BCE: one where Mycenaean objects are precious heirlooms. Odysseus wreaks revenge on the suitors who have infested his home for their hubris, and also because they have eaten him out of house and home (no palace storerooms full of produce) rather than bringing their own pigs to the wooing. The final coming together of Penelope and Odysseus takes place in a Dark Age hall, with a floor of earth rather than marble. So Odysseus' journey is also from palatial Troy to the subsistence world of Ithaca, 'good for goats'.

The wonderful, enchanting tales told to the king and queen in the fabulous palace on Phaeacia are different from the stories Odysseus tells elsewhere. Whenever he is asked the questions all Greeks asked, and ask today – *tis pothen eis?*, who are you (really) and where from? (what's your story about how you came to be that?) – he conceals rather than reveals his identity. He tells 'Cretan tales' (Cretans were famously incapable of 'telling true') to everyone, including to his goddess helpmeet, his old servant and, much more problematically, his wife and grief-stricken father.

The second half of the *Odyssey* is concerned with recognition: what of the Odysseus who went away is recognizable to those he left behind? And for what, as what, can he be recognized? A question for all in – and indeed outside – the story: soldiers and soldiers' families though the ages have similarly asked *tis pothen eis?* – who are you, who am I, *now*, returned from war?

Psychiatrists like Jonathan Shay who work with traumatized soldiers insist on the importance of helping soldiers to tell their stories. He says this 'transmutes the pain into something else: not relief, necessarily, or transcendence, and certainly not glory, but maybe a kind of understanding'. But they also understand that there is emotional baggage to be dealt with: the soldier's hypervigilance and aggression tend to transfer 'back home', can lead to an 'emotional shutting down. If the switch for the tender, softer, sweeter, more nuanced capacities for emotion remains jammed in the "off" position, then negotiating a life with a family, with a sweetheart or a wife, or with children becomes extraordinarily difficult.' (See Shay's 'The Trauma of War' in the *Voices in Wartime: the Anthology*.)

The intensity of the battlefield can make 'ordinary life' seem, well, ordinary.

So there is a double task involved in 'telling one's story'. One is to transmute the pain; as the swineherd says to the disguised Odysseus, 'tales are a way of turning pain to good: the suffering is metamorphosed into pleasure as the story is recounted for men's delight. Even a wanderer who has suffered greatly finds later enquiry and recall to be transformative.' The second task seems more problematic: it is to know who and what you are. One definition of 'identity' is 'the same yesterday as today'. In no sense is Odysseus the same as Penelope and the suitors remember him to be; in no sense is Odysseus the same in Phaeacia, in the swineherd's hut and in the hall in Ithaca – three of the places where he tells his stories.

Two of Odysseus' epithets are *polytropos* – of many ways: many wanderings and many forms of expression – and also *poikilomētis*, with a mind that is variegated, multi-faceted, shining variously. Odysseus can represent – re-present – himself in the way that will profit him most. But whereas a bard professionally distances himself from the stories he tells, Odysseus, very differently, is supposedly telling his own story. Psychiatrists treating returning soldiers say baldly that 'narrative is central to recovery'. But narrative can distance one from, can avoid, what one has seen, experienced and done.

Jonathan Shay also talks of the returning soldier's destroyed social trust, his new suspiciousness: 'Every interaction that person enters into is framed as, "I have to strike first." Or, "What's your gain? How are you deceiving me by expressing these good intentions?"'

Odysseus uses his crafty 'Cretan tales' to test out his interlocutors, including a process that Athene remarks on. She says, 'You are always so shrewd and so cautious! Any other man back from his wanderings would have dashed joyfully to his hall to see his wife and children, but you don't want to know or find out anything until you've tested out your wife.' It is difficult not to remember this as Odysseus holds out first on his son and then on the faithful Penelope, long keeping up his disguise.

The end of the *Odyssey*, Odysseus' hard testing of his grief-stricken father, leaves us with a question: can this testing frame of mind be a sign of damage as well as causing damage? That is also to ask, is being *poikilomētis* – being able to 'present' so variously – finally a sign of a loss of ability to form bonds of trust? Which takes us back to the question of identity which runs right though the *Odyssey*: who are you, Odysseus, now you have left Troy, now you are back, albeit temporarily, on Ithaca?

Books 1–4

Overview: Waiting for Odysseus

Telemachus and Penelope

T he *Odyssey* starts with the invocation to the Muse, to help the bard to tell the story of Odysseus *polytropos*: Odysseus of many ways, many turns, many stories,

who wandered far and wide, after the fall of Troy. Many the men whose cities he saw, whose minds he got to know. Many were his sufferings on the sea, trying to win through alive to a return, a *nostos*, for himself and his men.

The opening books of the *Odyssey* deal not with Odysseus himself but with what his absence means to those left behind. Odysseus has lost the battle to bring his men safe home from Troy and is alone with the nymph Calypso, who has trapped him in her caves. The story opens as the deadlock and inactivity on

Calypso's island and on Ithaca is about to be broken by the gods' intervention: Odysseus is about to be released from his very pleasant jail and go home.

On Ithaca, Odysseus' baby son of nearly twenty years ago is about to enter manhood. Both he and his mother, Penelope, are trapped by Odysseus' disappearance: like wives and children in all ages up to the social media connectedness of the present, those waiting at home without news are in limbo. Telemachus is neither son nor king, she neither wife nor widow. They cannot move on until they hear news of Odysseus' safety or death. Yet for both of them, time is moving on – he is approaching manhood, she is the magnet for any who want to take over Odysseus' position and property. In the course of the *Odyssey*, they both have to find a future for themselves without and independent of Odysseus, while understanding that future may be destabilized. Like warriors and their women throughout the ages, homecoming will not be easy for anyone.

The frame of the story's central books – where Odysseus tells of his adventures – is of those who are stuck. Odysseus is 'detained' by the lovely immortal nymph, Calypso (whose name means the coverer, the concealer). We are told both that she wants him for a life partner – later she complains that the male gods can take human partners at a whim but female goddesses have no such luxury – and that he is caught in a web of longing for return and his wife.

But a time of crisis is coming: we hear that Odysseus' return is prohibited by Poseidon, god of the sea, because of his blinding of Poseidon's son the Cyclops, but that Athene proposes they take advantage of Poseidon's absence at a feast held for him by the Ethiopians. The scene is set – Poseidon is seated at his banquet, the other gods meet to frame the story and decide what to do. Zeus starts by reminding all of the other big story of homecoming, that of Agamemnon, whose murder is here squarely attributed to his rival, Aegisthus (unlike the classical and tragic drama tradition of his killing by the adulterous Clytemnestra). From the start, the story that is to be told is of both the victorious Greeks' ongoing story once they have left the structured world of the battlefield and the disruption their return can cause to the new status quo established in their absence. This draws attention to the parallel but so different roles in their fathers' return played by Agamemnon's and Odysseus' sons, Orestes and Telemachus.

We then visit briefly the main characters in the story that is about to develop: Odysseus, stuck on Calypso's island, held by her love and by Poseidon's ongoing antagonism; and Telemachus, stuck in dependent adolescence in his father's palace. Here, in the absence of a head of the household, a swarm of suitors have settled in the house, devouring Telemachus' inheritance. From the perspective of Mount Olympus, the home of the gods, it is clear that it is time the stalemate is broken.

Hermes is dispatched to order Calypso to release Odysseus, while Athene, disguised as Odysseus' old friend, Mentas, goes to Telemachus to give him self-confidence. Athene's very arrival prompts Telemachus' first adult responsible act. Looking up from musing on his absent father, he notes with displeasure that a guest is not being attended to. He hastens to greet and entertain him, as is proper to the master of the household. The goddess sits down to advise him, recommending that he set out to find what has happened to his father. In the course of talking to the goddess, Telemachus grows from a despondent, unsure child to a young adult, encouraged by Athene/Mentas to take action in the same way that Apollo impelled the young Orestes to avenge his father King Agamemnon.

His new maturity is immediately made evident to Penelope, who is told to look to her handiwork and leave discussion to the men, and especially to himself, who is now master of the house. Similarly, Telemachus speaks sharply to the suitors – minor lords of Ithaca and of surrounding areas, who have during his boyhood moved into the palace in pursuit of Penelope and the kingship, in Odysseus' place.

Book 1 ends with Telemachus speaking sharply to the Suitors. Book 2 starts with him exerting himself over the Assembly, called for the first time since Odysseus went away. Those eligible to come to the Ithacan Assembly protest against Telemachus' complaints that for nearly four years they have eaten up house and home: it is Penelope, they claim, who is causing the delay. She has refused to remarry until she has woven a shroud for her father-in-law; a proper sentiment in a noble lady, showing concern for propriety and for her good name. But for three years she has woven by day and unpicked her work by night, showing herself to be cunning and resourceful, a worthy partner of Odysseus the 'resourceful/tricky-minded' spinner of tales. Her cunning has increased her desirability and reputation, making the suitors even more desperate to win a lady so wise, skilled and beautiful. If Odysseus manages to return, he will come back to a wife who has come to be valued in her own right, desired and famous for qualities developed in the twenty years of his absence.

Telemachus, helped by Athene, assembles stores and a team of young bloods and takes command of a ship to search for definite news of his father. He goes secretly, but by the time he returns, he will have assumed the status and learned the manners and duties of a prince: when Odysseus returns, he, too, will be a force to be reckoned with.

The emotions and character of the adolescent Telemachus are tellingly charted. At the start of Book 1, he is despondent and not self-confident, feeling his position to be difficult. Athene/Mentas gives him a sense of the stature of his absent father and the courage to act as one favoured by the gods. His speeches in the Assembly in Book 2, the first of his manhood, swing from self-assertive to self-pitying and back to decisive. When in Book 3 he arrives in Pylos in the Peloponnese at Nestor's palace, he is too embarrassed to approach his host because he doesn't know what to say. He is so overawed by the splendour of the Spartan palace in Book 4 that he whispers to his companion that it seems like the court of the king of the gods. However, from the old hero Nestor and from the powerful King of Sparta, Menelaus, and his wife, Helen of Troy, he learns how to behave, how to sacrifice and pray to the gods, to celebrate a feast, to entertain guests and to talk fittingly to his father's peers. He is also given for the first time a powerful sense of his father as a public man: of his cleverness, skill in speaking and effectiveness in council, of his strength, leadership and craftiness, of the impression he made on the great ones at Troy over the years of fighting. Finally, in his diplomacy in asking for a different, more wieldy parting gift from Menelaus, he is proclaimed to be his father's son.

He has journeyed to find out about his father; in so doing, he has found out about himself.

The portraits of adolescence, of Ithaca – where there is not enough grain or grass to pasture a horse – and of drunken guests outstaying their welcome, are portraits of a real world. Menelaus' court at Sparta provides a bridge into the heroic world of Troy: the Wooden Horse, the beautiful, divine Helen with potions that can give insensibility to the most terrible human tragedy, and King Menelaus, who only managed to return home after a fight with the Old Man of the Sea. The *Odyssey* constantly juxtaposes the real world of human relationships and human tragedy with the heroic and fabulous world of stories – stories which are in the main told by the heroes themselves.

Telemachus and Penelope at home in Ithaca

Telemachus

We meet Telemachus seated in the family hall, where the suitors are drinking, playing counters and feasting off Ithacan ox-meat. He is vividly described as day-dreaming of his father's return and of clearing out and taking vengeance on those infesting his home.

Athene has flown from Olympus, disguised as a visiting chief. Telemachus comes forward from the sidelines to greet the visitor hovering by the door of the high-raftered hall, welcoming 'him' graciously as a host should: offering food and entertainment before asking for an account of his needs and reason for his visit. He may be still a boy, but he takes responsibility like the prince he is, seating the goddess in a beautifully wrought chair with a footstool, away from the suitors' uproar. A handmaid pours water from a golden ewer into a silver dish for them to wash, while the housekeeper quietly lays out a feast, with delicacies and carefully carved meat, and attendants serve and keep filled the golden wine goblets.

The suitors carry on their feast. Under cover of the 'resident' bard, Phemius', song, Telemachus confides in the disguised goddess, contrasting the suitors' carefree feasting on his father's estate, his patrimony, with his care-filled life imagining the fate of that father. He asks whether the stranger is one who was a guest in the days when Odysseus welcomed wanderers and visitors from all over the known world. After giving an account of her pretend self, Athene increases the narrative's dramatic sense that change is coming, Odysseus will find a way home and Telemachus has a journey to make.

Telemachus is depressed and lacking in confidence, sure that Odysseus has died. He is anything but vaunting about his paternity: in answer to Athene saying that he is his father's son, he says 'so my mother says, but who can be sure of his fathering?'!

He talks of their present misery: how Penelope can neither declare herself a widow and accept one of the suitors, nor confidently tell them to go, and how he is ceaselessly but fruitlessly mourning his father, lost somewhere without the glorious rites and memorials of a fallen hero like those in the *Iliad* – Sarpedon and Hektor.

Athene reassures him, picturing the return of Odysseus as vengeful cleanser and restorer of his house. She then gives him a grown-up commission, to summon an Assembly

Athene

and order – as the *kurios* (responsible head) of the household – the suitors to disperse and his mother, if she wants to marry again, to go back to the care and arranging of her father.

Then he is to go to visit Nestor and Menelaus, safely returned home from Troy to their Mycenaean palaces in mainland Greece, at Pylos and Sparta. If they give him news of his father's return or death, he can act accordingly, either holding out and planning his part in his father's revenge or building a tomb and arranging his mother's remarriage. It is time to leave childhood behind and grow up. She offers him a model to follow – that of Orestes, avenging his father Agamemnon's murder by his father's supplanter, Aegisthus.

The next scene shows us Penelope, the 'ever thoughtful', hearing the bard Phemius' polished song of the Greeks' troubled return from Troy: 'She descended the high stairs from her chamber, accompanied by her two maids, drawing her shining veil across her face, and stopped by the hall's doorpost, framed by two handmaids.' In tears, she asks Phemius – 'you who know so many deeds of men and gods which can charm men's hearts' – to sing something less achingly full of grief for her, who forever holds her husband's face in her memory, 'he whose fame resounds through Greece'.

Telemachus intervenes, adopting a manly tone, saying it is not the bard's fault that sad songs are so pleasing, and – in a rare piece of insider information – that it is reasonable that the latest songs are the most popular. She is taking it too personally: Odysseus is not the only husband who did not come back, so she should 'go back to the women's quarters, supervise her maids and take up her work at the loom and the spindle. It is for the men to discuss and make decisions: all men, but I in particular, as I am the master here.' Any mother of a teenage son can relate to the next phrase: 'Penelope went back upstairs, in amazement at the words of her son.'

Telemachus speaks commandingly to the suitors, calling on Zeus to give him vengeance and the throne, which similarly amazes them. Then he retires to bed. The final domestic details are entrancing:

> With his mind full of thoughts, he went to his chamber high above the fine courtyard and his old nurse, the faithful Eurycleia, carrying a blazing torch, waited on him. Odysseus' father had bought her himself long ago for twenty oxen, when she was still young. He had honoured her in his palace as he honoured his loyal wife, never lying with her lest his wife should be angry. Of all the house slaves she loved him most, having been his nurse. He opened the door to the well-made room, and sitting on the bed took off his soft tunic, placing it in the wise old woman's hands. Folding and smoothing the tunic, she hung it on a peg by the wooden bedstead, and going out of the room closed the door by its silver handle, bolted it shut with the leather thong.
>
> There, all night long, wrapped in a woollen fleece, Telemachus planned in his mind the journey Athene had proposed.

Next day, Telemachus calls the first Assembly since Odysseus left, addressing all – seemingly those too old to go with Odysseus and those working the land – commandingly about the current situation. He demands that the suitors leave and calls for Ithacans to stop colluding: if it were the ordinary Ithacans who were taking advantage of Odysseus' absence and his minority, that would at least mean there could be an arbitration and compensation later, but there is no redress for the suitors' depredations. He speaks authoritatively and like an adult, until his voice breaks on the last words: 'I can no longer bear the pain you heap on me.'

The leader of the suitors, Antinous, answers robustly on their behalf. Rather than blaming them, he should rather blame his mother, who has kept them dangling for nearly three years: she has set up a loom to weave a shroud for her elderly father-in-law, and only when she has completed this task proper to a daughter-in-law, she has declared, will she be free to remarry. But deviously – a suitable attribute of Odysseus' 'other half' – she has spent each night unpicking the work completed the day before. Anything but passive, in being competed for for so long, she has been maintaining her stature and position.

Telemachus says it is not for him to criticize or turn against his mother. He calls on Zeus, who provides an omen: two sparring eagles, interpreted by the aged seer as indicating that Odysseus is even now plotting his vengeful return. Another leading suitor, Eurymachus, forcefully rejects this interpretation and is confident that should Odysseus return, one man against many, he would lose, and the then-widowed Penelope would have no choice left. (The question remains, why do the Ithacans not support Telemachus' demand that the suitors leave Ithaca? Is it because in the 'heroic' world, fighting is for heroes and those left behind are non-combatants? Or is it because in the Dark Age world of Ithaca, with a subsistence economy, all are concerned to either just feed their families or are benefiting by supplying the suitors?)

Telemachus reveals that he is going to Sparta and Nestor's palace at Pylos, hopefully to establish whether Odysseus is indeed alive or dead.

Telemachus in Nestor's Palace

Telemachus leaves the Dark Age world of Ithaca and arrives at the well-built, tall citadel of Pylos (where a Mycenaean palace has been excavated, visitable today). A huge sacrifice to Poseidon is taking place, with many thousand men drawn up in companies on the shore, each company sacrificing nine bulls to the Earth Shaker.

Telemachus is overawed, but Athene, in the form of Mentor, Odysseus' chancellor, reminds him that he is here to find out about Odysseus and encourages him to go forward. He is welcomed, sat on a thick fleece and offered skewers of meat and goblets of wine, before Nestor and his son ask the traditional question: strangers, who are you and where do you come from, how do you come to be what you are? The traditional answer is to tell the story of life's journey: the gift of the guest to the host in return for food and shelter. But Telemachus has only come from Ithaca and the story he needs is one for him to hear not to tell: that of Nestor, Odysseus and the other Greek heroes' return.

Nestor is pleased to talk, especially as he recognizes in Telemachus traits of his old, dear friend, Odysseus. He briefly reminisces about the end of the Trojan War and his own fairly swift return to Pylos, about others whose fate he has heard of, their return along the normal seaways, although sometimes blown off course though not off the map. There is little information about Odysseus, but there is much about the fatal return of Agamemnon to be killed by Aegisthus: a death avenged – Telemachus is to take note – by his son Orestes.

Telemachus indeed does take note: he asks the gods for Orestes' strength and requests more details. A fascinatingly different account of Agamemnon's wife Clytemnestra is given from that dramatized by Aeschylus in *Agamemnon*, the first play in the trilogy, the *Oresteia*. In the classical play, the murder is done by Clytemnestra, but here the dynamic is different: the beautiful Clytemnestra is 'good and noble', and it is Aegisthus who 'accomplished a monstrous plot'. For while Agamemnon and the Greek heroes were fighting at Troy, Aegisthus charmed Clytemnestra, despite the attendant bard whom Agamemnon charged with looking after her when he was away. Aegisthus took the bard and marooned him on a desert island for birds of prey to feast on. Seven years later, Orestes returned and avenged Agamemnon's death and the seven years' usurpation. Nestor warns him:

> So, dear friend, do not stay away long and far wandering, leaving overbearing men in possession.

Nestor recognizes that Athene's aegis encompasses Odysseus' son as well as Odysseus, and he proposes sacrificing a gilded horned cow to her. He leads the way to his 'glorious home', offering him a 'well-crafted bedstead in the fine open portico. Next to him sleeps Nestor's son, unmarried, while Nestor sleeps in the inner chamber with the lady his wife.' Next morning the cow's horns are gilded and sacrificed, while Nestor's lovely youngest daughter bathes and anoints Telemachus. With Peisistratos, Nestor's youngest son, as charioteer, Telemachus goes on his way to Sparta.

Telemachus at the court of Menelaus and Helen

> So they came to the hill country around Sparta with its deep gorges and reached glorious Menelaus' palace. They found him holding a wedding feast, to celebrate the coming marriages of his faultless daughter Hermione as bride to Achilles' son Neoptolemus, as he had promised at Troy.

The feast is deliciously described: acrobats, bard, kin and neighbours making merry in Menelaus' high-roofed hall. The strangers are welcomed royally, their horses attended to, and when they have feasted their eyes with gazing,

Helen and her maids

they enter the gleaming baths where the maids wash them and massage them with oil. Dressed in fleecy tunics and cloaks, they are seated near Menelaus; a maid pours water over their hands from a golden flask into a silver basin. The housekeeper quietly lays out a feast, with delicacies and carefully carved meat, while attendants serve and keep filled the golden wine goblets.

Telemachus is awed at the gleams of bronze, gold, silver and ivory in this echoing hall. Coming from Ithaca, he imagines that this is how Mount Olympus must look. Menelaus notices and hastily denies that his riches – gathered during *his* travels home from Troy from Cyprus, Phoenicia, Egypt and North Africa – are comparable to those of the gods.

This starts him reflecting on lost homecomings – his brother's murder and no news of Odysseus. At the name of his father, and like his father in Book 8, Telemachus starts to cry, which then leads his host to ask that traditional question – who are you and how did you get here, in all senses?

But the question is taken over by Helen,

who came from her tall, scented room, like a goddess; and her companions placed a finely-wrought chair, brought a soft wool rug, and a silver basket, a gift from the wife of an Egyptian king from Thebes. He had given Menelaus two silver baths, two three-legged cauldrons and ten talents of gold; his wife had also offered beautiful gifts to Helen: a golden spindle, a silver basket on wheels, with a golden rim now brought to her, full of fine-spun yarn; with the spindle wound round with dark, royal purple wool.

(It is notable that the tripods and precious objects that in the *Iliad* are given as prizes, won by extraordinary deeds, are here part of the royal gift exchange and royal domestic splendour.)

Helen recognizes Odysseus in Telemachus. As is traditional, after Menelaus as host has offered refreshment, feast and entertainment and a good night's sleep, he asks for the visitors' story: how and why they have come? Nestor's son confirms that this is indeed Odysseus' son, come for news and advice on how to rid his home of the suitors.

Menelaus remembers how close he was to Odysseus, how much he cared and cares. He starts crying, which starts a storm of grief in them all. Helen mixes them a special drink with *nepenthes* – hearts'-ease, banisher of pain,

which calms all pain and trouble, bringing forgetfulness of every evil. Whoever tasted it mixed with the wine would shed no tears that day, even if his mother and father lay there dead, even if they put his dear son or his brother to the sword before his very eyes. Helen, daughter of Zeus, had these powerful healing drugs from Egypt, home of drugs both medicinal and poisonous.

(Odysseus' voyage to the Lotus Eaters is dangerous not because they kill but because they cause Odysseus' men to forget – forget their homes. So Helen's *nepenthes* is a fearful drug: who can or should want to be unmoved by the death of a loved one?) Helen reflects that Zeus, like her drugs, can help or harm. They are to sit back and hear her story of Odysseus, brilliantly disguising himself as a battered beggar to get into Troy secretly, only recognized by Helen, who kept quiet until he had got safely back. His talk of Greece affected her, for 'I was already longing for home, and I sighed at the blindness Aphrodite had inflicted on me, inducing me away from my own dear country, abandoning daughter, marriage and a husband who lacks neither wisdom nor appearance.' Menelaus also reminisces, about his craft and endurance in the Wooden Horse; a strange detail is that Helen tested the hollowness of the horse by imitating the wives of the most prominent Greeks, including that of Penelope. It was Odysseus that hushed everyone inside.

First thing the next morning, in the 'rosy-fingered dawn', Menelaus goes to ask Telemachus what he needs from his visit to Sparta: which is, overtly, information about Odysseus' fate. But what Telemachus needs, and gets, is being recognized as, treated as, the heir of a Greek hero. He has said that no man knows his father – a joke or truism – but in a real sense he does not know, and needs to know, Odysseus.

Menelaus tells of his return, including his adventures blown off course to a mysterious island off the coast of Egypt: Egypt, home of secret knowledge, of magic and drugs. It was here that Menelaus had an encounter with Proteus, the shape-shifting (protean) 'Old Man of the Sea'. In disguise, in seal skins, Menelaus managed to hold onto Proteus as he squirmed and roared like a lion, snake, boar and rushing water, until he gave in and agreed to tell Menelaus about what he wanted to know: the fate of his comrades. He learned of Ajax's death, a story of his madness that has different elements to that dramatized so movingly by Sophocles, and also of Agamemnon's at the hands of Aegisthus, 'who might have been killed by now by Orestes or may be still alive for Menelaus to exact vengeance'. Finally, he was told about Odysseus, detained by the nymph Calypso. Though he was told about his own future – that as the husband of the divine Helen, he will after death go to the Elysian Fields – he heard nothing about Odysseus' future. Odysseus, and so his son and wife, are stuck.

Menelaus ends by narrating his own escape from Egypt – always a strange, mysterious and perhaps threatening place – after sacrificing to the gods he had offended and raising a memorial mound for Agamemnon. He then proposes that Telemachus stay to be royally entertained and sent on his way with lavish gifts – three horses, a shining chariot and a fine libation cup. Although Telemachus has not learned much about his father, he has learned how to behave as his son. He therefore diplomatically negotiates a more immediate departure and a more practical gift: Menelaus' most precious bowl, a Phoenician gift, made of solid silver with gold rim. We hear more of his departure later, in Book 15:

> Helen went to the chests holding richly-embroidered robes she had herself made. This most beautiful of women selected the richest and finest-worked of all, which lay at the bottom yet glittered like a star, and gave it to him: 'Dear child, I too give you a gift to remember Helen by, made by my own hands, for your bride to wear when the longed-for wedding day arrives. Let your dear mother keep it by her in the palace until then.' She placed it in his hands, and he received it with pleasure.

He is sent on his way with extremely precious gifts, linking him with and displaying his acknowledgment by the most powerful Greek family. His bride will have a god-blessed as well as a beautiful wedding dress: she will be dressed by and in some senses as Helen, the divinely beautiful. It is a ritually charged and potent gift for his transition to full manhood.

Back in Ithaca: the suitors

Back in Ithaca, things are coming to a head as Telemachus' absence has been noticed and the suitors plot to rid themselves of the threat he might pose if he takes up the role of *kurios*: acknowledged master of and fully responsible for both household and mother.

After the heroic world of Nestor's and Menelaus' palaces – with their historic and mythic links to Troy, Egypt and Phoenicia, as well as the wider Greek world – Ithaca must have felt very contemporary to the audiences of the 'Sons of Homer' performing and voicing this dramatic text. This is a place where, rather than

Penelope

the elaborate marriage games held for such as Helen, the suitors are criticized for not bringing their own food – their own pigs on the hoof – to cover their subsistence. They are literally eating all Telemachus' and Penelope's food. Compared to the great Mycenaean palaces with their vast store rooms, Ithaca is 'good for goats' … and not much else. It is a Dark Age subsistence economy.

Penelope puts her finger on the difference. Odysseus, like Telemachus' hosts, operated in a society bound by *charis* – reciprocity – signalled by exchange of gifts, obligations and support between equals. But the suitors flout all such proprieties, not ashamed to flaunt their outrageous behaviour, which is ruining Odysseus' household and Telemachus' inheritance.

Worse is to come, as Penelope hears that the suitors plan to ambush Telemachus on his return. She loses her usual self-possession and envisages a devastated future without Odysseus or Telemachus.

Wracked with fear and grief, she retires: 'Like a lion seized by fear, troubled by the tightening ring of men, so she turned all her anxious thoughts over and over till sweet sleep captured her.' A phantom comes, saying that Telemachus, like his father, has a powerful protector in Athene, but refuses to say if Odysseus is safe.

With such events hanging over Penelope, and over us, the narrative moves to Odysseus on Calypso's island. We are left with twin images: of Penelope like a lion surrounded by men plotting the kill, and a similar but sinister picture of Odysseus. Earlier in the book, Menelaus had likened the suitors to fawns brought by their mother to the lair of a lion. The mother suckles the newborns then goes out to forage for herself, but the lion comes back to his lair and 'visits shameful and outrageous destruction' on mother and fawns.

What kind of vengeance is Odysseus going to visit on the hapless suitors? Likening a returning warrior to a lion preying on doe and newborn fawns is a darkening frame for the narrative of return that will resume in Book 16.

Books 5–7

Overview: From Calypso to Phaeacia

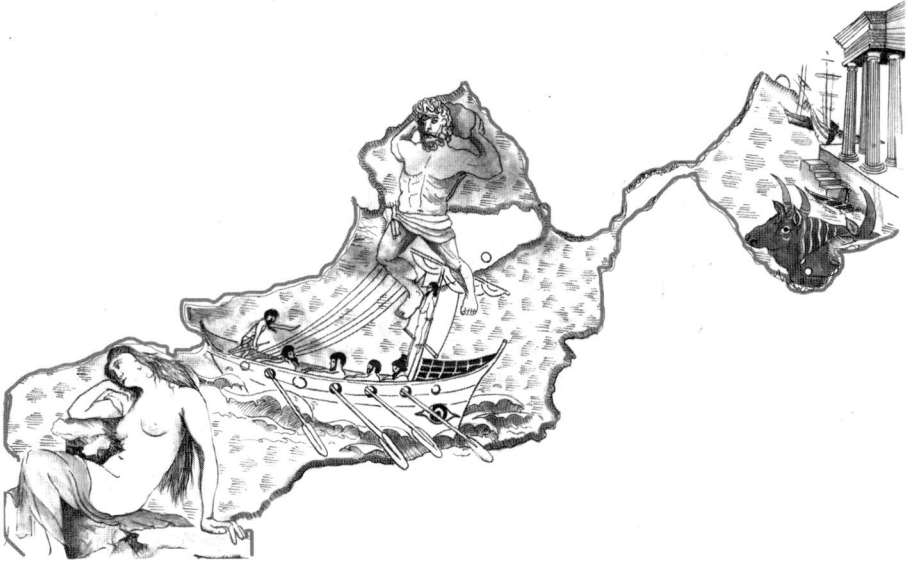

From Calypso to Phaeacia

The first half of the *Odyssey* falls into three parts – Telemachus growing up and Odysseus turning down Calypso, immortality and a home in paradise (Books 1–5); Odysseus as the unknown stranger in Phaeacia (Books 6–8); and Odysseus telling of his adventures among savages and immortals, who endanger his safe return to Ithaca either by threats or blandishment (Books 9–12). Phaeacia is a half-way house between the exotic worlds, dangers and excitements of his adventures and the very domestic world and relationship problems of Ithaca. Like Calypso though, the princess Nausicaa's hospitality, in offering an alternative home for the hero, poses a threat.

Book 4 ends on a dramatic note, with the suitors waiting in ambush to kill the returning Telemachus and clear the obstacle to Odysseus' throne and bed. The scene then shifts to Odysseus detained by the nymph Calypso, spending nights of love with the goddess and days of weeping for home. Hermes, alighting to tell Calypso of the gods' decision to help Odysseus return home, is enchanted by the beauties of the place – fountains playing in four directions, the all-important vine flourishing, sweet meadows and a luxurious variety of trees and birds. Yet Odysseus weeps for rocky Ithaca and his aging wife: he has been offered a paradise, the love of an ever-young nymph and immortality, but he has turned all this down. Instead, he will brave the dangers of the sea and the sea god's continued vendetta against him in the hope of returning home.

Calypso does not want to let him go. She complains of sexism on Olympus, such that gods can take any number of human lovers but goddesses' love affairs are punished and abruptly terminated. Nevertheless, she accepts Zeus' decree and shows Odysseus how to build a raft: he must use his famous resourcefulness to fashion his own means of escape from his desert island. When Poseidon's anger catches up with him and his raft is broken beneath him by the tempest, Odysseus reaches, literally, rock bottom: rather than dying nameless and tombless, he wishes he had died at Troy.

But somehow, resourceful even now, he manages to grab hold of a spar and, with the help of an amulet given him by the sea goddess Leucothea, he makes it to within sight of land. His joy at seeing land is described by a telling, touching simile of human love: it is as welcome as the sight of a sick father reviving from a long illness is to his attending children.

All journeys in the *Odyssey* are significant. This one takes Odysseus away from the nurture of the nymph who wanted to keep him for ever (whose name means the Coverer or Burier), and strips him of everything but his life. He left Troy with ships and men, which were successively lost, and this last battle with the sea casts him naked and half-dead on the shore of Phaeacia. Like a man saving the seed of fire by covering the last embers in ash, he saves his last spark of energy.

Happily, the princess Nausicaa decides to go down to the beach with her maids to wash the palace clothes so they are fine and clean for the wedding she has been dreaming of. Her youth, beauty and innocence, her wheedling of her 'dear father', are charmingly painted, as is her adolescent embarrassment at mentioning her forthcoming marriage. Yet when, while playing a ball game on the beach, she is faced with a battered, naked, rime-covered sailor, she acts with nobility and mature grace. Her acute consciousness of her attraction to Odysseus, and of the impropriety of being alone with

Nausicaa

Phaeacia

him, turns into a thoughtful strategy to get him received and tended by her mother, Queen Arete. Odysseus is saved from death from exposure and exhaustion by the care of a lovely girl.

Book 7 paints a full picture of the court of King Alkinous of Phaeacia. The Phaeacians used to live near the Cyclopes, but, harassed by them, they moved and now live 'far apart by themselves, very dear to the gods'. They are a powerful, independent and carefree people who are wary of strangers. They have automata of gold and silver designed by the blacksmith god Hephaistos – guard dogs and young serving men – and lush grass and fruit continuously ripened by the west wind independent of the seasons. They have the skill of seamanship to take Odysseus home if he can persuade them to – the sea god Poseidon is Alkinous' grandfather. However, Odysseus is hated by Poseidon, who will punish those who help him, so he must keep his identity secret. He must be accepted, but not too much – he cannot stay to marry Nausicaa, but must not slight her. When Alkinous says Odysseus is exactly the man he would like for a son-in-law and heir, Homer is showing us the other story that is in play, the stranger from the sea who proves pre-eminent and worthy of becoming the heir to this rich kingdom. It is an identity that Odysseus is sensible of, an alternative destiny, home and future like that which Calypso offered. It is a destiny and identity that he must negotiate.

Calypso

Book 5 starts with Athene reminding the gods of Odysseus' predicament, trapped in the care of the nymph Calypso. Zeus sends Hermes, the tricksy messenger god, to tell Calypso of the gods' purpose that Odysseus should escape to the Phaeacians, famous sailors, so that they can escort Odysseus home with honorific gifts:

> Hermes quickly fastened to his feet the lovely divine golden sandals that carry him swift as the flowing wind over the ocean waves and the boundless earth. He swooped over the sea, skimming the waves like a cormorant that drenches its dense plumage with brine, as it hunts for fish in the fearful deeps of the restless ocean.

As always when describing the various homes that Odysseus finds on his journeys – alternatives to Ithaca and Penelope – we have a wonderfully vivid description of both home and landscape:

> Around the cave grew a thick grove of alder, poplar and fragrant cypress, where birds with spreading wings made their nest, owls, falcons and long-necked, sea skimming cormorants. Over the cavern spread a mature trained vine, a canopy heavy with ripe grape clusters; four neighbouring springs were channelled in each direction and fed fountains flowing with crystal water. All around in gentle meadows, violets and wild celery grew.

Calypso's home is both delightful and fertile, with well-engineered watering system and well-tended crops.

Hermes is impressed, but Calypso wonders at this rare visit to her remote home by an immortal. After being wined and dined, he answers that not by his own wish would he come to this back-of-beyond place! But Zeus has insisted that she release Odysseus, who we have been told spends his nights as her lover and his days in tears by the seashore. Calypso 'shuddered, speaking winged words: "You are cruel, you gods, so quick to envy: you are only jealous if any goddess openly loves a man, taking a mortal to her bed. No problem when a god takes a mortal lover!"' She will obey Zeus, but her pain and generosity are palpable:

> You gods are so spiteful, jealous of me because I care for a man, one I saved from the shipwreck after Zeus had blasted with a lightning bolt his swift ship, as he made his way home with his remaining men on the wine-dark

Calypso

sea. I welcomed him with open arms, fed him, cared for him; I said I
would make him ageless and immortal.

But she will obey. She goes to Odysseus, who 'now the nymph no longer pleased
him was forced to spend the night loving her' (!) and is gazing out to sea, heart-
sore. She offers to help him as best she can to build a raft; she will provision it
and raise a favourable wind. He demands she swear the most sacred oath, by
Hades, that she will not try to harm him when he leaves. We get an intimate
glimpse of this strange relationship – it seems that she does all the giving and
he the taking – as she smiles at his demand that after everything else she swear
such an oath, then strokes his arm and says – admiringly or accusingly? – 'What
a rascal you are, very knowing: what kind of response is that? But I will do what
you wish, swear the oath, although my thoughts and plans are just those I would
have for myself; my intentions are honest, my heart is not made of iron; it is
tender and can feel pity.'

But once he is sat enthroned, surrounded by wonderful food and drink, she
tries to understand him and his intentions, the man of various strategies as she
here calls him:

Must you leave, like this, so soon? If so, let fortune go with you. Though if
your heart knew the anguish you are fated to suffer before you reach home,
you would stay and make your home with me and be immortal, no matter
how much you long, day in, day out, to see your wife.

She asks, bewildered, how he can leave her – a goddess – for a (now middle-
aged) mortal woman? He more graciously answers:

'Great goddess, do not be angry at what I say. I know that deep-thinking
Penelope is not in the same league as you, a goddess who is ever young.
But day after day I long to return home. If some god should strike me
down, out on the wine-dark sea, I will bear it as I have so often before.'

As he spoke the sun went down, and they both went into the deep dark
back of the cave and made mutually delightful love, staying in each other's
arms.

As soon as rosy-fingered dawn appeared, they dressed, Calypso in a
long, lovely, closely woven white robe, fastened by a fine gold belt.

Earlier, Calypso's island was described from the viewpoint of swiftly alighting
Hermes as a lovely fertile place, and now we hear of the resources of this
managed landscape:

Calypso led the way to the edges of the island where plantations of alder,
poplar and fir rose to the sky: dry, well-seasoned timber that would ride
high in the water.

Like the 'man of many devices' that Calypso called him, Odysseus fells twenty trees, trimming and smoothing them with the axe. The rest of the passage contains a host of shipwright terms – he uses dowels, mortice and tenon joints, deckboards, gunwales, rudder, mast and a yard arm, finishing the vessel with woven willow side screens and a brushwood decking, and using cloth from Calypso to fashion a sail and tackle. He can indeed turn his hand to anything.

Finally, lovingly, Calypso bathes, anoints and dresses him, provisions his rude boat with wine and delicacies, and sends him joyful on his way with a fair wind.

And so Odysseus leaves Calypso and seems to be headed for his homecoming. But the tempestuous voyage which follows – Poseidon renewing his hostility – is one which strips him of his last possessions and markers of identity and status. His landing on the shore of Phaeacia is unforgettably described:

> A long breaker suddenly lifts him, and he glimpses the shore. Just as a father's recovery from his sickbed is welcomed with joy by his watching children, so Odysseus rejoices. He swims on eagerly, but as he gets nearer he hears the thunder of waves breaking on rock. There was nowhere safe to land, just jutting reefs and rocky cliffs; his courage and strength drains away and a huge wave drives him onto the rocky beach. As he is swept by he clings to a rock with both hands, hanging there, battered by each wave as it comes in and out, the skin stripped from his hands as he clings on, like an octopus clinging in a crevice with its suckers.

With Athene looking on as ever, he manages to free himself from the surge and, swimming around, he comes to the mouth of a swift-running river, safe from wind and waves. He lies exhausted, mouth and nose streaming with sea water, but as his strength revives he remembers to unwind the sea goddess' veil from his waist and send it back to the ocean. When night comes on, he finds a gap in a thicket, and like a wounded animal he creeps in. The book ends:

> As a farmer on a lonely farm covers a glowing log with blackened embers, keeping alive the spark of fire, so Odysseus buried himself in the leaves.

Nausicaa

We have a vivid sense of what Odysseus meant to Calypso – as she says to Hermes, she wants a husband and partner who will live forever by her side.

Now Odysseus becomes part of another woman's story: this time the princess Nausicaa, whose destiny it is to bring into the family a foreign heir to the throne. (The throne goes with the woman, as Menelaus became King of Sparta by marrying Helen of Sparta, rather than being given by the father to his son.) The stage is set for Odysseus to be that man …

Nausicaa is lovely! The dramatic setting for her encounter on the beach with a brine-covered, naked Odysseus – the heart of Book 6 – is of her awakening to the sense that today is a special day. A thought, or vision from the ever-watchful Athene, spurs her to gather up the palace washing and take it down to the river. (Note the geography of Phaeacia is that they used to live near the monstrous Cyclopes and are now a liminal place between the magical and real, a sail away from Ithaca. The palace is also liminal – there are golden automata but the princess does the washing herself!)

The thought occurs to her that she will soon be married and will not only need to be dressed in lovely clothes herself, but to think about bridal attire for her companions and attendants. Her father refers to her upcoming marriage, and Odysseus' first words to her are in terms of how blessed her future husband will be. The anonymous stranger will be entertained as well as challenged to show his prowess in all kinds of manly competitions – this is a romance story where Nausicaa's dream and the omen both come true; the stranger from the sea wins the hand of the princess by beating the local suitors at the marriage games. But Odysseus does not fit neatly into anybody else's story. Odysseus the *poikilomētis* (of variously shimmering mind), in this as in all the situations he is going to describe, uses all his wit and craft to extricate himself tactfully.

Nausicaa

Reduced as he is to a naked, battered, begrimed middle-aged man, it is with trepidation that Odysseus looks around at this 'foreign shore'. Woken by hearing Nausicaa and her companions laughing and playing ball, he asks, 'Oh, what is this place? Are they cruel and wild; flouters or respecters of the laws of gods and society?' Are they *philoxenos* (bound by the obligations of host to guest)? The *xenos* (guest, stranger, outsider) arrives on a strange shore hoping for the god- and cosmos-validated laws of *xenia* (protective hospitality) to operate: that he will be welcomed and refreshed, his needs provided for and sent on his way safely, in the expectation that he will extend the same to stranger guests when he gets home and becomes the host (also called the *xenos* – the obligations of *xenia* are mutual).

All Odysseus' stories will be of perverted or vitiated *xenia* – of the Cyclops giving as guest-gift that Odysseus should be eaten last, for example, or the guest-gift of the bag of winds being opened by his men, with resulting destruction. 'Are they *philoxenos*?' is a good question. Given the tricky situation – a lovely

girl on the eve of marriageability – Odysseus has to use all the skills of his *poikilomētis* (tricky mind), his ability to shimmer, to present himself differently to different people and in different situations:

> He emerged from the bushes, breaking off a leafy branch to hide his manhood. He would have faced the crowd of flowing-haired girls, naked as he was. But, streaked with dried sea water brine, he terrified them, and all but Nausicaa ran away; she stood and faced him.

Odysseus has a difficult decision: he could formally supplicate Nausicaa – a ritual action of subservience and vulnerability, bending down and embracing the superior's or victor's knees – or as a beggar, ask for clothes and directions to the town. The first positions her as host, with all the above obligations; but he is naked, and jumping out of the bushes to hug her knees … could be misconstrued! But nor is he a simple beggar – he has the class and contacts to demand hospitality, peer to peer. 'He spoke to her crafty, honeysweet [almost lover-like] words', complimenting her and imagining how proud her parents must be and how blessed above all 'the man who wins the marriage competition with his gifts and leads her home as his wife'. He asks diplomatically that she lends him some of the washing so he can make his way to the palace, and concludes:

> May the gods grant you all your heart's desire, a husband and a home all in harmony, in all its beauty. Since nothing is finer or better than when a man and a woman of one heart and mind stay together, a joy to their friends, galling to their enemies, winning the very highest acclaim.

He displays *poikilomētis*, certainly, but also that attribute from the opening line of the *Odyssey*; a *polytropos* man, of many turns and also of many tropes and styles of speech. For this is eloquence, a polished and no doubt stock speech of compliment to the daughter of a host, even one appropriate to a suitor arriving for such marriage games.

How will Nausicaa, who dreamed of her future marriage, respond? First of all, with natural humanity and extraordinary sensitivity and sensibility. She calls her girls back, saying that it is unbecoming of them to flee, since all are charged with caring for strangers and beggars. Once he is bathed and clothed, her dream returns: 'This stranger now seems like one of the gods who rule the wide heavens. I wish such a man might be my husband, settling down here.' Her thoughtful intelligence and sensitivity are evident in the plan she proposes, that she enable Odysseus to supplicate her mother, Queen Arete, directly, rather than through her:

I wish to avoid slander and foul gossip; if I took you to the palace some man might say: 'Who is that tall and handsome stranger who has latched onto Nausicaa? Where did she find him? It's her future husband no doubt – some foreigner since we are too remote for neighbours to drop in! She clearly despises the Phaeacians and all her noble suitors!'

That would spoil my good name; I myself would condemn a girl who acted like that independent of her mother and father, before she was formally betrothed.

Directly and maturely as she speaks, there is a thrill of anticipation running through Nausicaa … and perhaps through us!

Odysseus at the court of King Alkinous and Queen Arete

Book 7 starts with a bustling townscape. Nausicaa and the mule-wagon with the washing arrive in the palace forecourt, while Odysseus explores the 'lovely city of the men famed for seafaring'. He marvels at the harbours, the stately ships, the assembly and market place where heroes gather, at the long walls crowned with a palisade.

Phaeacia is at the edge of the world, off the world's travel routes and suspicious of them: confident in their superb seamanship and charged with transporting travellers, they look warily on arrivals from outside. They control their border!

Athene advises Odysseus to supplicate Queen Arete, who seems to be a matriarch: 'The children and the people look to her as a god, greeting her as she moves around her city. She is infinitely wise and settles disputes and restores harmony in disputes, even among men. So if you can win her favour, there is every hope you can see your home again and the land of your fathers.'

Now Odysseus comes to the famous palace of Alkinous, which he will leave in Book 13 after hearing and telling some amazing stories. He arrives naked and, like Telemachus at Sparta, leaves with gifts and a fully worked-through, thoroughly performed identity. Books 13–24 will test that identity: how will, how can

Phaeacia

those experiences, those stories of dangers, suffering and losses endured, be brought home to those left behind?

Looking at the glorious palace, Odysseus stands lost in thought:

> The threshold was of bronze, the gold doors set into the bronze with silver newel posts and gold door handles, the inner walls topped by a blue enamelled frieze. Inside, elaborate, stately seats running along the walls were covered with beautiful fine-spun fabrics, where the high-born leaders would sit: living, eating, drinking lavishly.

Phaeacia is a blend of fantasy and reality: next to the covered seats 'carefully worked by women' are automata, 'immortal and ageless gold and silver guard dogs, which Hephaistos the smith god had fashioned with extraordinary craft and skill'. But also,

> golden youths stood on well-built statue bases holding flaming torches to light the banqueters in the hall. There were fifty slave-women grinding yellow grain at the millstone; others weave or sit twirling the yarn on the distaff; soft bleaching olive oil drips from the closely-woven linen. The Phaeacian men are expert at handling ships on the sea; the women are highly skilled workers at the loom.

The Phaeacians are expert in seamanship as well as in the finest and most beautiful arts and crafts.

The landscape is similarly a mixture of the utopian and the expertly managed:

> Just beyond the courtyard there is a large orchard, protected on all sides by a tall hedge. Tall pear, pomegranate and apple trees grow there, rich in glossy fruit, as well as sweet figs and dense olives. The fruit never rots or drops, winter or summer because all year round the west wind's breath brings on some while ripening others in the cluster, on the branch or on the vine. There is a fertile well-managed vineyard, one area for drying the grapes, another where the workers gather and tread the ripe grapes while some unripe grapes shed their blossom and others become purple-tinged.
>
> Beyond there is a kitchen garden with neat beds with every kind of plant, flowering all year round. Two springs are channelled, one to irrigate the garden and the other to provide water for palace and town.

Although the Phaeacians have been characterized as self-reliant and hostile to strangers and outsiders, Odysseus is treated in exemplary fashion when, as he has been advised, he supplicates Queen Arete. He asks for safe passage home, as the Phaeacians are bound to give. An elder calls for the visitor to be seated on a silver chair, wine to be brought for him and libations to be poured. He might be a god in disguise, after all!

Who are you? What is your story?

After the formalities, when the hall is emptied of feasters, the king and queen turn to Odysseus. Recognizing his borrowed Phaeacian court clothes, Arete asks for his story. She asks the standard, vital question: *tis pothen eis?* (who and from where are you?), which I translate as 'who are you really and how did you get to be that?'

There are two ways of responding. There is the externalizing way, paying the duty owed by guest to host of entertaining them and expanding their knowledge of the world's real and imagined societies. And there is the internalizing way, telling your story in order to understand and order it. Odysseus here responds that his story is too hard, too full of troubles, but he will answer the second part of the question literally, describing his journey from Calypso's island.

It does not take modern trauma psychiatry to discover that telling one's story is potentially and sometimes problematically cathartic. When in Book 15 Odysseus, still anonymous, holes up outside his palace in Ithaca, he asks his host, the herdsmen Eumaeus, for his story. Eumaeus replies:

> Stranger, since you ask, quietly enjoy your cup of wine and my tale. The nights are longer than even a god could tell: a time to sleep and a time to delight in hearing a story. We two will eat and drink and take pleasure in each other's memories of trouble and sadness, since a man who has suffered deeply and travelled far finds delight even in his sufferings when he later looks back at the details of the experience.

Suffering and tragedy are transformed not by distance and memory but by enquiring closely into the experience in order to relate it. The pleasure and delight are an aesthetic response that comes from the crafting of the tale. As Eumaeus says, the particularities, the details of the experience become transformed as they are worked into a story.

Telling your story is so important in therapy that there is medical training in helping to give a voice to those who cannot, whose stories are broken by trauma or an interruption like a psychotic episode. One definition of trauma is that which cannot be fully voiced, so that retrieving the memory brings not negotiation with but mere repetition of the traumatic experience. Someone who is traumatized by war or loss loses their 'narrative identity' – the story that holds them together, that tells them who they are, yesterday and tomorrow.

Eumaeus goes on to tell his story, to delight his audience over the long winter night and to validate and reinforce his narrative identity: he knows and can tell who he is and how he came to be that, here and now.

But Odysseus? His immediate answer to Arete narrows her question to the practicalities of his arrival, answering 'where from?' but not in any way 'who?'.

Book 8

Odysseus and the Divine Bard, Songs of Gods and Trojan War Heroes; the Effect

Odysseus in Phaeacia needs the two skills of the hero – effectiveness in council and effectiveness in contest. Both are tested when he is challenged to take part in a mini festival games, put on for his entertainment after the feasting and song. Odysseus is conscious that he is out of condition and out of training, and that it would be neither fitting nor politic for a married man begging safe passage home to shine in a contest designed to test and demonstrate the prowess of young men. He declines, but is abused as one more concerned with profit than excellence; his fighting spirit is roused by the insult and he makes a fearfully long discus throw. Behind the story motifs – the unknown hero challenged to demonstrate his mettle; the challenge of a potentially threatening pretender to the hand of princess Nausicaa – is the vivid placing of Odysseus, the hero-survivor of war, storm and hostile cultures, against this people who live apart, priding themselves on their seafaring, dancing and athleticism.

As Telemachus needed all his wits to deal with tricky social situations on his journey, so his father needs all his. Athene looks after both father and son in much the same way, encouraging them by appearing in disguise as a helper, giving them a sheen of vigour and grace. But whereas the point of Telemachus' journey was to establish his identity, to be accepted as his father's son, Odysseus has to avoid his identity becoming known prematurely. So the bards' stories of the Trojan War to which both are treated by their hosts serve very different purposes: Telemachus gains a sense of his father as a hero at Troy and of his cunning and subtlety when he hears the story of the Trojan horse, but Odysseus has to hide his face, acutely conscious of his tears and the heroic sensibility aroused by hearing his fame as a hero re-sung.

So this book is also the test of Odysseus in another way. He has come from a world where princes and leading warriors at rest are entertained by epic tales of the gods and of heroes. Here, the Trojan War is just such matter for song; his deeds have been worked up and crafted into a supreme bard's repertoire. Here, where he has only given a very basic account of his arrival, he hears songs about

Odysseus, the hero. He will have to decide what kind of account of himself, what kind of narrative identity, he is going to craft when the time comes to name, reveal and identify himself.

Accepted for what he is, as worthy of guest-friendship, he receives gifts, is promised return and given a final feast. He now can reveal his identity, an identity introduced to the Phaeacians by the bard who, at Odysseus' request, sings again of Troy, this time of the Wooden Horse. After this, in Books 9–12, Odysseus will become his own bard, telling the tale of his adventures.

Book 8 has a subtly double shape. Alkinous, king of a people charged with conveying travellers who bring them 'back from the edge', makes honourable preparations for Odysseus' return, manning and provisioning a new ship and providing lavish entertainment for him. But there is also a testing of this stranger. It is traditional to feed, refresh and renew with wine and song a guest, especially one who has arrived in such a sorry state, before then asking for his name and story; but Odysseus has avoided speaking in reply. Meanwhile, the potential threat he poses brings a strain to the narrative; the threat to the young princes of the land who would expect to compete for Nausicaa's hand and become Alkinous' heir combines with the potential threat any stranger brings – of blood-guilt, pollution, the gods' hatred or curse.

The stage is set. Alkinous calls an assembly and announces that, as is their duty and pride, he will make the arrangements to send the stranger on his way home, summoning a strong crew and provisioning a new ship. Meanwhile, he will offer a feast to all to entertain the stranger, and the divine bard will sing. Then there will be a competition, 'so this stranger when he is home can tell his friends how far we excel'.

But what is set up as entertainment, a demonstration of excellence, is also the opportunity for an overt challenge of the incomer from the restive princes:

> Indeed, stranger, you don't look like a man who competes in manly sports, more like the captain of a merchant ship, keeping a greedy eye on cargo and profit. You are no athlete.

In the *Iliad*, the desired response to this kind of 'hectoring'(!) is, 'who are you to call me a coward, I'll show you'. It is designed to rouse the hero to ever-greater feats. So this 'entertainment' has morphed into a competition between the local princes and the anonymous stranger. A provocation to take part, a test of status and a trial of worth in what are potentially Nausicaa's 'marriage games'. (It was at the marriage games for Helen of Sparta, won by Menelaus, that according to other Trojan War epics, the suitors swore jointly to avenge any slight to the winner.)

Odysseus is wily and experienced, but no less urgently competitive, even prickly, in words and deeds for all that:

'You speak rightly that men are graced with unequal capabilities; you for instance have a great body but a tiny mind. But, though I've suffered deeply, I will compete against you, since your words have stung me deeply.'

With this he leapt to his feet, still wrapped in his cloak, and seized a huge discus stone, much bigger and heavier than those normally used in competition, and whirled it in an enormous arc over the heads of the suddenly crouching Phaeacians.

Odysseus almost audibly crows. He effectively says, 'match that, you youngsters; when I'm minded I'll do it again and also will beat you all' (apart from his host, for it would not be proper to compete with him – and we feel he means, 'beat him hollow') at everything other than running, 'for the long, battering, cramped sea journey has weakened my legs'. With a spear and bow, he is 'best by far of all mortals', and anything else – bring it on!

He is not so much responding appropriately to the challenge as being pugnacious and boasting wildly. One feels that a nerve has been touched. Indeed, Alkinous, gracious as ever, almost apologizes for him, saying that he understands that he was taunted, and moves the agenda from competition to exquisite, delightful dancing; this is what the Phaeacians pride themselves on, not boxing or wrestling but speed and skill of ships and feet:

So come, you finest dancers among us Phaeacians, perform for this stranger, so he can tell his friends when he reaches home how we excel not only in swiftness of foot, and seamanship, but in dancing too, and in song.

Dancing

He calls for the peerless bard, Demodocus, who 'stood in the centre and round him a group of dancers, boys alight with radiance of near manhood, skilled in dancing, and Odysseus marvelled as he gazed at their flashing feet, striking the sacred dancing floor'.

The bard in the *Iliad* has a sacred duty, to record and disseminate the fighters' *kleos aphthiton*, imperishable fame, the only immortality a human can aspire to. In this book, too, Demodocus is 'inspired by the Muse to sing of the great deeds of men', but it is clear he is prized especially for his artistic and performance skills. He sings three 'showstoppers' in this book. The first is at the feast Alkinous and Arete hold for the stranger, where he sings of the quarrel at a feast between Achilles and Odysseus which

The Bard

delighted Agamemnon, a story nowhere else referred to. One can imagine how dramatic this scene was, with three so different and distinctive characters and the rich setting of the feast, although we have no details. The second song is a *tour de force*: a charming and irreverent tale of Aphrodite and Ares caught *in flagrante delicto* – caught literally, as Aphrodite's husband, the lame smith god Hephaistos, made a net trap, unbreakable and invisibly fine as a spider's web, that caught up and displayed them to the laughing gods. The third, although again we only have the outline, is no doubt the spellbinding story of the Wooden Horse (which, incidentally, doesn't feature in the *Iliad*).

There are two important bards in the *Odyssey* – Demodocus in Phaeacia and Phemius on Ithaca. Bardic song is important: it is, after all, the thing that the heroes of the *Iliad* fought for, to have their deeds celebrated in imperishable song. The Ithacan bard Phemius, in his plea for mercy, warns Odysseus of his importance: no-one can afford to mistreat the mouthpiece of their fame!

This section starts: 'Then the Muse inspired her bard to sing of the heroes' glorious deeds, part of that tale whose fame had risen to high heaven, the quarrel between Achilles and Odysseus.' It ends in the middle of the fall of Troy, with Odysseus heading for the house of a Trojan prince. After both songs, Odysseus cries, privately, covering his face with his cloak. Why?

Responding to the bard

Both Telemachus and Odysseus feel a complex response when hearing the bard sing of Odysseus in the Trojan War: as a hero passed into history, into song – 'heroized'. It is positive for Telemachus, who had seen his father's absence only as a problem or a source of potential shame. For Odysseus, the effect of hearing of his own deeds and now dead companions as passed into song is to induce overwhelming grief. Virgil writes of a similar upwelling of feeling in Aeneas when he sees Troy depicted on temple doors in the backwoods of Africa – *sunt lacrimae rerum et mentem mortalia tangunt* ('tears in the nature of things, the mind touched by human mortality'). To be heroized is not to be adored as a living star but to be canonized – accepted as part of that community of dead heroes whose deeds will be sung at feasts throughout the generations. It is a reminder that the only sort of participation in life for the hero is that of his fame on men's lips. Odysseus hears his deeds canonized in a way that distances him from them. In the same way, the sublimely comic story of Hephaistos entangling his wife and her lover in a net distances the laughing human audience from the gods, confirming them in their status as mortals, alive now round the feast hearth.

Odysseus praises Demodocus before and after his third song, first as singing *kata kosmon*, according to the order of things, and second *kata moiran*, according to the shape of things, according to both destiny and also the shape of the events. Order is beautiful, ordering is beautifying. I take singing *kata moiran* to refer to that tricky double aspect of art: the imperative that it is a true record and that it is a proper and appropriate rendering into actuality in art.

Odysseus still hasn't given an account of himself; in the next book he will become his own bard, singing of his experiences and travails, a fitting guest payment for these hosts. But before that, he hears stories about his past which make him cry, plausibly for many reasons. I am struck that neither of the songs refer to Odysseus' heroic achievements, although they do place him back in a heroic narrative, saying that when the Greeks poured out of the Wooden Horse, 'Odysseus and Menelaus were involved in the toughest fighting of their lives but also in the greatest victory'. Nor do they refer to the death of his friends or to the horror and heartache of war, though after the final song he cries,

> like a woman weeps who throws herself on her husband's dying body, fallen in front of his city and people, trying to ward off that evil moment from the city and his own children. Watching him gasping for breath in dying, she clings to him and screams aloud, while behind her the enemy beat her back and shoulders with their spears: then she is led into captivity to endure a life of toil and suffering, her cheeks wasted pitifully with grief.

He cries like a woman who has lost everything, including – as Andromache fears for herself and the other Trojan women, enslaved and raped by the victors, in Euripides' *Trojan Women* – her very identity.

There may be more to it. The imaginary is a world in which to invent oneself, to pretend or lay claim to an identity. There is a theory that the child needs to have his imaginary identity imaged and returned in order that it be validated; the child without such holding structures has no way of dealing with and forming a self in the apparent randomness and indifference of the world. So what might be the effect on a fully formed adult, stripped of identity by trauma and loss, of hearing scenes from one's past crafted into a polished piece of art? Might the imaginary identity when crafted into art have the opposite effect to the holding structures created between child and mother, effecting rather a final loosening of the structures of identity?

Narratives which shape actuality into story align it with and/or impose both *kosmos* – a beautifying order – and *moira* – the end point, the purpose, the shape of things that had to be. A narrative of identity imposes a shape and purpose to a life, gives it the 'sense of an ending', builds on the ordered past an imaginary future. Those halted by trauma lose both access to their past and their imagined future, their narrative self broken.

Narrative therapy is careful to help give voice to and rebuild, rather than further denuding, the identity of trauma sufferers by appropriating the narrative of who they are and putting words into their mouths. Odysseus the *poikilomētis*, the shimmeringly flexible-minded, the *polytropos*, man of many turns, can now be turned any which way a bard wishes to craft him. So, when Odysseus comes finally to answer Arete's question, *tis pothen*, who (really) are you, can he build for himself a narrative identity that is both *kata kosmon* and *kata moiran*? Can he construct the holding structures that keep at bay both fear of chaos – that the world out there has no structure, has no order – and loss of narrative identity linking past and imagined future and purpose?

How can someone faced with a blank canvas, the past taken away from him and no holding structures, build a shaped, holding narrative consonant with a sense that life has direction and purpose, that the cosmos is ordered and beautiful, that establishes a truth claim? How can Odysseus build a holding narrative identity to take back with him to Ithaca, where everyone will need to know who he really is?

When King Alkinous notices Odysseus' tears at the bard's song, he asks for four things of his guest. He asks for (i) the truth, not concealing anything 'with gain in mind'; and (ii) his name and that of his parents, lineage, land, people, city (so the ship can take him there). He also asks Odysseus (iii) 'to be precise and tell in detail about where you went off course, to which lands, peoples and well-built cities you were driven, both those wild, cruel, lawless and godless and those respectful of gods and the rights – and rites – of hospitality'. This is because the Phaeacians have been warned against conveying dangerous or polluted people, and may be punished by the gods for being too easy to offer passage to all. Finally, perhaps most difficult of all, he asks Odysseus (iv) to explain why he was so moved by the bard's singing about the Trojan War and fall of Troy, when those things have now passed into material for song. Did he lose someone he was close to then?

Before Odysseus leaves Phaeacia, he fully answers (iii) about his travels, and sketchily (ii), though perhaps not precisely (i), since he says that he must leave with honour-validating princely gifts. He leaves it to us to answer (iv): why did he cry?

A bard is unaffected by his material, distanced from it, focussed as he is on his crafting and performance. So, as we delight in Odysseus' adventures, we ask with Alkinous how has he been affected by what he has experienced? And how will, how can, how should Odysseus shape and transpose his experiences of loss and catastrophe into a tale worthy of such a host?

Books 9–12

Overview: Odysseus' Stories

Wondrous worlds, terrifying peoples; *nostos* (return) threatened and *xenia* (host obligations) perverted

Odysseus' tales are both delightful and resonant with significance, as befits a master story teller. Throughout the *Odyssey*, listeners take pleasure in and are moved by the stories they hear and by the subtle timing and placing of stories for effect. The Cyclops, Scylla and Charybdis, the Lotus Eaters, the enchantress Circe who turns Odysseus' men into swine – these are stories well known and delighted in through generations. Odysseus shapes them into a well-constructed narrative. The first set, comprising the Lotus Eaters (a threat to the return through enchantment), the Cyclops Polyphemus (a man-eating monster in a cave), Aeolus (the wind god's island, the safe return vitiated by Odysseus' men who open the bag of winds while Odysseus sleeps) and the Laestrygonians (man-eating giants), is neatly paralleled by the second set – the Sirens (a threat to the return through enchantment),

Odysseus as Bard

Scylla (a man-eating monster in a cave) and the whirlpool Charybdis, Helios (the sun god's island, and the safe return vitiated by Odysseus' men who kill the sacred cattle while Odysseus sleeps) and Scylla and Charybdis again. Between the two sets comes the major figure of Circe, who first detains him as her lover and then sends him on his way (via the Underworld), a figure paralleled by Calypso, who finally sends him on his way to Ithaca via Phaeacia.

In the course of his travels, he visits every sort of location on the earth and under it – clashing rocks, a floating island, a whirlpool, the Underworld. He experiences every sort of society – people who live in caves (Calypso, Cyclops),

Odysseus' Travels

in a hall in a forest (Circe), pastoralists who don't practise agriculture (the Cyclopes), who feed off flowery blossoms (the Lotus Eaters), who work a day shift and a night shift (the Laestrygonians), whose fruit ripens regardless of season (the Phaeacians), those who practise incest (Aeolus), who don't have assemblies, laws or ships for travel (the Cyclopes) and who are served by automata (the Phaeacians). In each new place, Odysseus has to find out whether the inhabitants are 'churlish and tyrannous or pious and hospitable' – what kind of society, what kind of agriculture, what kind of laws. Most importantly, he must discover whether they respect the god-validated universal law of hospitality, whereby strangers must be cared for, entertained and given guest presents. Odysseus finds out in this instance that the Cyclopes are anything but hospitable: Polyphemus' offer of a guest gift to Odysseus is to eat him last.

The satisfaction of the symmetry and order of the well-crafted tale is appropriate to Odysseus the crafty, the various-minded, the resourceful. Perhaps because of the teller, perhaps because the tales – themselves archetypal folk and sailors' motifs – seem to signify more than lies on the surface, the story of the journey of Odysseus intrigues the mind as well as satisfies the ears. The Sirens do not just sing sailors to their deaths on the rocks, as mermaids do in many cultures; they entice by promising knowledge of 'everything that happens over all the generous world', by the ability to see, among other things, 'everything the Greeks and the Trojans did and suffered in wide Troy'. The sailor is lured not by song but by access to the material from which they can make immortal song, an access that only the all-seeing, omniscient Muses have.

Similarly, the pleasure of the childlike joke of Odysseus calling himself 'Nobody', so that the Cyclops yells 'Nobody is hurting me', is deepened by the running questioning of who Odysseus is now he is no longer one of the famous heroes at Troy. To the Greeks and Trojans of the *Iliad*, Odysseus' name, his reputation for prowess and cunning, was his identity. But in the worlds he now inhabits, anonymity is safer. The consequence of his vaunting his triumph over the Cyclops by shouting out to him from a safe distance that 'Nobody' was a pseudonym, is that the victory and, it turns out, Poseidon's punishment, can be fixed firmly to 'Odysseus'. As he travels, he is gradually stripped of his companions from Troy: to the Cyclops, Circe and Calypso he is a human body; he goes down to the Underworld away from all living creatures; and ends up alone, naked, dependent on Calypso (the goddess) and then Nausicaa and Arete (the maid and the mother). There is development as well as symmetry in the stories: a unifying onward thrust of narrative as Odysseus moves from being the hero at Troy and leader of many men, to a leader of a small band using his wits to get out of one situation after another, until he ends up on Calypso and Nausicaa's islands as 'but a man'.

There is a strong thread running through the *Odyssey* that memory and recognition are the two stable markers of identity. So the Lotus Eaters are as dangerous as Poseidon to him, because they have the power to make men forget home. The magic root given to Odysseus by Hermes protects him from being turned into an animal with human consciousness (horror of horrors – remembrance without outward form) but does not protect him from the power of Circe's bed, which entices him to forget about home. Unlike Calypso, who wants to keep him as her husband as well as lover and is willing to change him into an immortal in order to do so, the bond between Circe and Odysseus is explicitly and solely sexual. He needs protection from the gods to prevent her 'unmanning' him when he is naked, and he needs to master her in bed before she will release his companions from her spell. The sexual union of Circe and Odysseus is a form of self-forgetfulness – his men have to remind him of home. Losing himself sexually is followed by a visit to the Land of the Dead: a linking of sex and death. In the Underworld, Circe's spell of forgetfulness will be finally broken, his identity and purpose reasserted: he is recognized as Odysseus by his former companions at Troy, and is vividly reminded of his home by meeting the shades of his parents. It is this theme of Odysseus' loss and reinvention of his identity that binds the well-loved tales into the *Odyssey* as a whole. They take their place between Telemachus' search for identity at the start and the final books, which deal with the complex process of Odysseus gaining recognition and a renewed identity on Ithaca.

The Cicones, the Lotus Eaters, the Cyclops

Book 9 starts with Odysseus shaping up to the task of delighting his audience, accepting the obligation as guest which may be reciprocated later:

> It is a fine thing, in truth, to hear a bard such as this, with a godlike voice. I say myself there is nothing more delightful than when all the people feel this joy, and the banqueters sit in their rows, listening to a singer in the

Odysseus' Travels

feasting hall, at tables loaded with meat, bread and frequently refilled wine cups. It seems the loveliest thing of all to me.

But you are prompted to ask of my sad troubles; how shall I start and end my tale? First let me give you my name, so you all know, and if I escape from pitiless fate later, I will play host to you in turn.

Then begin the ever-fascinating, ever-retold stories of monsters and witches, a floating island and clashing rocks.

There are two places where the story is marked as 'going off course', from recognizable geography to sailors' tall tales. The first is after the initial encounter after leaving Troy: they attack for spoil the city of the Cicones, but instead of carrying off the 'women and riches' and escaping, they carouse on the stolen wine and slaughtered sheep and cattle until the Cicones and allies regroup. The survivors get away but are blown off course 'as they are in sight of the bottom of the Peloponnese'. Nine tempest-tossed days later, they arrive – off the map? –

The Lotus Eaters

in the fabulous land of the Lotus Eaters. The storytelling is of two strands put together: firstly the marvellous and dangerous affordances of each land and people – what kind of society, what kind of exploitation of the land – and secondly what specific help or hindrance is each stop to Odysseus' return.

The Lotus Eaters – who need no agriculture as the Lotus drop their fruits untended – are dangerous because those who eat the Lotus forget their purpose, their direction in life, which in the *Odyssey* is represented by the return to home, the *nostos*.

The next, perhaps most well-known and loved, encounter is with the Cyclops. It is a beautifully constructed as well as an unforgettable story!

The Cyclopes are placed against all social norms:

The Cyclopes are a lawless, aggressive people, who never lift their hands to plant or plough, but rely on the immortal gods. Wheat, barley, and vines with richly clustered grapes grow there without ploughing or sowing which Zeus' rain makes flourish. The Cyclopes have no council meetings or law code but live in echoing caves on the mountain slopes; each man lays down the law to his wives and children and takes no account of or responsibility for his neighbours.

Odysseus gives a very critical account of the Cyclopes' wanton refusal to maximize potential:

They never lift their hands to plant or plough but rely on the gods [actually beneficent weather] for crop and vine ripening. There are no flocks and no ploughed and tended fields: though there are rich, well-watered meadows there where vines would never fail and there is level, fertile land which if ploughed would reap a rich harvest.

Despite there being 'a safe harbour with no need for moorings, where ships can be beached safely and easily until the wind and the spirit incline the sailor to travel on', they shockingly 'have no shipwrights or crimson-prowed ships to enable them to travel to other men's cities': no craftsmen that is who might also have turned it into a fine colony.

Odysseus spots an excellent natural harbour where he beaches his ships and kills the wild goats flourishing there. The morning after a day spent feasting and drinking, Odysseus takes a handful of men to explore the Cyclopes' cave dwellings and find out the essential features of this new society. They scope the Cyclops' homestead – a deep cave overhung with laurels at the cliff's edge, where herds of sheep and goats are penned – and then they see the Cyclops: a monster more like a man-mountain than a man, tending his flocks, pens crowded with lambs and kids, with newborns separated from the older ones, pails for milking and pans for separating whey. Odysseus' men want to steal the cheese and escape back to the ship, but Odysseus refuses to listen because he wants to find out about the Cyclops and see if 'he would offer *xenia*'.

They light a fire in the cave and feast on the cheese, waiting for him to return. Polyphemus arrives carrying a cartload of firewood, herding in the flocks for the night. He rolls a huge rock across the cave entrance, penning both livestock and men in for the night, and settles down to milking the ewes, curdling and storing half the milk and keeping the rest for drinking. Then he sees Odysseus and his men and asks the customary question: who are you and where do you come from (*tis pothen*)? Polyphemus addresses them as *xenoi*, but by this does he mean stranger or guest?

> Odysseus, though terrified, answers as guest to host, identifying them as Greeks returning from Troy, blown off course, now asking for 'a guest gift as is customary and right, a right watched over by Zeus'. The Cyclops replies that he, protected by Poseidon, has no interest in Zeus' ordinations. He grabs two men, bashing their heads together 'as one kills puppies', eats them and then sleeps off his meal. But before he sleeps, he completes his travesty of guest-host relationship: after drinking Odysseus' rich wine, he asks for Odysseus' name, so he can give him a guest gift in exchange. Odysseus says: 'Cyclops, you asked my name, so in return for the guest gift I will tell you: it is Nobody. Nobody is what my father, mother, and friends call me.' The Cyclops replies: 'Then this is my gift: I will eat Nobody last of all!'

This is Odysseus the tricksy (*poikilomētis*). The trick is that when the Cyclops later cries out for help, his appeal is received as a pointless riddle – if nobody is attacking you, why should we help? No-body, no-person: Odysseus is refusing to identify himself: *he* is perverting the guest-right in his turn.

The next morning, the Cyclops goes about his morning care of his flocks and prepares his breakfast: two more men. Odysseus the *polymēchanos* (man of many stratagems), trapped with his men when the Cyclops leaves and rolls the huge boulder door back after him, plots their escape.

What he devises is famous in countless representations, including on earliest Greek vases, such as a painted amphora from Eleusis dated to the middle seventh century BCE, used to hold the ashes of a person who no doubt had heard one of the regular performances of the *Odyssey*. Odysseus blinds the one-eyed Cyclops with a sharpened wooden pole and escapes with his remaining men by holding onto the woolly underbellies of the Cyclops' rams as he sends them out of the cave to pasture. Once safe on board and under way, but just still within hailing distance:

> I began shouting to the Cyclops, though the men clustered round me, trying to shut me up: 'Why do you recklessly provoke the wild man to anger? He just threw a rock the size of a mountain top and drove us back to the shore! If he had heard you and thrown another jagged rock, he'd have crushed both us and the ship.'
>
> But they could not daunt my great, heroic spirit. 'Cyclops, if any man asks how you were blinded, say it was at the hands of Odysseus, sacker of cities, son of Laertes, a native of Ithaca.'

The Cyclops

Disaster! He has identified himself, claiming as a heroic deed the maiming and duping of ... Poseidon's son.

There is a nice balance of sympathy here. Of course, the man-eating, guest-host bond-flouting monster is the stuff of nightmares. But Odysseus' men clearly feel he is courting danger, and we might feel that the heroic claiming of victory over a fallen opponent of the battlefield is hubristic vaunting, when it is the trick as much as the maiming that Odysseus is claiming.

And when the blinded Cyclops tenderly runs his hands over the last of his herd, the ram under which Odysseus is hiding, it is difficult not to feel for him.

My fine ram, why leave the cave like this, last of the flock? You're always the first to step out proudly, to graze on the tender new grass, always first to reach the flowing river and first to tell me you want to come back home. But today you are last of all: it must be that you are grieving for your master's eye, blinded by a wicked man when my wits were fuddled with wine.

Last of all, the Cyclops laments that the prophecy that he would be blinded by 'Odysseus' has come true, but says, 'I always expected some great, fine, mighty man, not a feeble little weakling.' He has the last laugh, however: he cries out to his father Poseidon for vengeance. Odysseus has roused the anger of the god of the sea.

We can go back to Odysseus' ever-present question, which he asked here as he set out to explore the Cyclopes' island: 'Let us go and find out whether they are cruel, savage and lawless, or good to strangers, and in their hearts fear the gods' – whether they respect or outrageously flout social bonds, laws and *xenia*, the bond and reciprocal obligations between guest and host? We should perhaps ask how Odysseus measured up to those criteria: was he cruel, savage and hubristic, or respectful of *xenia*, others' society and the gods?

The bag of winds, the Laestrygonian cannibals

First in Book 10 we have Odysseus entertained for a month on Aeolus' floating island, which has:

> A surrounding wall of unbreakable bronze on sheer cliffs, within which the God of the winds lives with his six daughters that he married to his six fine sons. All day long the courtyard resounds and the Great Hall is full of savoury smells as they feast with their dear father and mother. At night they each sleep by their spouses, on well-covered, well-strung beds.

In return for Odysseus telling him the whole tale 'according to the shape of things' of the Trojan War and the Greeks' return, Aeolus gives him a precious guest gift – a leather bag bound by a silver clasp in which he has placed all the winds except the beneficent West Wind.

For nine days and nights they sail, until within sight of the fires of home. So near and yet so far; Odysseus allows himself to go to sleep and his men take disastrous advantage of his lapse of attention. Suspicious and rebelling against Odysseus' privileges, they decide to share the silver and gold they presume to be in the leather bag Odysseus has been keeping so close. They are blown straight back to Aeolus' island, where the welcome is very different; despite Odysseus' explanation, they are sent on their way without any following wind and have to row.

The next land they are washed up on is a high citadel of the giant Laestrygonians, a land where day and night are one, so 'the man who needs no sleep can work a double shift'. Odysseus sends out two men to see 'what kind of men there are who eat bread here'. They find a huge girl who points out the palace, where the giant queen, 'massive as a mountain top', terrifies them. She

Odysseus' Travels Fragment

calls for her husband, who promptly grabs one of Odysseus' men and prepares to eat him. The others escape, but some of the giants lob huge boulders at the ships from the cliffs and others spear the men like fish and take them back to eat. Only Odysseus' ship gets away, later arriving on Circe's island.

Circe

The *Odyssey* began with Telemachus growing into a position where he could take Odysseus' place as Penelope's *kurios* or legal guardian. We had Penelope poised between widowhood and new marriage, between grief and loss, and becoming the focus of male rivalry. Then the narrative moved to Calypso, the goddess on a secluded island, hiding Odysseus away for nine years until ordered by the gods to allow him to escape, and Nausicaa, the bride-to-be and heir to the glorious Phaeacian kingdom. Now this group of Odysseus' women is joined by Circe 'of the lovely tresses' – the witch, guarded by tame wolves and mountain lions, who sings at the loom (singing and weaving being the two bewitching activities) and will entice Odysseus into bed and there unman him, unless Odysseus the *polymēchanos* can contrive an equal and opposite enchantment.

Before this encounter, we have the view of Circe as seen from a lookout point, smoke rising from a hall. The scouting party Odysseus then sends out finds

Circe's house of polished stone, in a clearing in the forest glades. Round it wolves and mountain lions prowled, which instead of rushing to attack my men, rose on their back legs, wagging their tails, like dogs greeting their master home from a feast. Gripped by fear, they stood there at the gate of the goddess with lovely tresses; they could hear Circe's clear voice singing inside, as she went to and fro working at the loom at the fine, shining, beautifully made weaving.

They go inside her great hall, are seated on chairs and served honeyed wine. The cautious Eurylochus – quite rightly! – refuses, as it was indeed drugged, 'so that they would forget completely their native land'. Circe taps his companions with her wand, turning them to pigs but still, horror of horrors, retaining human sensibility.

Here we have, after Calypso the coverer, Circe the enchantress, both stories of fable (the goddess taking a human lover and hiding him away in her cave, and the witch who enchants with her body as well as her drugs). For the dramatic encounter between Odysseus and Circe comes in a trial of strength in the bedroom. Odysseus is told by Hermes that she will try to drug him and fail, due

Circe

to a magic protective root, 'moly'. He must threaten her with his sword, which she will resist by enticing him to sleep with her, which 'he must not refuse'.

It all happens exactly as predicted:

> I stood at the shining doors of the goddess of the lovely tresses and called to her. She immediately invited me in and, anxious, I went inside. She brought me a beautiful, richly made, silver-embossed chair and footstool and gave me a drink, which she had drugged, in a golden cup. When I drank it down – though without any ill effects – she struck at me with her wand and cried: 'Off to the sty with you, and join your friends.'
>
> But I drew my sharp sword and threatened to kill her, but with a cry she slipped beneath the blade to clasp my knees in supplication. Weeping, she asked, 'What man are you and where are you from? What city? Who are your parents? You must be extraordinary, to drink my potion and not be bewitched.'

She has asked the crucial question – who are you, where are you from? (*tis pothen eis?*) – but does not wait for Odysseus to identify himself:

> 'You must be Odysseus, the man of many ways, the *polytropos*, who Hermes told me would come here in his swift dark ship on his way home from Troy. Come, sheathe your sword, and let us go to my bed, so that in lovemaking we may establish a bond of trust.'

Odysseus, however, is suspicious that 'once he is naked she will unman him' – again, what witches do! – and makes her swear a great oath before they go to consummate their new bond.

After that trial of strength – the fabulous hero and the enchantress – Circe makes both Odysseus and his men wonderfully at home:

> Her four handmaids, water and tree nymphs, threw linen covers over the chairs, spread fine purple fabrics over them and drew up silver tables. Another laid out golden baskets; a third mixed honeyed wine in a silver bowl and served it in golden cups, while a fourth fetched water and heated it in a great bronze cauldron. When it boiled, she drew hot water for me, pouring it over my head and shoulders till she drew the soul-consuming weariness from my limbs. When she had massaged me with oil, dressed me in a fine tunic and cloak, she led me into the hall, and seated me on a beautiful, richly crafted, silver-embossed chair and footstool. Then another handmaid brought water in a lovely golden jug, pouring it out over a silver basin so I could rinse my hands and drawing up a shining table, on which the faithful housekeeper loaded bread and delicacies.

But his bewitched men weigh on Odysseus' mind, and once Circe understands she immediately releases them. They cling to him 'sobbing so that the walls echoed and the goddess was moved to pity', and are treated similarly: bathed, anointed, dressed in fine clothes and feasted. Odysseus, meanwhile, gathers up his men left on the ship, who had feared the worst. Seeing Odysseus, they cluster round him like 'calves released from their pens in the farmyard round their mothers returning from the pasture'.

Circe is the most gracious as well as most understanding of hosts! Their time with her refreshes and revitalizes Odysseus and his men. In a similar way to Helen, she can wipe away all traces of their suffering, saying they are 'dried up in spirit and in body from the memories of what they have suffered' and should 'eat and drink until each regains the spirit they had when they left their homes on harsh Ithaca'.

After a year (!), the men remind Odysseus of that home, and he accepts he must leave Circe and her abundantly rich dwelling. He goes to their bed and asks her to help him leave, which she immediately does. But first he must go down to the Underworld and consult Teiresias, the seer.

The Underworld: revenge and judgment

Odysseus, though he does not know it, has a new ghost to follow: his companion Elpenor, who broke his neck in the night. This is a narrative reworking of the traditional human sacrifice needed as a prelude to raiding the Halls of Death; no golden bough, but blood and the promise of more sacrifice make Odysseus able to talk to the dead. The first, very personal encounters in the

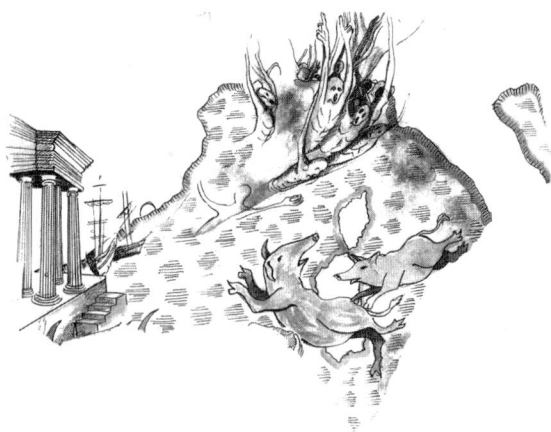

Odysseus' Travels: The Underworld

Underworld are with Elpenor and his mother, neither of whom he expected to see here. But, prudent as ever, he keeps his mother away from the blood until he has consulted the great prophet Teiresias. From him he learns of the need to punish the suitors in his palace, and that his return will be made very hard because he has offended Poseidon by tricking and blinding his Cyclops son. Finally, he learns how to make peace with Poseidon by travelling inland until he can find a people who know nothing of the sea, and learns too about his own death, which will come from the sea, in prosperous old age.

Many of the scenes are vivid stories from myth – of women who bore the gods' children, of men who suffer in the afterlife for sins committed on earth. But the majority of the encounters are woven into Odysseus' story. The dead souls warn him about women long left to plan revenge on absent husbands (Clytemnestra – will Penelope really be different?) and show him exemplars from myth about judgment and punishment (Minos, Tityus, Tantalus, Sisyphus), about suffering and endurance (Herakles), all of which he will draw on when he returns to Ithaca.

In an extremely moving scene with his mother, he also learns about death itself. He tries to embrace her, but three times she evades his grasp 'like a shadow or a dream, which broke my heart. I begged her to tell me why we couldn't embrace, and find some relief in lamenting together? But she showed me that this is what is left after death – the spirit flees and flitters like a ghost.'

She who gave him life shows him the insubstantiality and irreversibility of death. This lesson is strengthened by Achilles (who in the *Iliad* is obsessed by heroism, the risking of death for eternal glory), whom Odysseus greets as pre-eminent in the Underworld as he was pre-eminent on earth. But Achilles replies that he cannot be reconciled to death: he would rather serve as the serf of the poorest peasant and be alive on earth, than be lord of all the lifeless dead.

Human life looks different from the Underworld. Only Telamonian Ajax is intransigent, turning away from Odysseus as the man who 'stole' Achilles' armour, keeping enmity in death as he did in life.

Homer has the listening Alkinous break into Odysseus' narrative of the Underworld to praise his art as a master storyteller of grace, order and understanding. This is a reminder that this section contains many stories stitched together (the Greek for a travelling singer/storytelling performer is a *rhapsode*, someone who 'stitches together' tales). In the Underworld, Odysseus meets many figures of myth – like Tantalus, Sisyphus and what is clearly a 'catalogue of extraordinary women': Alkmene, Megara, Jocasta, Leda, Phaedra and Ariadne – whose stories have come through to later generations of storytellers and playwrights. Likewise, many of the second set of adventures, such as the clashing rocks, can be mapped onto stories of Jason and the Argonauts.

The Underworld is a place of stories, like those mythical exemplary punishments, and also of the ends of stories. Odysseus learns about the fate of those from whom he has been long parted – like Achilles, Ajax and his mother – and hears the story of Agamemnon's tragic return from Troy. He also learns about his own end: how he must appease the angry sea god Poseidon by taking another journey, somewhere so far from the sea that there is a people

Circe weaving

who do not recognize what an oar is –
an extraordinary thought for a Greek! –
and there he must make a final sacrifice.
So beyond this story told by Odysseus
to Alkinous and by Homer to us there is
another story – that of Odysseus' death.

Circe is the turning point in Odysseus'
narrative of return. After he returns
from the Underworld, Circe will finally
send him on his way home. She refreshes
and revitalizes him, predicts the future
and prepares him for the second half of
his amazing journey. Circe has a story
of her own: there is a lost epic, perhaps
the last in the many cycles of 'the return
from Troy' that we know of, which tells
of her three children by Odysseus, and
one of them, Telegonus, has an extensive
story of his own when he reaches
manhood (including that he was fated
to kill Odysseus; a story dramatized by
Sophocles in a lost play, where an oracle
told Odysseus he was to be killed by his son, which he presumed to mean
Telemachus).

The Underworld divides the two parallel sets of Odysseus' adventures, the
second informed by his experiences there. In the Underworld, Odysseus gains
knowledge and sense of self; he also gains distance on the heroic ethic that
powered the society in Troy. Instead, he is shown figures of myth bound to suffer
appropriate punishment for their crimes: Tantalus punished for infanticide and
cannibalism by eternally being nearly within reach of food and drink; Sisyphus
punished for vaunting tricksiness by forever pushing a rock up a hill, only to
have his efforts defeated just as he is about to succeed. In the books that follow,
we see Odysseus put what he has learned into sometimes harsh practice.

The Sirens, Scylla and Charybdis

All through his wanderings, as he approaches each new world, there is the
challenge and danger of what customs, what practices, will be current there.
The later set of adventures are a darker version of the earlier: the Sirens of Book
12 offer not just happy forgetfulness of self and home, as the Lotus Eaters did,

Lotus Eaters

but access to the record of the hero's doings that only the Muses, who can see and record everything, hold. To turn that down is to turn down all remaining access to the (now lost) heroic world of Troy. Odysseus the all-experiencing does not turn anything down easily: following Circe's warning, he has blocked up his men's ears but allowed himself, lashed to the mast, to hear the blandishments. His men are oblivious both to the Sirens and to Odysseus' pleas to be freed, and so all survive.

In this second set of adventures, Odysseus asserts his cunning and uses experiences gained in the Cyclops' cave to cheer his crew; he conceals the human 'toll' that Scylla will extort and, despite Circe's advice, he arms himself to do battle with her on their behalf. His comment on his pain at their death show the reflective distance he now has:

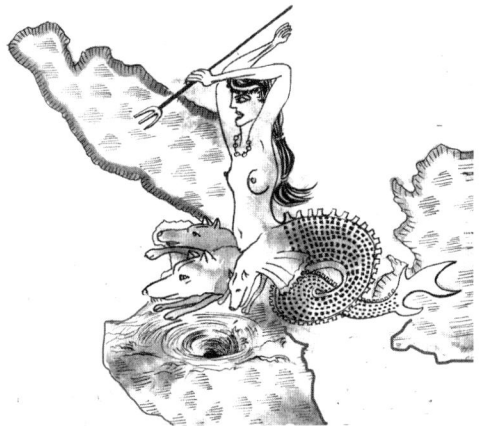

Each of Scylla's heads dragged a man writhing towards the rock. In anguish they cried out my name one last time, then at the entrance to her cave, as a fisherman on a jutting crag casts his bait to lure small fish,

Scylla and Charybdis

lowers the long rod into the sea, and catching a fish flings it ashore, she devoured them. They shrieked and reached out their hands to me in their dreadful death throes, the most pitiable sight of all that I saw exploring the pathways of the sea.

This thread – of Odysseus as leader coping with the loss of his men – is counterbalanced by the other theme, of his return vitiated by the folly, greed or envy of his men. Earlier, it was the bag of winds that they opened while Odysseus slept, and this is paralleled in this second set by their going hunting on the sun god's island while Odysseus slept, despite all instructions, killing the sacred cattle.

The adventures end with Charybdis depriving Odysseus of his last remaining companions, leaving him clinging to a fig tree. He is described as waiting for the whirlpool to vomit back a spar from his wrecked ship like a judge listening to civil cases: that time of day when a judge who handles young litigants' endless quarrels rises from court to find his supper. Stripped of his last warrior companions, experienced, cunning and vengeful from his various adventures, he moves now to civil rather than heroic life.

At the end of Book 12, Odysseus finishes his story with his arrival on Calypso's island, from where he landed on Phaeacia, bringing his story up to date. After this he accomplishes the final part of his journey to Ithaca swiftly and painlessly, with gifts and in a ship provided by the Phaeacians. The transition is almost magical. Like at other crucial times, he falls into the deepest, 'sweetest sleep, like that of death', but this time the punishment falls after his safe landing – when Poseidon turns the Phaeacian ship to stone, as a punishment for giving passage to someone he hated. Nausicaa will presumably find her husband and Alkinous his heir, just as presumably Calypso will continue to grieve … or find another lover. The spotlight of Odysseus' storytelling has switched off.

Books 13–14

Odysseus Returns to Ithaca: Disguise and Lying Tales

Odysseus as 'master storyteller of grace, order and understanding'

On Phaeacia, Odysseus clearly fulfilled one of the obligations of a guest – bringing the world outside to those at home, and like the pre-eminent bard, delighting the host with rich and well-crafted storytelling. But there is the other side of the obligation, which is to 'tell true': to shape the narrative not just beautifully but according to order and the way things are. Odysseus *polytropos* – of many wanderings, but also of many modes – is seemingly very ready to make use of other people's stories as well as his own. A bard is precisely a rhapsode, a stitcher together of stories. But did Odysseus answer the question: *tis pothen eis?* (who are you, where from?). Was he concerned rather to do something different in these books which follow on from the games at which he proved so competitive, now also competing with Demodocus to be crowned best bard?

To answer 'accurately and in detail', as Alkinous requested, 'who are you, where have

Odysseus as Bard

you come from and *how did you become that person*?' takes self-reflection as well as self-narration. To tell one's story is to shape, and own, an identity – a self formed by and continuous with the past and which shapes the imagined future.

Odysseus is returning from war, from loss, from shipwreck, from being reduced to clinging naked to a rock by his fingernails. Who is Odysseus now? Can he in any way tell his story, shape and present to his wife and son an identity? We have become much more understanding now that those returning

from warfare, who have seen and done 'unutterable' things – things that can't be described – need to be helped to make sense of them in order to heal. But we also now understand how difficult that is: that terrible experiences traumatize and fracture the self, often leaving discontinuities that can't be simply left out or skated over.

And from the other side, those returning from war or trauma can seem not just unrelatable to but also in some essential way unrecognizable to those left at home.

Homer clearly marks the discontinuity between the Odysseus on Phaeacia and what he will be on Ithaca. He lands in a deep, obliterating sleep and when he awakes, it is to a new self – no longer returning from Troy, but returned; no longer Odysseus whose 'deeds reach the heavens' like the heroes of Troy, but a stranger in his own land. How will he be recognized, and as what will he be recognized? A father, a husband, a son, a king? Or, as an avenging judge of the outrages and crimes committed in his absence? In what guise is he returning? Until he has decided, 'Athene poured a mist over him so he was unrecognizable to his wife or his townsfolk'.

But it is a two-way estrangement, for not only Odysseus but his homeland is unrecognizable. There is a strange but to modern ears resonant impression of the newly arrived Odysseus waking up as if from an induced sleep or coma, not remembering what has happened or recognizing where he is, startled into anxious questioning:

> Oh, what is this place? Are they cruel and wild; flouters or respecters of the laws of gods and society, respectful of the rights of strangers?

These are the same questions he has asked every time he has landed: on Phaeacia or in the land of the Laestrygonians or the Cyclopes. But whereas, in the retelling anyway, he there sounded adventurous and curious, here he groans and laments. This time it is not a matter of a reconnaissance, bringing back to base knowledge of the affordances and customs of a strange land, but the difficult and perhaps painful task of reuniting a past knowledge with what is in front of the newly returned … stranger. It is getting to know the people and place from which he set out, as if for the first time.

His second concern is with those guest gifts, conferring honour and prestige, marking him out as not a vagabond but a visiting dignitary. He fusses over them, wishing the Phaeacians had not just left him, worrying where to store them, worrying in case the Phaeacians had taken advantage of him by taking some back with them. Of course this is practical, but it is also a mark of what material goods have come to mean for him or for Homer's audience since the *Iliad*. There, the spoils of raids were distributed as prizes, in recognition of extraordinary heroic feats. In the Mycenaean world of great palaces such as those that Telemachus visited, gifts are precious not only in intrinsic worth but as carrying a story of their own with them. In Book 4, Menelaus gave Telemachus, upon leaving, 'one of the richest and loveliest treasures of my house, a finely-fashioned solid silver bowl with a rim of gold, made by the Smith God, Hephaistos, himself. The famous Phoenician King Phaidimos made me a present of it, when I was a guest there and now I wish to present it to you.' In the tales told by both Odysseus and Eumaeus, the swineherd who hosts him, Ithaca appears to be part of a later, Dark Age network of trade and exchange, pirates and enslavers; an impression that will be borne out by Eumaeus' account of the effect of the suitors on what is clearly a subsistence rather than a Mycenean Age palace culture.

His first, anxious words on Ithaca are, remarkably, to himself, but when he had counted his 'surpassingly beautiful tripods' (one of the most prized rewards for fighting at Troy) and cauldrons, gold and fine weaving, and was satisfied that none was missing, he enters into conversation with a disguised Athene. He asks the important questions: 'What land is this? What people dwell here? Is it an island or part of a deep-soiled mainland?' Athene has to introduce him to his homeland:

> It is a rugged island, narrow and not fit for herding horses but not completely unproductive: with good rainfall it grows corn beyond measure and a rich wine-harvest as well. The land is good for pasturing goats and cattle; there are plentiful pools and springs and trees of every kind.

Odysseus, being Odysseus, checks his immediate joy at being shown the land of his fathers and 'concealed the truth, repressing certain words and always turning over in his mind what would work best and be most profitable'.

He conceals his identity in a long 'Cretan tale'. It centres on treasure: his story is that he and his wealth, spoils from Troy, have been landed on

Athene

Ithaca after an adventurous journey escaping from Crete, where he had killed a man who was trying to steal it. He had paid for transport in a Phoenician ship, which had been blown off course and landed here; he is careful to note that they did not take advantage of him but landed him with all the treasure intact.

Athene is overjoyed at his tricksiness, his subtlety, his alikeness to her – his 'flexible presentation' (*poikilomētis*) or 'conman' skills:

> Even if a god encountered you he would need to be wily and devious to outdo you in cunning. What a man you are, never tiring of intrigue, even in your own country you will always be full of guile and the lying tales you love so much.

Odysseus is still cautious, asking for reassurance that Athene isn't deceiving him and that this really *is* Ithaca. Not that he does not recognize, remember, know again his homeland. Athene again salutes him with what are perhaps backhanded compliments:

> You are always so shrewd and so cautious! Any other man back from his wanderings would have dashed joyfully to his hall to see his wife and children, but you don't want to know or find out anything until you've tested out your wife.

Athene tells him that Penelope is faithful – he will not face Agamemnon's homecoming, killed at the hands of the deceitful Clytemnestra – and equally cunning in keeping herself free from the suitors' advances; also that Telemachus is safely returned from a journey that has won him renown on his own account.

She helps him hide his treasures in the cave of the nymphs. (There is a cave on Ithaca which is claimed as the very cave: pottery inscribed with eighth-century BCE writing, including dedications to Odysseus, was found there.) Remembering their old fighting partnership – she is a warrior goddess – she will help and glory in the blood-letting of the suitors that she encourages Odysseus to plan.

She disguises him as an old beggar, so that like a cunning Sherlock Holmes he has a guise in which to present himself to the Ithacans and the suitors without attracting attention: battered, rough, on the lookout for titbits and handouts. This raises the question: why does he not go in with a fanfare to say that he, the great Odysseus, is back and resuming his former roles of king and *kurios* (overlord/guardian) of the family? Is it because he now has been reduced to exactly how he appears – battered, roughened, old, concerned with his goods, marginal? Perhaps he cannot 'just' reassume those roles. He will have to construct a new narrative as well as a new relationship with Telemachus, since neither of them knows the other.

In any case, he is also taking on the role of the 'Judge in Disguise', known from the Bible and many folk tales, where a lord returns in disguise in order to judge how his servants and underlings have behaved in his absence. He is 'pretending to' a role: claiming the role of avenger that he will fully and bloodily inhabit when he, like the 'Avenging Judge', throws off his disguise and distributes rewards and punishments accordingly.

With Eumaeus the swineherd

Looking like the old vagabond that in some sense he really is, he goes to find a faithful old servant, Eumaeus the swineherd. As always in the *Odyssey*, we first get a description of the approach, landscape and habitat – a hut with a wide aspect, surrounded by a well-maintained wall and wattle- and thorn-fenced sties which Eumaeus had built for the sows, piglets and hogs he fattens for the palace.

Eumaeus draws the dogs off: note that here Odysseus needs to be protected from ordinary, familiar dangers and that the dogs have no sense that he is the returning king, attacking this

Odysseus Disguised

unknown outsider. In keeping with this simple home and lifestyle – barking guard dogs, not the golden automata of the Phaeacians or Circe's fawning lion – the swineherd receives him with the simple hospitality due to strangers:

> Stranger, it would be wrong for me to turn a guest away, even one more broken than you, since every beggar and stranger is from Zeus, and a small gift is welcome.

It will be necessarily small because, as he explains, times are tough, with the suitors taking all the food they produce.

From Eumaeus we get a stark, Dark Age account of the suitors' offences: they are eating too much in a poor country with not enough food, literally consuming Telemachus' inheritance, which the good Eumaeus sees as against gods' law. The listening Odysseus sits quietly, 'devising evil in his heart for the suitors', as perhaps not just avenger but Zeus' avenger.

In this world, Odysseus' mastery of narrative can be turned to good account. Eumaeus greets the conclusion of Odysseus' story with 'well begged', and he is warned that he will find Penelope sceptical about accounts of the wider world, because so many travellers have been well rewarded for bringing 'deceitful tales' and mentions of Odysseus. He is warned because 'you too would invent a tale fast enough, old man, if it brought you a tunic and cloak'. There is much further talk about reward for news of Odysseus. The stranger begs such a reward, but says that he is happy to wait for the 'fine tunic and cloak' until his message is proved true.

After eating, Eumaeus asks the traditional question: *tis pothen eis?* – who are you and where from? Odysseus replies that, given enough food and wine, he could talk for a year describing the hardships that have oppressed his spirit. He then embarks on his second 'Cretan tale': that raised and adventuring in Crete and thereafter the Trojan War, his restless feet took him to Egypt but – like Odysseus himself – his men took to plundering while he was away and were killed or enslaved. He 'stayed for seven years collecting wealth', then was duped by a Phoenician and taken to be sold in North Africa, but was shipwrecked off north-west Greece, where the king said he had recently hosted Odysseus. The story goes on, through deception, slavery and escape, albeit with nothing but rags on his back.

Eumaeus accepts all but the assurance that Odysseus is coming home and orders a fine hog roast dinner prepared. As a storm gets up, Odysseus decides to hint at his need for warm clothing by recounting a tale of his and Odysseus' cunning, to which Eumaeus responds that he has taken the implication and that as soon as Telemachus returns, he will give Odysseus the warm cloak he has begged. The reunion is coming ever nearer.

Book 15

Telemachus Returns: the Swineherd's Story

Meanwhile, Athene goes to Sparta to bring Telemachus home. The trap set in Book 4 by the suitors, who have gone unchecked while Telemachus was a boy and Odysseus absent, is now gradually closing in on the suitors themselves. Athene represents to the newly mature Telemachus that his mother may not always remain locked in the past. With his adulthood comes the possibility of her independence. Building up her own possessions and material worth from the suitors' gifts, she may choose to reward the most persistent of her suitors.

Telemachus skilfully negotiates his departure, turning down both the horses and chariot that would impede his journey home and Menelaus' offer that they embark on a long guest tour, collecting gifts from each host. The parting gifts he does accept include a lovely, shining, elaborately worked robe from Helen for his future bride; he arrived like a boy, but leaves as

Telemachus

a hero among heroes. On his return journey, he accepts the supplication of a fugitive, after a long account of why he needs protection – another tale stitched in. He is now able, in his own right as the man in charge of the household, to offer sacred guest-friendship and his protection. As he makes his way back to Eumaeus, his return is elevated by portents and by Athene's guidance.

In the meantime, Odysseus proposes to Eumaeus that he go and try his luck in the palace, which horrifies the swineherd, who warns him of the suitors' outrageous violence. (A telling comment is that Odysseus won't be welcome, since those who wait at the 'polished laden tables' are a different kind altogether – bright-faced young men, well dressed and groomed.)

Odysseus asks Eumaeus for news of his (or rather, of course, the absent Odysseus') mother and father: news he already has from the Underworld is now told to him on earth. Whereas in the Underworld, Odysseus' mother was gracious and loving, only at the end admitting that it was longing for him that had brought her there, Eumaeus' very personal and affecting account would have been more difficult for Odysseus to hear. Eumaeus reveals that Odysseus' mother treated him like a son and describes her death as wretched, in grief for her noble son, a death he would not wish on anyone. He clearly is still grieving for her. But what about her actual son, Odysseus? His father Laertes is still alive, but is 'wasting away praying for death, in grief for his wife and son'. Although the narrative moves on, the question of Odysseus' emotional responsiveness and familial bond of attachment has been raised.

Odysseus goes on to ask a question about Eumaeus' childhood, which Odysseus asks him to tell 'in strict detail'. In a vivid reference to the world of those who listened to Homer's stories, Eumaeus agrees: there's nothing else to do in the long evenings other than listen to stories or sleep the hours round. Besides, tales are a way of turning pain to good, the suffering metamorphosed into pleasure as the story is recounted for men's delight. Even a wanderer who has suffered greatly finds later enquiry and recall to be transformative.

And Eumaeus' story is fascinating: it rings true but also lights up an exotic world of trade and bargains. He was a prince of an eastern area of the Mediterranean with a Phoenician nurse who was seduced, 'as women are wont to be', by a smooth-talking Phoenician trader who offered to take her back with him to her parents, who were still alive and rich. The woman agreed, swearing him to secrecy (presumably she was a valuable slave) and offering that when they have sold their wares and are ready to sail home, she will bring not only treasure but the king's son, who will fetch a high price. When it was time, a cunning messenger came to the house, offering a gold and amber necklace for sale that the women of the household could not tear their eyes away from, and she slipped out with the young, 'clever and inquisitive' Eumaeus. On the voyage back, she died, but he was sold at the next stop to Odysseus' father.

This account focuses the narrative on fathers and sons, and on Eumaeus as a bridge between the world that Odysseus left behind and the one he has come back to and with which he must now engage.

Book 16

Father and Son

Eumaeus' hut is the halfway place between shore and palace, the intermediary between father and son. There is no simple coming together between this boy who has had to grow up without a father and this man whose identity and qualities have been those of an individual hero: they have to negotiate a relationship while learning to establish their new identities on Ithaca.

The first sign of Telemachus' arrival is the fawning of Eumaeus' dogs (the dogs that were ready to attack Odysseus). Telemachus belongs here. Eumaeus is overjoyed:

> He leapt up in amazement, and the bowls he was using to mix the bright wine fell from his hands. He ran to meet his young master, kissed his forehead, sparkling eyes and his hands, while the tears ran down his cheeks. 'Telemachus, sweet light of my eyes, you are here! I thought I would never see you more, after you sailed away. Come in, dear boy, and let me gladden my heart by gazing at you, home now from distant lands.'

Telemachus calls Eumaeus *Atta*, 'Dad' – a respectful and intimate term. Similes in Homer are used frequently to point to an unusual yet striking similarity (Odysseus clinging to the rocky shore in Phaeacia like an octopus). But when Eumaeus greets Telemachus, Homer says:

> He hugged and kissed him endlessly as if he were back from the dead, as a loving father greets a son returned from a far-off land after a nine-year absence, a dear and only son for whom he has suffered much pain.

The point of this simile is that it is a simile: Eumaeus is *not* Telemachus' adoring father. The simile wonders at the gap between the emotions of the biological father – who demonstrates none of the natural sentiment of the simile and who observes his son coolly from the shadows – and the kind, tearful old man who has served as his emotional base all these years.

He introduces Odysseus as the Cretan that Odysseus claimed to be, whom Eumaeus assured Telemachus would take under his protection. But this is a problem for Telemachus, aware that the household structures of his youth are disintegrating and that events at the palace are moving too fast for him to be able to receive and protect a guest. Odysseus questions him about his helplessness and almost reproaches him (a very acute and timeless exchange between ageing father and fully grown son: 'I could have done something about it at your age'). His helplessness in the face of the situation he vividly describes at the palace shows what Odysseus will have to negotiate. Eumaeus going off to reassure his grandfather, who has not eaten and drunk since Telemachus has been away, shows the chasm that separates Odysseus from those he left nearly two decades ago.

Athene rejuvenates Odysseus, to the astonishment of Telemachus, who now thinks Odysseus to be a visiting deity. In the *Iliad*, the gods' intervention often mirrors the independent decisions of the fighters, a double determination: action seen from inside and outside, both according to the shape of the epic narrative and as part of

Odysseus rejuvenated

an individual drama. Something similar happens in the *Odyssey*, when Athene 'beautifies' Penelope as she arises after a long refreshing sleep determined to present herself to the suitors as the desired queen she now feels herself to be. Athene also intervenes to disguise Odysseus as an old beggar and then as a radiant hero. This vividly illuminates the double identities that Athene – or circumstances – offer Odysseus: the battered wanderer or the man who returns from taking part in the greatest heroic venture.

How can Odysseus inhabit an identity which bridges both? His wanderings have dislocated his heroic identity as warrior, and he is in no sense the young man who left his new wife and new baby to fight in the great war. And how can, or will, that wife and son recognize him? What will Odysseus be recognized *as*?

The epic narrative has Telemachus amazed and a little fearful of this powerful, godlike figure. Odysseus brusquely denies that he is a god and abruptly reveals who he is, saying: 'I am your father; it is because of me that you are so oppressed and subject to the violence that makes you cry.'

Odysseus, the all-enduring, is suddenly overwhelmed at the suffering his absence has caused Telemachus, and, weeping, tries to embrace him. Telemachus keeps his distance, still taking him to be a god in disguise come to test him – in his wariness showing himself truly to be his father's son. When Telemachus suspiciously continues to keep his distance, Odysseus reproves him: it is not proper to doubt his father, and he restates his identity in a strange formulation, saying 'no other Odysseus will ever come here'. We remember that Athene wonders at Odysseus holding back from the reunion with his family until he had 'tested them out'.

When Telemachus does finally believe, they weep together like birds of prey whose fledglings have been stolen away from them by man, shedding common tears for the loss of the years spent separately. Those years are lost, but they can establish a bond of common purpose, proposing and rejecting first steps in their objective of ridding the palace of the suitors and bringing the household to trial.

Odysseus answers Telemachus with the truth about his journey (as distinct from the 'Cretan tales' he tells everyone else, even Athene!) and sends him back to the palace to put the first part of their secret plan into action. Here he must endure whatever ill-treatment the suitors mete out, just as they may also ill-treat Odysseus, now again disguised.

The narrative switches to the suitors, whose ambush of Telemachus has been unsuccessful. They too talk of things coming to a crisis: Telemachus' coming-of-age brings the need for Penelope finally to make a choice.

The book ends with Eumaeus' return from the palace. A great deal has happened in his absence, although Athene reverses Odysseus' rejuvenation so the scene in the hut appears the same. Telemachus and Odysseus are now bound in common secret knowledge. Eumaeus is uncertain about the figures he has seen on what Odysseus and his son know was the suitors' failed ambush ship. When he hears this, Telemachus smiles as he secretly catches his father's eye: they bond in their common secret knowledge.

Book 17

Odysseus at the Hall

In Book 17, we finally arrive at the reality of Odysseus' home, presented as both an immediate goal – the place to be reclaimed and cleansed – but also somewhere irreparably lost. Odysseus' return is heralded by a telling scene, with the first to recognize Odysseus being his old dog, Argus, whom he trained for the chase before leaving for Troy, and who is now lying on a dunghill dying of old age and neglect. The mistreatment of the once fine, prized hunting dog is distressing, a symbol of the suitors' ravages, and points to the sort of treatment anyone helpless will receive at their hands. Infinitely moving is the old dog's summoning of his very last energy to wag his tail and prick his ears in recognition of his long-absent master, before dying. It is also a mark of the distance between the noble household and position Odysseus left and what he will find – a riotous food hall that is anything but noble. It is commonplace that there is a gap between the 'home' of memory and actuality; the mutual

Telemachus and Penelope

recognition of dog and man over time, age and degradation provides a spark that crosses and shatters one vision of the past.

The book starts with Telemachus' return to Penelope, who has been worrying about him. This emotional return is vividly anticipated from the adolescent's point of view: he must go, he says, to show that he is safe, as she won't have stopped worrying and crying since he left. Penelope does indeed create the 'scene' Telemachus feared: bursting into tears, she flings her arms about her dear son, kissing his head and both his beautiful eyes, crying out in delight that he has come back safe when she thought she would never see him again

Telemachus uses his new assurance to hold her off, saying that she should not stir up his anxiety now he is home safe. She should collect her womenfolk to see to the ritual thanksgiving, while he goes to call an assembly and see to his suppliant, the seer Theoclymenus. He does then relent, telling her the high points of his trip and assuring her that Odysseus is alive but detained. Theoclymenus reinforces this message, saying that Odysseus is not only alive but already on Ithaca. For the first time, Penelope does not dismiss the possibility.

The action is moving from the hut to Odysseus' hall (*megaron* – standard word for a Mycenaean feasting hall and central hall of a palace), where the suitors are very much at home. Called in by the steward from where they have been throwing practice spears and discuses, they throw their cloaks over their chairs and settle to butchering sheep, goats, fatted calf and pigs.

It is into this scene that the disguised Odysseus comes, with a beggar's wallet and a knobbly walking stick. We rapidly hear that although there is no respect for social order among the suitors, they have very clear ideas about lower classes! Melanthius, one of the most hostile, sees Eumaeus and Odysseus coming in:

Here comes wretch leading wretch, like with like. You miserable swineherd, tell me where you're taking this vile pig, nuisance, ruiner of feasts? He's the type of beggar that scrapes his back against every pillar, whining for scraps. If you handed him over to me to work on the farm, muck out the pens and hump fodder for the goats, he'd get some muscles. But as he's feckless and work-shy, he'll just beg; he'll have problems if he tries that in Odysseus' house!

This refrain is taken up by the other main suitor, Antinous: 'Have we not enough vagabonds and miserable beggars, eating your master's substance, without adding to them?' Eumaeus has a great answer, distinguishing between 'good' and 'bad' strangers:

No-one invites strangers into their homes unless they are masters of an art that serves some public good: a prophet, physician, architect or a divinely inspired bard; certainly not beggars [and who are you to talk about wasting Odysseus' substance!]

The theme of the avenger in disguise occupies the centre of this and the next book. In incident after incident, Odysseus is abused and ill-treated, although his bodily strength beneath the shabby disguise causes many a suitor to rue the insult. The motif of the poor stranger who appears in a household and who eventually throws off his disguise, rewards the worthy and generous and punishes the uncivil, is a common folk motif. The stranger is often (as Telemachus and one of the suitors suspected) a god in disguise.

Odysseus' qualities of cunning, endurance and bodily strength can be displayed as a beggar as much as a king: this is a different world from the *Iliad*, where the noble are all brave and all beautiful, and only the low-born, foul-mouthed Thersites is ugly. In this world – that of a local chief and subsistence economy rather than of a Knossos or Mycenae palace with infinite store rooms – Odysseus can harp on a commonality between the highest and the lowest, in that both are subservient to the needs of the belly. Here, Odysseus the tricky-minded with the multifaceted persona is recognizably himself whether fighting a beggars' duel, standing up to the suitors' blows or begging his food with cunning stories. To Antinous he says that someone who looks so like a king should be as generous as a king, and he will in exchange sing his fame over the wide world. He tells another 'Cretan tale' of his identity: as a prosperous householder he went off raiding to Egypt, where he was enslaved and sold to Cyprus and on to Ithaca.

The folk story of the disguised judge is interwoven with the narrative of the double process of recognition: of Odysseus being recognized as himself and of Odysseus learning who he now is, in the non-Iliadic world of Ithaca. For his dog Argus, recognition was simple; no words or explanation were needed – the relationship between master and hound is unchanged by twenty years. For others, Odysseus has to establish himself, to be recognized not *as* anything but *for* what he now is.

Book 18

Odysseus, Penelope and the Suitors

Odysseus as Beggar

A t the end of Book 17, the long-awaited meeting between Penelope and Odysseus is anticipated but is then, dramatically, postponed for a whole book. In the meantime, there is a mock duel between Odysseus and Irus for the position of 'official' beggar, with the suitors putting forward Irus as their 'champion' for the prize of a blood-pudding. Irus, like Argus, is an illustration of the rottenness of the palace hall as now infested by the suitors. His downfall is welcomed as just, prefiguring the more general punishment Odysseus will mete out, and the episode is a lively burlesque of a heroic encounter.

Penelope's attendants (and Athene) urge her to have a beauty bath, but Penelope yet again insists that her shining beauty was destroyed when Odysseus left, leaving her wasting the years away in tears. But she accepts the need to show herself, and has a deeply restoring sleep from which she awakes as if reborn.

There is a sense of matters coming to a head. Odysseus' return coincides with and precipitates the new independence of both his son and wife, while Penelope's reaction both to her son's maturity and to the now more authoritative reports of Odysseus' safety is carefully described. Homeric psychology maps easily onto the modern world – any modern novel could convincingly translate this scene, where Athene puts it into the heart of Penelope that after years of waiting and mourning she should now smarten herself up and show herself to the suitors in order to demonstrate her desirability to her husband and son … and herself.

Although Penelope and her nurse Eurynome are frank about the ravages worked by time and dull grief, a beauty bath and a reviving sleep contribute, with Athene's help, to her radiant appearance. When she shows herself, shining through a veil, the suitors tremble with desire. She is establishing herself as a gracious independent woman, valued for her own sake. Eurymachus – a leading suitor, offering the best presents, and the leader in the plan to ambush and remove Telemachus – expresses their common sentiment: 'You exceed all other women in beauty, body and intellect.'

Penelope says several times that Odysseus took with him her bloom and value as a woman. Here she says again that her 'excellence' – she uses a term that a warrior would use of his fighting skill – was destroyed when

Penelope

Odysseus sailed away; if only he would come back to her, her reputation would be re-established and be greater than ever. With Odysseus listening, although she does not know that, she is using heroic terms. As a man demonstrates his *aretē* in contest, in battle, in the assembly and by the prizes that accrue, so a woman demonstrates hers by the dowry she can command and by the gifts she can inspire:

> Antinous presented a fine, richly-embroidered robe, pinned with curving-clasped, gold brooches. Eurymachus brought a cleverly made gold chain, strung with amber stones that shone like the sun. Eurydamas offered triple-clustered earrings with gracefully glowing mulberry-shaped drops, Finally Peisander brought a precious necklace.

Odysseus, from his beggar's seat, sees both her and the suitors' reaction. He is going to have to compete against the others to re-win Penelope, a wife whose status and desirability have been reasserted. But she has talked of the Odysseus who left all those years ago, who she remembers telling her to look after his father and mother and, if he doesn't come back, to remarry when his son and heir reaches adulthood. The gap between the world he left and the one he is coming back to is emphasized by Penelope's reflections about the proper behaviour of suitors in those past days: when suitors wished to pay court to a noble woman, daughter and heir of a rich man, they would arrive not just with gifts but with animals for the feast, rather than infest the house and live off its wealth.

Odysseus, watchful in the background, cannot react directly to the suitors, but he threatens the uppity maid, Eurymachus' mistress, with savage violence which 'shakes the women servants, making their knees tremble' and warns us of what his vengeance may be like.

Telemachus has resumed his role as Penelope's not-quite-of-age son. When in unrecognized concern for Odysseus she had upbraided him for not looking after the stranger better, he says she is in the right of it: 'If only the suitors could be defeated in the same way as the stranger [the disguised Odysseus] defeated the beggar Irus!' It sounds like a boy's empty wish; but plans are afoot.

Book 19

Odysseus in Disguise Tests the Suitors: Penelope is Intrigued

Telemachus and Odysseus are coming together as men, albeit an older and a younger man. Telemachus carries out Odysseus' plan to get at the weapons, pretending he's worried by their proximity to the hall, where smoke might affect them and the suitors might start a late-night drunken fight. The nurse Eurycleia helps her old charge, getting the servant women away while Telemachus and 'the stranger' move the weapons.

Telemachus is now assured enough to feign helplessness in front of the suitors when it will serve his and his father's cause. For the first time, too, he speaks out against their carousing – he sends them to sleep it off and goes to bed himself, leaving the palace quiet for the meeting of Odysseus and Penelope in the half-shadows of the empty hall.

Penelope comes down from her chamber, 'looking like Artemis or golden Aphrodite,

Odysseus as Beggar

goddess of love, and sat in a chair inlaid with ivory and silver'. In one last delay, Odysseus has to fight for his place once more, this time against the wicked maidservant Melantho, who though brought up by Penelope has now joined forces with the suitors and has, as Eurymachus' mistress, set herself up against Penelope. The disguised Odysseus challenges her on her aggression to someone whose appearance is so ignoble, though many wanderers like him used to have homes that were welcoming to strangers. Penelope calls her a shameless bitch for intruding on what she knows Penelope wants to be a private talk. When it comes, Odysseus' purge will extend to the servants who have consorted with the suitors as well as the suitors themselves.

When Penelope and Odysseus-as-stranger finally come together, their exchanges are in character but strike common resonances. Odysseus addresses her as one whose fame goes up to heaven, like a king ruling as a lord (Odysseus elsewhere has cried like a woman who long missed her husband). There is a sense of recognition, not of Odysseus' identity but of some kind of like-mindedness. He is 'too full of grief' to tell his tale; Penelope represents herself, again, as one whose *aretē* or excellence has been destroyed by longing. Her question, *tis pothen eis?* – who are you and where do you come from? – also reveals a like sense of suffering. Odysseus says the recalling of his troubles is too painful, while Penelope responds with her own griefs and by talking openly and intimately about her life.

She says, again, that Odysseus took with him her bloom and value as a woman; that if only he would come back and cherish her, her story would resound to the heavens. But, beset by the suitors, she cannot properly care for strangers, suppliants and heralds, and wastes her heart in longing for Odysseus. She has come up with a cunning strategy to keep them at bay: she set up her loom to weave a shroud for her elderly father-in-law, Laertes, as is proper if she is to become part of a new family. But each night she unpicks the day's work: a ruse that the tricksy Odysseus – *polymēchanos* – surely listens to appreciatively. However, one of the shameless maids has caught her unravelling the weaving, so now she is forced into facing up to moving on: her son is now of age and is capable of becoming the lord of the land and household.

Turning to Odysseus, she asks him for his story. He responds with another 'Cretan tale', inventing a lineage and home, where he says he hosted Odysseus: 'He spoke false just like true' – the storyteller who can make deceiving fiction affect the listener as if real. Tears run down Penelope's cheeks as she listens. 'As the snow on the high mountains melts when the east wind thaws it, filling the streams till the rivers overflow, so her lovely cheeks were drenched' as she wept for her husband, who was actually sitting next to her. But although Odysseus feels his wife's distress, he keeps an impassive face, keeping up his disguise and repressing tears.

Deeply affected as she is, Penelope is cautious – she has been duped before – so she stops her tears and tests him: what was Odysseus wearing? Odysseus can of course answer this perfectly, describing the fine clothes and unusual cloak pin he was wearing when he left, again cementing Penelope's image of the Odysseus that used to be. He swears that Odysseus is on his way home, visiting Zeus' oracle and collecting wealth. In this way, he establishes a bond between himself and Odysseus; one that moves Penelope to tears. He has passed the test, and through his beggarly appearance she has accepted him as a worthy link to her husband. He has offered one further link with Odysseus: he says he has seen his stockpile of rich gifts amassed on the way home. (He would have been home long before, but has travelled to accrue wealth: a harsh statement but one which likens him to a suitor amassing wedding gifts.) Penelope will not accept such proof of his survival, but the story has brought to her mind the Odysseus who left, the young hero; has it also brought to mind Odysseus as he must be now, battered by experience and like the man in front of her?

Perhaps because she is subliminally conscious of the stranger's similarity to the Odysseus who left, she makes a strange request: that he should be bathed and massaged, so he is ready to sit by Telemachus' side in the hall and so is no longer an easy target for the suitors' abuse. How else, she asks, can he judge whether Penelope really does surpass other women in intellect and judgment, if he is reduced to eating in rags?

There is definitely something being built between these two long-parted spouses.

Penelope's state of mind is sensitively described. Coming round from her beauty sleep, she had wished she could stay in that soft sleep for ever and never awake to the grief and longing that has been her life for nearly twenty years. Yet when she is fully awake, it is as if she is reborn to another life. She acknowledges her son's beard as a rite of passage for her too: she offers to marry but demands proper wooing gifts. Although she says she cannot believe reports that Odysseus is alive and coming back, now – following her long talk with Odysseus – she dreams of his return. She has 'one last thing to share before it is time for sleep'. She spends the nights tossing and turning, grieving over Odysseus, but also aware that Telemachus is growing up and the decision whether to remarry is urgent. She had a dream she wants the stranger to interpret, that she was feeding her pet geese when an eagle came and killed them all. While she was grieving over the bedraggled corpses, the eagle spoke in a man's voice, saying that he was Odysseus and would return and wreak vengeance on the suitors.

Odysseus cannot see a problem with the interpretation: it is a portent that Odysseus would return and kill the suitors! But Penelope introduced the dream saying her grief was like that of a mother turned into a nightingale after accidentally killing her daughter; the suitors are her pets, all of them killed by a huge-taloned eagle in the guise of Odysseus. Odysseus' return may be a consummation devoutly to be wished, but it is also a threat to her newly found status as a woman.

The scene is set for the denouement, but before that there is an important development. Before their late-night talk, Penelope calls the old nurse, Eurycleia, to bathe the stranger's feet: 'No doubt Odysseus' hands and feet look like his now, since hardship ages men quickly.' Eurycleia grieves over the present man and the fate of Odysseus, because 'we have welcomed many a long-suffering traveller but never one so like Odysseus, in looks and voice, even your feet'. She, like Penelope, feels the connection.

But immediately there is more: she recognizes a scar which has a tale to tell about an incident on Odysseus' first boar hunt, that connects the present man with Odysseus' childhood. As with Argus, the recognition is simple: Odysseus for her is in some sense the same as the boy she suckled, who went on that first boar hunt, the scar a witness to the continuity. The scar tells a full, direct and non-'Cretan' story of a past experience, a past danger, past companions.

Eurycleia imagines the man in front of her as Odysseus and weeps for both. Her recognition of the scar brings to her and us a vivid evocation of his naming ceremony and young manhood. Like fond carers through the ages, she sees the man but remembers and is bonded to the boy; like sons through the ages, Odysseus is conscious of, and perhaps threatened by, the chasm that separates him from his early self. He threatens her with violence, which strikes an odd note in what might be expected of a man reuniting with his old nurse, and prevents her from revealing who he is to Penelope: her recognition will be fuller, more complex and more difficult to achieve.

It is interesting that Odysseus and Penelope react differently to Penelope's description of her dream. Odysseus says no interpretation is needed as the dream carried its own: the voice of Odysseus saying that 'the geese are the suitors and I, your husband, am the eagle returned to prepare a dark fate for them all'. He says shortly, 'there is no way of twisting this dream to give some other meaning'. But in her dream, her maids came and found her sobbing for the death of her pet geese.

Penelope counters Odysseus' brusque response by saying that 'dreams are difficult as portents; some come through the gates of ivory and others of horn and no-one knows which will come true'. She dismisses the promised return.

Axes

But this vision of carnage and vengeance in the return may have served finally to dissolve her dream of Odysseus as he was, and make her focus on the present. A decision has been made:

> The crucial day is drawing near that will cut me away from the house of Odysseus. I will declare a contest; whoever wins I will go with, leaving this lovely house where I was first a wife, filled with riches, a house I will always remember in my dreams.

She sets up a bridal contest: she will marry whoever can match Odysseus' feat in stringing his huge bow and shooting an arrow through a line of twelve crossed axes. Her new husband must match and will replace her old.

Book 20

Odysseus: Testing and Recognition

We get very little direct access to Odysseus' state of mind in this extraordinary homecoming. In the last book he aligned himself with the vengeful returning husband and threatened anyone who opposes him or who has been complicit with the suitors. But most of all there has been a sense of discontinuity with the man he was rather than disquiet at how he is to bridge that gap.

Book 20 starts with Odysseus tossing and turning, woken by the carousing suitors and the servant women. This is a vivid picture: his heart and mind in turmoil, his anger boiling like a sizzling blood pudding

Odysseus Disguised

tossed on a barbecue by a frantic chef. He boils over, crying to the heavens; Zeus obliges with a great thunderclap, which a late-working mill-woman interprets as a validation of her urgent wish that this would be the last day for the suitors, who have caused her so much back-breaking work.

So the sign that this is the day of vengeance goes out from Odysseus to the heavens and then to the land and its labourers.

Meanwhile, Telemachus is conscious of his new responsibility and maturity, and of his father. He surveys the arrangements for the 'stranger', because his 'mother tends to be lax in such matters'. Eurycleia reassures him, and the narrative turns to the morning preparations: the maids sweeping, washing and polishing the cups for the feast and drawing water, the labourers splitting logs and the swineherd driving in fattened hogs. A cowherd – who had brought a heifer and goats over on the ferry, so had not met the disguised Odysseus – warmly and sympathetically greets this wanderer, saying that the future will

bring better fortune for him. He too sees the resemblance to Odysseus and wells up at the thought.

Meanwhile, the suitors start carousing early. They are irritated by Odysseus' presence and one of them sarcastically offers him a guest gift: an ox hoof flung hard at him. It misses, and Telemachus takes umbrage: lucky for him, Telemachus says, that the stranger dodged it, because otherwise Telemachus would have killed him outright in vengeance. He is his father's son! He warns them that he is no longer a child and only tolerates their outrageous behaviour because he is one against many.

The book ends with the suitors laughing almost hysterically, Telemachus and Penelope looking on, and the narrator reflecting that the banquet that Odysseus and the vengeful goddess Athene were preparing for the suitors would be less appetising.

Telemachus

Book 21

The Trial of the Bow of Odysseus

B ook 21 is a tense, exciting, self-contained book of the bridal contest for the hand of Penelope: the trial of the bow. Penelope takes out from the treasure chest the huge bow, weeping over this attribute of Odysseus, now a symbol of his power and loss. Its history points up its significance: an heirloom given to Odysseus before its owner was murdered while Herakles' guest, during a venture to resolve a difficult dispute on which Odysseus had been sent by his father, though he was still quite young. The bow has a story of its own, is a memorial to a murdered friend and is so potent a mark of Odysseus' skill and so precious that Odysseus left it behind when he went to Troy.

The suitors are ambivalent about the test: worried that they might fail and prove themselves inferior to Odysseus, yet secretly hopeful of being the bow's master. The narrator points to the baselessness of their hope; they will die at the hands of the bow, safely back in its rightful owner's hands to avenge the abuse of hospitality.

We have a vivid picture of the scene. Penelope, lovely and gracious, in a shining gauzy veil standing by the hall's wooden pillar, issues her challenge:

Hear me, proud suitors, your prize stands here before you, clear to see.
The test is godlike Odysseus' mighty bow: whoever best strings the bow
and shoots an arrow through the rings of a dozen axes, with him I will go,
leaving this lovely and luxurious house, that I came to as a bride and will
always remember in my dreams.

She orders Eumaeus, in tears at the sight of his master's bow, to set out the axes with their handle-rings of grey iron. Antinous, one of the leading suitors, upbraids the swineherd for yet again bringing to Penelope's mind Odysseus as he was. He himself remembers Odysseus as he was when they were both young, and doubts any of them can compete.

Telemachus is in that position between boyhood and manhood: formally now his mother's guardian but standing on the sidelines while she speaks. Now he springs forward, setting the axes in a straight line in a long trench, stamping the earth in around them (note that the hall, unlike the marble-paved Mycenaean palaces, has an earth floor). He is also inbetween being his mother's son and his father's rival. He imagines trying the bow himself, entering the competition:

If I can string it and shoot an arrow through the iron rings, I will not be disturbed by my dear mother's departure for another house, since I myself will be a man as capable of winning fine prizes as my father.

If he succeeds, he would establish himself as as much of a man as the young Odysseus to whom the bow was given, and would also symbolically replace his father as his mother's lord and guardian. Dramatically, Telemachus attempts to string the bow:

Three times the bow quivered in his hands as he made a strong effort to string it; three times he had to let go, though he wanted so much to succeed in shooting an arrow through the iron handle-rings. Now exerting all his power and strength he might have strung the bow, had Odysseus not shaken his head and checked him.

Through tact, cunning and/or inhibition, he pretends to be too young and weak. He steps back and invites the suitors to try. The first was a seer, whose 'smooth and delicate hands failed; he set it down, saying "This bow will break the heart and spirit of many a man here. Still, it is better to die trying, than live on without winning the prize that brings us here each day, in endless expectation."' In many folk stories of marriage competitions (such as that for Hippodomeia or

Odysseus and his bow

Turandot), the entrants wager their lives. In a way the suitors do not anticipate, the seer's words are prophetic.

They try all kinds of tricks, warming and greasing the bow with tallow to make it more flexible. Meanwhile, Odysseus takes the two most loyal herdsmen aside, asking if Odysseus were to come back, would they help him against the suitors? When both affirm their support, Odysseus reveals his identity and shows them the sure sign of his scar from his boyhood boar hunt.

Back in the hall, the chief suitor tries and fails, acknowledging the ignominy of being so demonstrably weaker than Odysseus. The final contestant consoles him, and himself, by pointing out that this fateful day is that of Apollo the archer. Of course they will fail (and Odysseus succeed) on such a day. When the bow is laid aside, Odysseus proposes that he try the bow,

> so I can see what strength is in my hands: if I still possess the power I used to have when my limbs were supple or whether deprivation and endless wandering have reduced it.

Surely this is a real, not feigned concern? The stranger's proposal is met with outrage, despite his carefully emphasizing that he is not entering the competition, and the accusation that he is drunk. A warning story of the vengeance wreaked by a maddened centaur when his passions were aroused by alcohol misfires, pointing as it does to the terrible fury that Odysseus will wreak on them.

There is continued tension between Telemachus, Penelope and Odysseus. Telemachus leaps to assert his authority over the bow and tells her to take her distaff and go back to the women's quarters where she belongs. He has had it in his power to win her himself: he now feels able to stand as an independent man in front of his mother (and perhaps of his father). The stringing of the bow has indeed been a test of manhood.

The book finishes with the long anticipated sight: Odysseus lovingly checking over, flexing and easily stringing his great bow,

> like a master bard stretching a new string onto his lyre's tuning peg. Then grasping the bow in his right hand, he plucked the string that sang sweetly at his touch.

He sends an arrow surely through the twelve crossed axe-heads.

For most of this epic, Odysseus has been the master storyteller, the bard who entertains the Phaeacian court, the teller of lying, identity-obscuring 'Cretan tales' to gods and humans. Now, stringing it like a bard but not as a bard, he will let his great bow do the talking.

Book 22

Odysseus' Vengeance

O dysseus has become the protagonist of two folk motifs: that of the victor in a marriage games where the losers die and that of the avenging judge, returning from a long absence to punish the transgressors. With Book 22 comes the vengeance – a complete cleansing of the suitors and their consorts, Odysseus purifying the palace with fire and brimstone. The deaths are described with delight in the skill and appropriateness of the shot or stroke, and perhaps with a certain bloodthirstiness that, despite its battlefield setting, is less a feature of the *Iliad*.

Antinous is shot through the throat in the act of drinking, blood mixing with the wine in his drinking cup, and as he falls he overturns the banquet table: a fitting start to the punishment of the suitors' greed. Odysseus at last fully reveals himself:

> You curs! You thought I'd never return from Troy so you laid waste my house, raped my maids and wooed my wife in secret though I was still alive. You did not regard the gods who rule the wide sky or think that mortal vengeance would find you. Now the net of fate is thrown over you all.

Antinous is killed by Odysseus in the guise of the stranger-beggar who was insulted and buffeted; after declaring who he is, he kills the other suitors as the returning, vengeful lord. He refuses the supplication of the other main suitor, the Ithacan Eurymachus, who blames the incomer Antinous for everything and offers to make good all the damage. Odysseus is in no mood, any more than Achilles in the *Iliad*, to accept generous reparations.

Now Telemachus can act openly as his father's helper, killing one suitor in the act of attacking his father, and together with the two loyal retainers he gets to the armoury. Odysseus carries on killing with his great bow:

> He kept shooting steadily, killing the suitors one by one until the dead were heaped high. But when the arrows were gone, he propped the bow by the doorpost, picked up two sturdy bronze-tipped spears, slung across his

shoulders a shield with four layers of hide, and set a mighty helmet on his head, its horsehair plume nodding threateningly.

Melanthius the collaborator tells the remaining suitors where the armoury is, which momentarily dismays Odysseus. Telemachus admits a fault in leaving the door open, and sends Eumaeus to close the trap. Melanthius is horribly tortured for the role he has played. He is, literally, strung up: limbs twisted and bound, he dangles from the roof timbers all night, waiting to be finished off and mutilated. Odysseus' henchmen repay the insults to their master – the man who threw an ox-hoof at Odysseus now has an answering 'gift', which is death.

There is now a pitched armed battle between Odysseus, Telemachus and the two faithful herdsmen, and the remaining suitors, who are said to stampede like a herd of cattle stung by the horseflies in spring. Odysseus and the others attack them, like vultures with crooked talons and curving beaks swooping down from the mountains on smaller birds that try but fail to get away. They set about the suitors, striking down one after another. Horrible cries ring around the hall and the floor is drenched with blood.

Some sue for mercy. Leodes, who acted as a seer for the suitors, pleads non-involvement in any harm to Odysseus' households and indeed that he acted to restrain his fellow suitors. His supplication is denied on interesting grounds: he must have prophesied, and therefore in some sense envisaged, Odysseus' death in his wish to marry his wife.

The poet Phemius has a more persuasive argument and is allowed by the poet Homer to make it very powerfully: the bard is in charge of heroes' reputations, and Odysseus' fame is in his and his brethren's hands. He is allowed to live when Telemachus vouches that he sang for the suitors only under duress.

With Athene's help, all the rest are killed like fish caught in a net. Odysseus is drenched in blood from head to foot, like a lion feeding on an ox, up to his haunches in gore.

In a troublingly ghastly episode, the twelve maidservants who have been consorting with the suitors are made to clean up the slaughter in the hall and then are led out and killed by being strung up by the neck on a cable, their feet not touching the ground, like long-winged thrushes or doves caught in a snare as they go to roost in their thicket. They writhe for a while in the noose, but their feet soon stop kicking. We remember Penelope's dream, of Odysseus as a cruel eagle killing her pets; we think of all we know of female servants and slaves in the hands of powerful men, and know how little choice such have other than to 'collude'. But choice is not the point – Odysseus is cleansing the house from contamination. Nevertheless, that cruel image – of the girls' twitching feet – haunts the rest of the narrative.

Melanthius is now finished off in equally gruesome fashion. He is led outside and his nose, ears and genitals are hacked off and given to the dogs. Still working off their rage, Odysseus and Telemachus cut off his hands and feet.

In blackly comic contrast, the old nurse refuses to fetch fire and brimstone to cleanse the gore of the mass killing, until she has first brought Odysseus a cloak: it is not proper that the master should go round in rags (the last shred of his assumed identity). The book ends with the faithful women servants embracing him in joy at having him back, a recognition which brings tears to his eyes.

Odysseus and Penelope

Book 23

Odysseus and Penelope: Recognition and Reunion

Book 23 is the final twisting together of the stories of the *Odyssey*: Odysseus' eventual recognition by his wife, Telemachus' establishment as a grown son within a two-parent household, and Odysseus' final narration of his adventures – this time to his wife.

Now only Penelope, sunk in the deepest sleep she has known since Odysseus' loss, does not know of his return. Deep sleep like this – such as Odysseus' sleep on landing on Ithaca – marks a kind of rebirth and a new chapter in the narrative. She will wake to a different world and to a different identity: as Odysseus' wife.

Eurycleia, chuckling, flies upstairs with the speed of youth to tell Penelope that her husband, so longed for, is alive and here. But there is pain here too. The reversal is too sudden for her to take in: it feels like a cruel joke played on someone who had at last resolved to free herself of her grief and move on. Eurycleia – as Odysseus' mouthpiece? – describes Odysseus triumphant and blood-drenched, standing over the corpses of the suitors. Does Penelope remember her dream, of Odysseus as cruel eagle killing her pet geese?

Her psychology is sensitively described:

As she went down, she was considering whether to remain distant and question the man who was said to be her dear husband, or whether to run up to him, hug and kiss his head and hands. She sat down by him; he was sitting with his eyes on the ground, waiting for his wife to speak. She sat there silently for a long time in wonder, gazing intently at his face, trying to recognize him through his ragged appearance.

Telemachus is outraged:

Why do you distance yourself from my father like this, instead of sitting by his side, plying him with all kinds of questions? No other woman would harden her heart like this, sitting apart from a husband who had just returned to her and his native land, after twenty years of bitter exertion.

This is reminiscent of Athene's critical observation about Odysseus on landing on Ithaca: 'You are always so shrewd and so cautious! Any other man back from his wanderings would have dashed joyfully to his hall to see his wife and children, but you don't want to know or find out anything until you've tested out your wife.' But whereas Odysseus' wanderings have offered him all kinds of alternatives – homes, partners, futures – which he has finally turned down, Penelope has been tied to and identified with house and family. Until now, when the ties to both have suddenly been loosened. All the references to Odysseus have been to the man who left, a hero in the prime of life, but Penelope has been gradually drawn to and found herself being protective towards this man, older and battered by life, who now is suddenly hailed as a returning avenger.

Penelope – whose epithet is thoughtful, cautious – is only with difficulty convinced that it might indeed be Odysseus: even the scar, she points out, might be faked by a god! This reserve, this caution, this insistence on putting the stranger to the test, is what marks Penelope as Odysseus' 'other half'. Precisely because it is how Odysseus would have acted, he is both amused and understanding. In answer to Telemachus' anger at his mother's 'flint hard heart', he says that Penelope will take time to see past the way he now appears.

For the dog Argus and the nurse Eurycleia, Odysseus is recognizable as the same man who went away, while for the loyal herdsmen, he is the returning master. For Telemachus, he is eventually accepted as the father he never knew and happily acknowledged as senior partner in the plot to reclaim, cleanse and restore the household. But for Penelope least of all, is the recognition one of simple continuity of identity: she has to remake a relationship, retake him as a husband.

Meanwhile, Telemachus is given a job to do: he is to arrange the festivities of his mother's wedding, to create the impression that Penelope has accepted the suitor who succeeded in the bow competition (as in a very real sense she has). The shape of the narrative was of a marriage competition, with the winner wreaking destruction on the losers. The household bathes and put on their best clothes and the bard plays his lyre for dancing, so the wedding sounds cover the traces of the slaughter. The great hall resounds with music and the noise of dancing feet, so that anyone passing will think that Penelope has failed to be constant to her absent lord and has taken a new husband.

Odysseus is bathed, massaged and dressed in new clothes, as a bridegroom should be. But what about Penelope? She has taken decision after decision about her future as an independent woman: rather than the marriage games being set up by a father, she has herself set up the trial of the bow. When she heard that Odysseus was back and had killed the suitors, her first reaction was joy, but her second was to check details and demand proof.

Sitting opposite her, Odysseus says exactly the same as Athene had said to him on arriving – 'no-one else, after twenty years, would keep back from your spouse'. He asks that a single bed be made up for him.

Penelope responds that she is neither proud nor dismissive, but is overwhelmed. The man she knows well is the Odysseus who left Ithaca. As if it were a *non sequitur*, she asks the nurse to bring the bed out of the master bedroom and make it up for Odysseus.

Odysseus understands: this is the final test. For this man who has used every exchange to make trial of his interlocutors, it is a test too far. He bursts out angrily, saying her words have grieved his heart. The bed, as only they two know, Odysseus fashioned with infinite care out of and around a living olive tree that he had enclosed to make the marriage chamber. So either someone has taken an axe to his wedding bed, or Penelope is putting him to the test.

The details he gives of the process of building and decorating the wedding bed is the final proof; his careful craftwork links him in some way to the multifaceted wily stranger Penelope has come to know. Penelope's whole body relaxes and all tension is released. Crying, she hugs and kisses him and asks him to forgive her hardened heart:

> Her words stir him to tears, and weeping he embraces his dear wife. As welcome as the sight of land to shipwrecked sailors, who swimming to shore to escape the angry waves are overwhelmed with joy when their saltwater-caked bodies touch land, saved from drowning: so welcome was the sight of her husband.

Once more, there is reciprocity: Odysseus is as welcome to her as the sailor washed up safely onto shore … that Odysseus so recently was. Penelope cannot take her eyes from him, never taking her white arms from round his neck.

Odysseus reveals that this is not the end of their trials, but proposes they go to bed before facing up to the future. However, Penelope, characteristically, wants to hear about this future trial. Odysseus is reluctant – why anticipate pain? – but reveals what Teiresias told him in the Underworld that in order to make peace with the god of the sea and finally resolve Poseidon's anger at Odysseus' treatment of the Cyclops, he has a strange journey still to carry out. He must take an oar and wander until he finds a people so ignorant of seafaring – impossible to imagine for a Greek! – that they ask why he is carrying a winnowing fan (a blade for tossing wheat and chaff into the air). There he must sacrifice to Poseidon – bringing worship of the god of the sea to an agricultural people – and he will then die, in old age, from the sea.

In some sense, then, here is the conclusion to the story of the return of Odysseus. They make love, exchange stories of their sufferings and sleep in each other's arms. It is as if all the suffering and losses are redeemed by becoming the medium of intimate exchange.

Book 24

Completing Stories

Afterstories: Agamemnon and Achilles in the Underworld

However, there are several other stories still to be finished. First, there are the families of the suitors who are expected to demand vengeance for the murder of their leading men. We have followed the story from Odysseus' point of view, as an avenging judge, cleansing his house from the pollution of an 'infestation' of rivals. But in a pre-judicial revenge culture, where 'blood will have blood', the suitors need vengeance of their own.

At the start of Book 24, Melanthius' story is woven into those of the other Iliadic heroes of Troy, and the narrative follows the souls of the suitors down to the Underworld. In Book 24, for the first time, we move away from Telemachus gathering stories of his father and Odysseus as storyteller and bard. We remember that those 'Sons of Homer' who performed these and other epic cycles were called rhapsodes: stitchers-together of stories. And now Odysseus has told Penelope a very short version of his adventures, the rhapsode has turned to delight his audience

Agamemnon

with an exchange between two other great characters, whose stories were dramatized by the great tragedians: Achilles and Agamemnon.

The dead heroes are given voice by the narrator and can talk to one another as if for the first time. In the *Iliad* there is a foreshadowing of Achilles' death, but, like the fall of Troy, it happens outside the narrative. Yet here, Agamemnon tells Achilles about Achilles' funeral:

> The sea nymphs wrapped your body in an imperishable shroud and lamented while the nine muses sang sweetly in counterpoint, which

moved all the Greeks to tears. Immortals and mortals, we mourned you for seventeen days and nights, and on the eighteenth we gave your body to the flames, clothed like a god and richly covered in oils and honey. We sacrificed fatted sheep and cattle round you, and the Greek heroes, warriors and charioteers streamed past your pyre making a vast noise. At dawn we gathered up the ash and bone, steeped them in oil and wine and placed them with Patroclus' remains in the gold two-handled urn your mother gave us, made by the smith god Hephaistos himself. Your goddess mother provided fabulous prizes for your funeral games, and on a headland jutting out into the Hellespont we built a grave mound, so it might be seen far out at sea by men who live now and those to come.

This description serves as a pendant to the death of the suitors here in the *Odyssey*, but also to the *Iliad*. The first words of the *Iliad* are of the 'rage of Achilles which brought the souls of many heroes to the underworld and gave their bodies to the fire' – the end of his rage comes when he officiates and adjudges Patroclus' funeral games – and the last words are the making of Hektor's grave mound.

The other major story of the 'return from Troy' which has come down to us as dramatized by the Athenian tragedians is that of Agamemnon. He has just revealed to Achilles his 'eternal fame granting' funeral and grave mound, which will keep his story alive as sailors point it out as they pass on the busy trade route. Agamemnon contrasts it sadly with the way his own dead body was treated after Clytemnestra killed him.

Achilles

There has been a running contrast between Odysseus' story and that of Agamemnon and Menelaus. Telemachus was adjured to live up to Orestes' example in ridding his household of rivals to his absent father's bed; Penelope in her constancy was compared favourably against Clytemnestra, and in her prudence and chastity against Helen. Now, in the news of Odysseus' avenging homecoming being brought by the suitors to Agamemnon in the Underworld, these stories are stitched together. The end of Odysseus' story told to the heroes of Troy forms a fitting conclusion to both the *Iliad* and the *Odyssey*.

Odysseus and Laertes

After the conclusion of Odysseus' return, with love making and exchange of stories, there are still 'leftovers': other wanderings, other stories. There is one last thread: Odysseus has yet to be recognized by his father, Laertes, who is living in the country like a poor peasant. At this end of the *Odyssey*, there is what feels to be a leftover habit: testing, probing this elderly father, half-dead with loss and neglect. We know that his wife died of grief at Odysseus' absence and that since then he has lived alone on his remote farm, and we see Odysseus' response when he sees his father 'dressed in a wretched filthy patched tunic, old and worn and burdened with grief':

> He debated in heart and mind whether to clasp his father to him with kisses and tell him the whole story of his return home; or whether to make trial of him with questions. On reflection he thought the latter was best, to try him with testing words.

Why does he do so? As always, Odysseus observes, tests out and deceives before revealing himself. Tests, and proofs like the scar, are traditional motifs in oral poetry through the ages (e.g. those collected and analysed by Harvard's Milman Parry, such as 'The Returning Husband'). But with his father? The narrative has a subcurrent about the competition between father and son – Telemachus could but does not string Odysseus' bow – but is there a hint here of Odysseus testing to destruction his father? As with Penelope, though, the habitual distance between himself and those to whom he tells 'Cretan tales' is disturbed by his emotions, but he keeps to his plan to tell how he entertained Odysseus, years ago. Laertes presumes his son dead. The effect on Odysseus of his father's distress is physical; he drops his pretence and reveals himself. Again as with Penelope, the declaration is too sudden a turn to be believed: Laertes needs physical proof and identification. Odysseus shows him the scar, the mark of his boyhood hunting trip with his grandfather, and reminisces about the planting of the trees which Laertes gave him, now full-grown.

Laertes is rejuvenated by this, metaphorically and actually, and takes his place as a hero among his people. The *Odyssey* ends with the three generations of heroes reunited, facing the suitors' vengeful kin, before Athene intervenes to end the killing, and Laertes tells Telemachus to be worthy of his lineage.

The household is complete.

Afterword

Others' Stories, Women's Stories: Circe, the Women of Troy, Helen, Calypso … and Dido

The *Odyssey* ends with the three generations fighting together. Odysseus has returned and been recognized, in many senses, by his own: his people, place, family. But throughout the later books he has been testing his son, wife and father, a testing to near destruction not just of his family, his near and dear, but of generational bonds and the consolidation of the centrality of his place.

Both the *Iliad* and *Odyssey* weave in other stories. In the *Iliad* Book 2, the catalogue of ships mentions many heroes whose stories we pick up in Greek tragedies, while Odysseus 'borrows' several of his adventures from those which are attributed to Jason in other epic cycles.

Sappho

But there are three women whose stories have a life of their own, before and after they are woven into those of Homer's heroes: Helen of Troy and Sparta, and two of Odysseus' partners, Circe and Calypso.

In the story of Odysseus' return, he has come into the lives of, been cared for and dependent on many women, such as Nausicaa and Calypso. He has woven them into his story; appropriated their stories into his epics. And Odysseus has come home to Penelope, but at their reunion – their second wedding night – he has told her that that is not the end of his story: there is another journey to come for him. But what of Penelope?

The Chorus of women in Euripides' *Medea* sing triumphantly about women's *kleos* being taken over, reappropriated, from male mouths. Natalie Haynes' *Pandora's Jar* is just one of those who have taken up that chorus' challenge; Margaret Atwood has reimagined Penelope's story in *The Penelopiad*, and

Madeline Miller that of Circe. Both these women already had stories of their own, told in other poems and other epics. Perhaps most extraordinarily, the last epic of the Trojan War cycle, the *Telegony* (now lost, but in antiquity attributed to both an eighth- and a sixth-century BCE poet), told not only of Odysseus' future but of the problematic after-story of Circe, Odysseus, Penelope and Telemachus.

Circe

The *Telegony*'s story continues that of Circe, the fascinating enchantress. It is clear in the narrative that despite his magic herb, she does bewitch Odysseus, in bed and out: after a year, it is his men that force him to remember he is supposed to be going home! In epic tradition, their story continues: Circe had at least three sons by Odysseus, and her later narrative continues to intertwine with his. The remarkable story of her eldest, Telegonus, was told in the *Telegony*, the outline of which survives. When Telegonus was a man, he went in search of his famous father – a man who had tested his own son and father – and dramatically and tragically caused his death. He also brought back to Circe's island Penelope and Telemachus, closing the cycle and bringing back Circe into an after-story of 'life after Odysseus'.

The Women of Troy

Though, or because, the *Iliad* starts with a girl as a prize, exchanged and substituted, women's voices run as a critical underflow through the epic.

In Euripides' devastating play of that title, the Trojan Women stand for all time as the victims of the violence of (male) war. Andromache is torn away from her son, the little prince Astyanax (lord of the city), to be allotted as bed-mate to one of the victors. Hecuba, going to serve Odysseus, is left to bury her grandson, who lies, after being thrown from the walls, in the crook of his father Hektor's shield and arm-strap, sweat-stained hide against bruised baby skin. The women of the chorus, meanwhile, lament their fate as allotted to one master or other.

The play ends with a lament for the city, one of three traditional, powerful lament forms – for the lost hero, the lost city as well as for the human condition as encapsulated by a particular death: 'Troy is no more!' But each performance is a recall, a revivification: Troy *is*, exists for as long as it stands as the archetypal ruined great city.

Euripides' play was produced during the winter of 416/415, at the height – or perhaps nadir – of the Peloponnesian War between Athens and Sparta, described by Thucydides in almost tragic terms, as the winter after the fall of the besieged island of Melos, after which the Athenian forces slaughtered all the males and took into slavery the women and children. Thucydides tellingly describes this as a newly inhuman act of war: some years before, a similar punishment had been decreed for Mytilene, one of a few 'non-contributing' states of the Athenian alliance who made overtures to Sparta, rebelled, were besieged and forced to surrender. In book 3 of his *History of the Peloponnesian War*, Thucydides narrates the decision-making process: the speeches that swayed the Athenian Assembly – a participant not representative government – to vote for the absolute destruction of this enemy state. He also tells of the impact: the next day, a further Assembly was called where an argument against such exemplary punishment was mounted not on the grounds of compassion, but of Athens' self-interest. The first decree was overturned and a second trireme was sent to overtake the state galley, whose rowers 'were laden down by their unprecedented message': these were Greeks, former allies, whom the first decree had sentenced to be killed and enslaved.

In the bitter last years of the war, Melos, long neutral in the Peloponnesian War between Athenian and Spartan allies, was similarly besieged and reduced. A shorter debate in the Assembly similarly decreed the absolute punishment on the grounds of the *Realpolitik* of empire, with rule maintained by might not right. But this time there were no second thoughts.

In a very real sense, Euripides' play is the 'Melian Women': the chorus of Athenian citizens performed to an audience of Athenian citizens, sitting in the Theatre of Dionysus in the same blocks as in the Assembly where they voted for the enslavement of the Melian women and children. These were the same fellow Greeks that they now had the opportunity to buy as housekeepers and slaves or to use in the male and female brothels. The chorus assume the mask and envoice the Trojan Women, as the Melian Women, as the victims of war through the ages.

Helen

The women of Troy are literally fabulous: Helen, the most beautiful woman in the world; Hecuba, the greatest queen; and Andromache, the iconic wife and mother. These figures resound through later retellings, but behind their working into the *Iliad* we can see the shadowy figures of previous story-tellings, poems and epics.

Helen of Troy is literally the stuff of legend, 'the face that launched a thousand ships'. As the old men sitting by the Trojan battlements say, chattering in the sun like cicadas, who could blame the Trojans and bronze-greaved Greeks for fighting so long and so hard for such a woman, who has the devastating beauty of a goddess?

Helen

All kinds of stories about Helen have come to us. She fascinated ancient authors and poets, and references to her come in works such as Herodotus' *Histories* and Plato's dialogues, while the geographer Pausanias' travels in the second-century CE took him to many sites associated with her. The cycle of epic accounts of the Trojan War – the 'other Iliads', now largely lost but surviving and retold in the world of Alexander the Great – contain stories that flower in the romances of the Hellenistic authors and the Roman love poets, the 'classic' texts of medieval and Renaissance imagination, and beyond. As Homer has Helen reflect, it is an evil destiny to be the subject of poetry and stories for generations to come.

Her backstory – told as elsewhere in the first of the now lost cycle of Troy stories, the *Cypria* – has three goddesses arguing over 'who is the fairest of them all', with the Trojan prince Paris appointed as judge. Each goddess offered a gift from her particular domain as a bribe: Hera, kingship of Asia and Europe; Athena, wisdom and prowess in battle; Aphrodite, as goddess of love, the most beautiful woman in the world, Helen, wife of the Mycenaean king of Sparta.

The chorus in Aeschylus' tragedy *Agamemnon* sing of the origins of the Trojan War, of the outrage of Paris' rupture of the all-important bond of trust between host and guest, carrying off the queen. They link Helen's name with 'drawing to destruction': Helen the archetypal destroyer of ships, of men.

Euripides' *Trojan Women* has a formal debate about Helen's responsibility for starting the war. Paris' mother, Queen Hecuba, disputes Helen's passive role in this male account – 'you fell for my son's beautiful body, no force or immortal intervention needed!'

But the *Odyssey* starts, in contrast, with a gracious Queen Helen, presiding over the court at Sparta with her husband Menelaus, entertaining Odysseus' son, Telemachus. She comforts the young man with a magic potion: *nepenthes*, meaning 'no more pain'.

So we have Helen of legend, Helen the love prize, Helen the Spartan queen, Helen the destroyer and Helen the witch. Archaeology also provides evidence of Helen the patron deity of Sparta. But we have another Helen who, like Odysseus, can not only reflect on her multi-faceted persona but also control her narrative: the Helen who blinded the poet Stesichorus for his vilification of her. Odysseus tells his own story, but Helen punishes her detractor.

Helen of Sparta

From the advent of Paris, Helen becomes Helen of Troy. But it is clear from many thousands of cult objects that for the people of Sparta she remained Helen of Sparta, to be worshipped, supplicated and prayed to, with her superhuman power and beauty extolled and emulated.

In the *Iliad*, Helen says how she regrets leaving her home, her daughter and her girlfriends in Sparta. We know of the close bonds between male Spartans – the system of male 'dorms' – and see Sparta as the highly regulated martial and masculinist state described by fifth-century BCE Athenian writers, a 'Spartan' way of life brought in after the subject population rebelled.

But Helen balances this – later – image of Sparta as an entirely male warrior society, and shines a light on the continuity of girls' and women's prowess, and worship of a female deity. We have references to Spartan girls dancing and training in athletics, and from the eighth century BCE onwards we have finds, dedications and references to Spartan girls' festivals involving athletics, dancing, choral singing and even chariot racing. So, unlike Athenian girls, Helen as a girl had a strong female community, meeting socially and to train for a wide variety of performances.

For the severe Sparta, a male citizen quasi-police state, we have a date, a founding father – Lycurgus, a late eighth-century BCE lawmaker – and a cause, the need to keep down the 'helots' (subject peoples who worked the land of much of the southern Peloponnese) after they rebelled. This image – or, some Sparta authorities say, 'mirage', created or at least sharpened by Athens – has boys and men living apart from their families in all-male barracks, speaking laconically (Lakonia, the land of Sparta), frugal in speech as in diet, with all frivolity stripped away, enduring rigorous training for war and the subjugation and policing of the subject population. All this has nothing to do with women: marriage was for mating and the bearing of future Spartans, with the husband visiting for that purpose.

But we know from poetry and pottery that Sparta at the time of Homer was a rich and richly cultural place, with fine ceramics, palaces and metalwork. Finds at shrines – inscriptions, representations on stelae and votive figurines – testify to the ongoing importance of Helen as a demi-goddess; a sort of patron saint for Spartan girls, reputedly able to transform an 'ill-formed' baby into a famous beauty. From at least the eighth century BCE, we know of girls training to excel physically in races and to take part in female rituals and celebrations, including, it seems a Heleneia: Helen's Festival.

The first story we have of the young Helen is of her on the dancing ground by the River Eurotas; raped like her mother, Leda, in her case by the visiting elderly King of Athens, Theseus. The stories of her as a girl have her as the embodiment of female doubleness: of *erōs*, the irresistible force of passionate love, while the forcefield around her prompts *eris* (strife, as in the apple of *eris* that Paris reputedly awarded to Aphrodite). Theseus' rape, like Paris', causes strife: the breaking of bonds, here of propriety but also of *xenia*, the bond between host and guest, palace and palace, envoy and king.

The next 'non-Homeric' story we have is around arrangements for her marriage to Menelaus. In a long fragment of the 'Hesiodic' Catalogue of Women, we have a list of suitors and their 'many bridal-gifts, by which to surpass all the heroes'. We hear of the participation in a bridal competition by many of the main Greek figures of the Trojan War, who in the legend – though markedly not in Homer – were fighting because as suitors they had been bound by Helen's father into an oath of brotherhood to uphold the rights of the successful suitor. So we hear of Achilles and Odysseus both hiding to prevent them becoming embroiled; of Agamemnon, despite coming late, winning the competition with extraordinary gifts, on behalf of his brother, Menelaus.

We have many references to such betrothal competitions: the Peloponnese is named after Pelops' betrothal race, traditionally the origin of the Olympic Games. In this cursed race, the father Oenomaus – not wanting to allow his daughter, Hippodamia, to supplant him by marrying and bearing a child to the new king presumptive – raised his spear to kill his would-be son-in-law as he was about to win the race. The outcome is intensely indicated on the Olympia temple pediment, where the old seer, head on hand, is looking across Hippodamia, her parents and suitor to her father's charioteer. Pelops had bribed him to replace her father's bronze chariot axles with wax, which melted just before the finishing line, killing Oenomaus and entangling the charioteer in the traces. With his dying breath, he cursed Pelops and all his line: a curse that echoed down the generations and through Aeschylus' drama, the *Oresteia*.

The *Odyssey* has re-versioned and brought into Odysseus' story two bridal competitions. The first is for Nausicaa, held after the prophecy that Nausicaa was to marry 'out'. (Though as we've seen, Odysseus tactfully avoids competing for Nausicaa: her story, like all those who become involved with this arch storyteller, does not follow its natural path as Odysseus can't compete for a wife because he has Penelope waiting.) The second competition is for Penelope: overtly set up for the suitors to win her, Odysseus and Telemachus enter the competition to string his bow, shoot an arrow through the axe loops and win the bride. After a nod from his father, Telemachus bows out and leaves it to his father to re-win his mother,

These are resonant stories told as part of the competition winner's story – Pelops winning that for Hippodamia, Menelaus winning that for Helen,

Odysseus re-winning Penelope. But the most notable feature of the story is the evidence that in pre-classical times, the royal line goes through the female: Menelaus, Pelops, and also notably Oedipus and, as dramatised by Euripides in the *Ion*, Xuthus, become kings of Sparta, Elis, Thebes and Athens respectively as consorts of the royal princess.

Helen and Menelaus

Helen's palace which amazed Telemachus in the *Odyssey* remains a tantalizing image of the poetic imagination, although finds at the late Bronze Age and archaic religious site in Therapne – along and overlooking the River Eurotas, a site traditionally called the Menelaion – did in the eighth century BCE have a sign saying 'Helen's Shrine', and as late as the fourth century CE, Helen was referred to as the 'Bride of Therapne'. The excavations by Heinrich Schliemann and others have been woefully destructive, but there is evidence for a cult from at least the eighth century BCE onwards: 300 terracotta figurines, some of women on horseback, female dress brooches and two objects inscribed 'For Helen'.

But there is still no palace, unless the few stones of the adjacent late Bronze Age building are all that is left, not of Menelaus' palace but of that of the queen of Sparta.

Helen and Paris

The story told and retold of the start of the Trojan War is that it was fought for Helen, who fled with or was seduced or was abducted by the beautiful Trojan prince Paris while he visited Mycenae: 'stolen from the nest' (the chorus in *Agamemnon*). This of course was a domestic outrage, but it was also the breaking of the bonds that hold nations together: Menelaus as husband, Menelaus as king of Sparta through his wife and Menelaus as host of a guest prince from another country are all compelled to extract punishment for the outrageous act and to appeal for support to Zeus as upholder of oaths and sacred bonds.

Paris

Paris' hostile act is also a diplomatic incident. Homer's narrative is set in the Mycenaean world, which controlled trade across a wide area of the Greek world, which interacted with neighbouring major powers like Egypt and the Hittites, whose legal and diplomatic documents give us rich information about trade and society. With modern 'pretexts' for war in mind – oil or mineral wealth, for example – some historians see Paris' abduction of Helen as merely an incident which could be used to put together an invading Mycenaean force bent on expanding their empire into Anatolia by taking the city that controlled the Dardanelles and trade up into and from the Black Sea. Archaeology shows that thirteenth-century Bronze Age Troy, like many other cities in the great Hittite empire's sphere of influence, was a hub of trade and diplomacy, the area (Wilusa) regularly appearing in the abundant Hittite tablets. As well as Mycenaean Greek and Cypriot, Assyrian and Babylonian finds, documents show that heads of state, chancelleries, scribes and envoys, as well as traders, regularly came and went. Women – all kinds! – feature heavily in the records: priestesses, prostitutes and princesses.

The Hittites maintained their huge empire by a system of marriages, with secondary wives assuring a network of family alliances between the Hittite and neighbouring, vassal or subordinate states. We have a 'Tawananna', a sovereign queen, arranging such dynastic and diplomatic relationships (we remember that Hecuba as queen of Troy presided over a court of Priam's fifty children) and diplomatic incidents. Intriguingly, a fragmentary tablet we call the Aleksandru Treaty suggests that Prince Aleksandru of Wilusa, a dependent state round about Troy, though the son of a concubine, had a claim to succeed; in Homer, Paris is usually called Paris Alexander.

There are also many instances of and laws about what happens when such an arranged marriage breaks down – including for the return of a second wife – such as what happens to the dowry. (We remember Menelaus, ever concerned with property, going into the duel with Paris insisting on exemplary restitution and damages.) But if the lover came between a man and wife, he faced punishment, including death.

Was Helen a victim of the gods or of an expansionist dynasty looking for a pretext to reduce a rival trade power? In the digest of the lost *Cypria*, we have a suggestion of the gods' involvement: that the Judgment of Paris was part of the plan to bring about a sort of world war.

Helen the goddess

Homer's epics contain the retelling of age-old myths (*muthoi*, stories), some fixed as in the Mycenaean world of palaces and royal dynasties, and some 'Dark Age'

(Ithaca and Phaeacia are visualised as places where food can run out, where the princess does the royal washing), layered and woven into a coherent narrative. Similarly, Homer's Olympus is an organized place of gods and goddesses with distinct spheres of influence; they tell stories of the past – when Hephaistos was lamed, for example – but they are very much stories around the feasting table. But there are glimpses in the narrative: in biographies of 'nymph born' heroes or victims, of Hera's sometime preeminent power, as matriarch not only Zeus' consort, of a world of female power.

And, from references in poetry, cult objects and fragments of lost epics, we have Helen as a powerful figure in her own right, touched by divinity. From the 'Hesiodic' Catalogue of Women, we have her birth:

> Philoctetes sought her, a leader of spearmen, most famous of all men at shooting from afar and with the sharp spear. And he came to Tyndareus' bright city for the sake of the Argive maid who had the beauty of golden Aphrodite, and the sparkling eyes of the Graces; and the dark-faced daughter of Ocean, very lovely of form, bare her when she had shared the embraces of Zeus and the king Tyndareus in the bright palace.

In the similarly influential though now fragmentary Trojan War epic *Cypria*, a 'contents list' has:

> Zeus plans with Themis to bring about the Trojan war. Strife arrives while the gods are feasting at the marriage of Peleus and starts a dispute between Hera, Athena, and Aphrodite as to which of them is fairest. The three are led by Hermes at the command of Zeus to Alexandrus on Mount Ida for his decision, and Alexandrus, lured by his promised marriage with Helen, decides in favour of Aphrodite.

In this digest of the lost *Cypria*, we have the gods' involvement in her story: the Judgment of Paris was part of the plan to bring about a sort of world war. So here we have a Helen who was connected to the gods rather than a victim of power politics or male rivalry.

The second-century CE historian and travel writer Pausanias visited a shrine which preserved the egg that Helen hatched out of – the extraordinarily beautiful Spartan princess Leda, raped by Zeus in the form of a swan, having given birth to two sets of semi-divine twins, Helen and Clytemnestra and Castor and Pollux. Such a 'relic' sounds strange and visiting it naive; the Mycenaeans traded and prized ostrich eggs, but the linking of Helen with an egg cult points to her as connected to or the focus of a fertility cult – like Oestra/Eostre, the pagan goddess who gives us our Easter egg tradition – in the same way as Artemis of Ephesus was linked to Cybele, the great eastern mother goddess.

Indeed, the main cult site of Sparta was that of Artemis Orthia, a conflation of the Olympian goddess of hunting, virginity and childbirth with the incoming Dorians' Orthia, goddess of renewal and fertility. The sanctuary of Artemis Orthia was famous in the classical world as the scene of male coming-of-age endurance competitions. Boys competed to reach the altar braving the whips of older boys; often several of the winners died, flayed alive. Steeped in male blood it might be, but the sanctuary was much visited by women from at least 700 BCE: over 100,000 votive figurines of girls dancing or riding have been excavated, surely offered to Helen (the Heleneia, her festival, seems – possibly uniquely – to have been celebrated by girls driving chariots), along with various finds of girl musicians, girl dancers and female side-saddle riders together with cosmetics, mirrors, combs, perfume bottles and sixth-century BCE stelae. All this points to Helen's various cult sites as known from the poets. Certainly from the eighth century BCE, or even earlier back to the early Bronze Age, there were cultic buildings on the site just outside Sparta at Therapne known as 'Helen's shrine'. More than 300 figurines, some of women riding horses, and dress pins have been found on the site, perhaps dedicated by girls on the eve of marriage and womanhood.

Nearby was the small island in the River Eurotas, the traditional site where Helen danced as a girl. The Spartan poet Alcman speaks of all-female orgiastic initiation rites taking place here, when girls on the eve of womanhood were gathered together, dancing wildly overnight into womanhood. He wrote *parthenaia* (virgin songs) in praise of female beauty, practised privately to be performed in choral contests which were surely thought of as presided over by the most beautiful woman in the world, patron goddess and heroic ancestor.

There are references in the Homeric Hymns, such as 'To the Dioscuri', to the birth of two sets of semi-divine twins, Castor and Pollux but also Helen and Clytemnestra: doubly emblematic of womanhood, storied as seducers and destroyers of men.

Doubly storied, did she, as Tyndareus' daughter the princess of Sparta, choose her consort Menelaus, or was she traded for the richest gift? Did she, as the personification of beauty and divine Eros, fall in love with the beautiful prince, or was she abducted by an unscrupulous guest?

Medieval German cathedrals have representations of the literally double-sided *Frau Welt*: divinely beautiful and/or corrupt, she is an allegory of womanhood's double nature. Helen similarly is a figure of double representation: divine or human, quintessence of *erōs* and *eris*, ultimate prize for or ultimate destroyer of men? The Hesiodic Catalogue of Women even has her fathering as ambiguous or double: Leda 'bore her when she had shared the embraces of Zeus and the king Tyndareus in the bright palace'.

Such rich questions can be raised about Helen because of her ambiguity, her doubleness. She has been used as the topic of sophisticated as well as sophistic argument: debating autonomy, responsibility, guilt; about human or divine status; about the personification or victim of sexual passion.

Extraordinarily, this has taken place not only in poetry and drama but in philosophic debate. One of the first of the foreign 'professors' who came to Athens in the middle of the fifth century BCE, who were collectively called 'wise men' (sophists), the Sicilian Gorgias, advertised his arrival and touted for pupils in an outrageous showpiece of persuasive oratory that set out to defend the indefensible. The speech was called 'In Praise of Helen', the text of which was preserved and served as a model piece of rhetoric. Wonderfully, when Hecuba in the *Trojan Women* undertakes to cross-question Helen as the cause of the war, Helen defends herself using the best possible brief – Gorgias:

> First of all, you should direct your accusations at her. It was she, Hecuba, who gave birth to Paris and it was then when our troubles began. The destruction of Troy, and mine, came because of Priam, her husband, who should have killed Paris when Paris was a baby. [...] No-one can resist the gods. [...] Greece benefited from my tragedy. How? Because the Greeks are not ruled by barbarians which would have happened if Paris had chosen one of the other two goddesses. Greece gained happiness while I gained misery. Because of my beauty, I was sold ...

The Chorus respond with both 'her speech was strong, persuasive, forceful, eloquent' and that Hecuba must 'destroy it because she is the cause of something dreadful'.

Helen and the 'what if' narrative

There is a fascinating story about a sixth-century BCE poet literally 'recanting' – re-singing – Helen's place in history as the shameless wife who went off with the beautiful boy and started an East–West world war. The story is that Helen – with a goddess' power to punish those who speak against her – struck blind the poet Stesichorus for singing this traditional 'guilty' version. He then composed a take-back (*palin*) ode, a palinode, to exonerate her, and got his sight back!

Of all Helen's double positioning, this is the first instance of a truly extraordinary tradition: that there were two Helens, one Helen the wife of Menelaus, whom Aphrodite spirited away to Egypt, and second, a virtual-reality Helen who went with Paris to Troy. All those heroes thus fought and died for ... a phantom.

According to later references, the Palinode argued that 'Helen and Paris were driven ashore on the coast of Egypt and that Helen was detained there by King Proteus. The Helen carried on to Troy was thus a phantom, and the real one was recovered by her husband from Egypt after the war.' This fantastical story – although Pausanias and other travellers dutifully went to Helen's temple in Egypt – gave rise to an extraordinarily moving play: Euripides' *Helen*.

In this, Helen speaks the prologue:

And now let me tell you the dreadful pains I have suffered. Hera was so very angry that she had lost the golden apple contest, that she handed over to Paris, king Priam's son, not me in person but a breathing wraith that looked exactly like me, a phantom she shaped out of the aether. My name, not my body became a trophy between the spear of the Greeks and the bravery of the Trojans.

But here I am, safe and sound, whereas my poor husband Menelaus gathered an army and went off to the high towers of Troy to hunt for me and take me back to Sparta. I am the cause of many deaths of men around the streams of the river Scamander, and though I have suffered so much, men curse me, thinking that I have betrayed my husband and that it was I who brought this dreadful war upon Greece.

She also reflects on what it is to be Helen:

Women and friends, what is this destiny to which I am fastened? Was I born a monster among mankind? [...] I wish that like a picture I had been rubbed out and done again, made plain, without this loveliness, so the Greeks would never have been aware of all those misfortunes that are now mine. [...] My name might be disgraced in Greece, but my body shall keep its honour here!

Ajax's brother, Teuker, arrives in exile and sees Helen:

Great gods! What do I see here? This is the murderous form of a most hateful woman, a woman who has ruined me together with all the Greeks!

In the course of explaining why Helen is so hated, he updates her on the deaths that 'her phantom' is responsible for, including that of her twin brothers; Menelaus is believed lost. Helen is distraught, but takes care to save this one Greek. Teuker leaves, saying:

You look very like Helen in form, dear lady but you are certainly far different to her in heart. May she die a painful death and never reach her home by the streams of Eurotas!

Left alone on stage, Helen turns to expressing her grief, summoning the chorus to join her lament. We are made to feel desperately sorry for this most guilty but also most fascinating woman of all time: the embodiment of *erōs*; the bringer of *eris*.

This double-edgedness gave rise to both the original recantation and the original sophistic double-take; a duality as divine and all-too-shamefully human that has been explored in literature from at least Euripides' *Helen* onwards. But maybe Helen has the last laugh: her story is told and retold, *kleos aphthiton* indeed.

Calypso … and Dido

In the *Odyssey*, Calypso – the coverer or burier – upbraids the male gods for malicious interference in her and female divinities' love lives. Her after-story exists 'in translation', because from her, and from the historical figure Cleopatra who similarly 'detained' Antony, Virgil created Dido.

Out of Hektor, Odysseus and Achilles, Virgil created Aeneas; from the *Iliad* and *Odyssey*, he created the great Latin epic poem, the *Aeneid*. We can trace the structure of this translation. In Book 1, Aeneas lands on Queen Dido's North African shore as Odysseus lands in Phaeacia, and in Books 2 and 3 he tells her the story of his storm-tossed wanderings after Troy, just as Odysseus does to the Phaeacian Queen Arete. In Book 4, Mercury lands in Carthage to release Aeneas, as Hermes orders Calypso to release Odysseus. After a visit to the Underworld, Aeneas lands in the part of Italy that he is destined to make his own. For Aeneas has an overarching mission, to found the dynasty that will lead to the Julii and so to the Emperor Augustus.

As Augustus translated Athens into Rome ('I found Rome a city of bricks and made it a city of marble,' he claimed, according to Suetonius), the plan seems to have been for Virgil to translate Greece's two foundational epics into one, to become the foundational epic of a new era: an Augusteid.

The schema has Aeneas transferring 'classicism' from Troy to Rome, building into the foundation of Rome and its Imperial dynasty a narrative of god-given destiny. But whereas Odysseus in the Underworld is shown those for whom he cares, his mother and his fellow heroes, and learns what his journey home is going to entail, Aeneas sees not his own future but that of Augustus. Aeneas leaves the burning Troy not only with his father and his family gods, but also with Augustus, on his back.

But the *Aeneid*, like all truly great works of art, escapes its schema. Just as Calypso detained Odysseus – as that great North African queen Cleopatra detained Augustus' arch rival, Antony – so Dido, queen of Carthage, detained

Aeneas. There is therefore no doubt about the effect that Mercury's speech to Aeneas should have had: like that of Hermes to Calypso, there will be a 'coming to the senses', an acceptance of the god's words as a correction of the onward arc which is Odysseus' return and Aeneas' onward journey to Italy.

But whereas Calypso remonstrates with Hermes, Aeneas is literally struck dumb, the words sticking in his throat. Aeneas leaves Dido with a stilted explanation: he is leaving her at the gods' and history's will, not his own. Whereas both Calypso – and we – know that Odysseus has spent at least some of his years on the island thinking of home and Penelope (Calypso tackles him directly about wanting to leave a goddess for an ageing, mortal wife), we have watched both Aeneas and Dido grow and bloom in deep, new-found happiness. Aeneas is in the right place, supervising the new city's building programme, a cloak woven by Dido round his shoulders. And whereas, once her complaint has been made, Calypso accepts the diktat and helps Odysseus build a raft, Dido's complaint echoes endlessly, forever unanswered: in Book 4 of the *Aeneid*; in letter VII of Ovid's *Heroides* (reworked for the lockdown theatre stage by Stella Duffy); and in Act 3 of Purcell's *Dido and Aeneas*. Hermes and Homer do not stay to address Calypso's feelings and fate, but in her guise of Calypso, Dido's lament for all betrayed women echoes tragically and affectingly down the ages.

To read the *Aeneid*, as I cannot but do, as a fascinating, superb and problematizing translation of the *Iliad* and *Odyssey*, is to find the effect of two 'translations' in particular continuously troubling. The first is that of Calypso into Dido, holding Aeneas in Carthage, impeding his mission. The second (and strangely relatedly) is that of Books 21 and 22 of the *Iliad* into Books 10 and 12 of the *Aeneid* – places where, after the deaths of those dear to them (Patroclus and Pallas), Achilles and Aeneas become killing machines. Aeneas like Achilles is possessed by a terrible fury (*furens*), maddened by the death of someone for whom he was responsible. But whereas Achilles explains to Lykaon that after Patroclus everything has changed – his heart, his understanding of the human condition, his future – Aeneas kills Magus while he is still supplicating, interrupting and silencing him; the voice of pleading and protest is excised from the narrative. These two silencings – of Calypso/Dido and Lykaon/Magus – are deeply disturbing, suppressing not just the *Aeneid*'s characters but their Homeric forebears. Or do they, somewhere, sound a note of resistance, pull against the tight construction of the poetry?

Like Achilles, Aeneas becomes overwhelmed after the death of someone to whom he is very close and for whom he is responsible. But unlike Achilles, Aeneas is not free to consider only his own values and heroic path: he must protect his son and the sacred objects he brings from Troy, and it is his son's – and Augustus' – future that he must achieve. Like Hektor, he is trammelled:

Hektor by *aidōs*, Aeneas by the need to exemplify the Augustan signature values – especially that of *pietas* (which, like *aidōs*, could be translated as 'respect for social and emotional bonds').

In the section on 'the wrath of Achilles', I argued that the cause of his wrath, *mēnis*, can be equated with that fundamental rupture in the bond of trust that Jonathan Shay identified in his Vietnam veterans who 'lose it' and go 'berserk'. I distinguished Achilles' *mēnis*, mad bloodlust, from the '*memaōs*' state of battlefield arousal – an acceptable and even proper state for a warrior. Not so Achilles' rage; he is criticized within the narrative for his bloodlust, by the river and by the gods.

But Aeneas seems to feel no such sense of a fundamental rupture. He accepts the god's and Rome's will and leaves Dido without compunction if not without regret. It is the killing of Pallas, like the killing of Patroclus, that tips him over the edge: burning with rage (*furens*), he replays Achilles' vengeance on Lykaon and the killing of everyone in his path, including a priest, while – extraordinarily to our ears – being called *pius* (pious, deeply respectful). *Pietas* is one of Augustus' four mission values, connoting respect for bonds between allies, fathers and sons, gods and men. Aeneas' often repeated self-identifying statement '*sum pius Aeneas*' (I am *pius* Aeneas) reminds and replays Hektor's cardinal attribute of 'bound by *aidōs*'.

Do we, should we, feel that Aeneas, like Hektor, is impeded by his *aidōs*, his *pietas*? It makes uncomfortable reading that Aeneas is continually required to serve the future that he is told of but will not himself see. Unlike Hektor, we feel that his *pietas* is insensible obedience, subservience to what is finally an imperial, and imperialistic, project.

Every reader has to puzzle this out for themself. Should we, and does Virgil, criticize that obedience? Why do Dido's accusations, which sound so strongly in our ears, go unanswered? Calypso's complaint is against the gods, but Dido's is against Rome's mission; Virgil's *Aeneid* was written for the ears and appreciation of the emperor who had rejoiced in the destruction of his rival contender for power, Antony, by just such a North African queen as Dido. Did Virgil the poet himself 'lose the plot', allowing Dido to grow in character and sympathy beyond what was intended? Does the poem give voice through Dido to the complaint of Calypso and of all those betrayed by the pursuit of an imperial mission?

For my part, I would like to think that Dido is present in, and influences, the very end of the *Aeneid*.

The fighting in the second half of the *Aeneid* is formally similar to that in the *Iliad*: as Achilles attacks Troy, so Aeneas attacks the land that will become Italy. As in the *Iliad*, to win is to dispossess and displace the loser, here Turnus, the leader of the Latins. But the Iliadic fighting is woven into an Odyssean structure. Aeneas' reception in Italy is parallel to Odysseus' in Phaeacia, with the king of the Latins offering his daughter, Lavinia, to Aeneas. But unlike Nausicaa's mother, Queen Arete, Lavinia's mother, Queen Amata, is extremely hostile to Aeneas. Lavinia has been long promised to the Latin leader, and Aeneas is going to have to fight for both land and bride. Aeneas and Odysseus are both older, veterans of the Trojan War, and both have full-grown sons. But Aeneas may not gracefully avoid the marriage alliance as Odysseus did in Phaeacia; he rather has to fight Turnus for Lavinia in exactly the same way as Menelaus and Paris fought for Helen. Unlike Helen though, we are not given access to Lavina's feelings, as now she is suddenly presented with this ageing stranger, Aeneas, having been brought up with Turnus as her intended husband and successor to her father the king.

In the course of the to-and-fro of the war, of attacking and defending the city and the camp, there are individual battles which replay various of the Iliadic encounters. In the course of one such, Turnus kills Pallas, the young son of Aeneas' ally, whom Aeneas had promised to look after and protect. So the stage is set for the final replay, as Aeneas, *furens*, goes out to get revenge. When Turnus finally comes up against Aeneas, time stands still just as it does when Hektor meets Achilles. Nightmare-like, he freezes, can't move or cry out; like Hektor, he turns for support, only to find himself alone. This recalls Hektor, but also Priam – for the end of the *Aeneid* telescopes both the death of Patroclus and the end of the wrath of Achilles in *Iliad* Book 24. Turnus, accepting defeat, supplicates Aeneas, begging him to think of his own father and return him or at least his body to his father's home. For the Italians have acknowledged Aeneas as victor; Lavinia and the future kingdom are now his.

This is the end of the epic; Aeneas must lay down his *furor* as Achilles had done his wrath. It is not in keeping with Stoic values that a hero should ever so lose control, and certainly not at this decisive time. And *pius* Aeneas must respect the conventions governing proper treatment of the vanquished, for whatever Augustus' actual practice, he claimed clemency, *clementia*, as one of his cardinal virtues. But at that moment, right at the end of the war, the epic and the project, Virgil has Aeneas catch sight of Turnus' wearing of Pallas' sword-belt; he snaps and kills him. Unlike the end of the *Iliad*, the end of the *Aeneid* is savagery not reconciliation: the last words are of the dead Turnus' protesting soul.

Why does Aeneas snap? My answer is that Virgil has Aeneas, time after time, accepting and submitting to fate and to the demands of the narrative. Virgil does not allow Aeneas to really answer Dido or Magus in the way that Odysseus did to Calypso or Achilles did to Lykaon. Finally, Aeneas is given as the prize – or price – of victory a young girl long betrothed to Turnus. Not his wife, whom he was forced to leave in Troy: unlike Odysseus his Penelope; and not Dido, with whom he had a made a deep bond of like-mindedness or *homophrosunē* (Odysseus' word for Penelope); but Lavinia. Is that, the memory of all the losses, why Aeneas snaps? Do Dido's accusations ring in his ears?

The final words of the *Aeneid* are not about Aeneas, but of Turnus' soul, fleeing unreconciled to the Underworld. If the final question of the *Iliad* is whether undying fame, *kleos aphthiton*, is worth the human cost, the final words of protest of the *Aeneid* make us consider whether the imperial mission is worth the human cost.

Bibliography

Primary

Homer, *Iliad* and *Odyssey*. Many full translations available, including the free online poetryintranslation.com, which has a very useful hyperlinked index on the homepages.

Homer, *The Iliad: The Fitzgerald Translation*, narrated by Dan Stevens (Audible Audiobook).

Homer, *The Odyssey* (trans. Robert Fagles), narrated by Sir Ian McKellen (Audible Audiobook).

Homer, *The Iliad of Homer*, translated into verse by Alexander Pope.

Homer, *The Odyssey*, translated into verse by Alexander Pope.

Parker, Jan, *The Iliad and the Odyssey: Translated by George Chapman* (Wordsworth Classics of World Literature, Ware, 2000).

Virgil, *The Aeneid* in various translations, e.g. by Robert Fagles or Frederick Ahl.

Background and Further Reading

British Museum, *Troy: myth and reality* (Thames and Hudson, London 2019).

Cartledge, Paul, *Ancient Greece: A History in Eleven Cities* – Cnossos, Mycenae, Argos, Sparta (Oxford University Press, Oxford, 2011).

Haynes, Natalie, *A Thousand Ships* (Picador, London, 2020)

Hughes, Bettany, *Helen of Troy: Goddess, Princess, Whore* (PBS DVD; book, Alfred A. Knopf, New York & Pimlico, London, 2005).

Shay MD, Jonathan, *Achilles in Vietnam: Combat Trauma and the Undoing of Character* (Simon & Schuster, New York and London, 2005).

Shay MD, Jonathan, 'The Trauma of War', in *Voices in Wartime: the Anthology* (ed. Andrew Himes) (Andrew Himes, Seattle, 2005).

Strauss, Barry, *The Trojan War: A New History* (Simon & Schuster, New York and London, 2006).

Wood, Michael, *In Search of the Trojan War*. Film, DVD, book (BBC, 2005).

Index

Index A

People of the *Iliad* and *Odyssey*

Gods

Aphrodite, winner of the Golden Apple contest, Paris' supporter, 12, 25–6, 29–30, 35
  Aeneas' mother, 38, 131–3
  v Diomedes, 38–9
  Aphrodite's 'cestus', 87–8
  Caught with Ares, 215
  and Helen, 281
Apollo, 95
Ares, 92, 94, 135
Artemis, 38, 45, 101, 130, 135, 139, 252, 279
  Orthia, rites and sanctuary, 280
Athene, 21, 31–2, 38–40, 43–4, 49, 53, 55, 57–8, 71, 92, 94, 116, 135
  and Achilles, 17, 19, 55, 67, 126, 128, 138, 141, 145
  and Diomedes, 35, 38–40
  and Odysseus, Telemachus and Penelope, 187, 190–6, 203, 206–207, 209, 212, 236–8, 241, 244, 249–50, 258, 263, 266–7, 270
Hades, 62, 94, 130
Hephaistos, 130, 135, 138, 203, 210, 215
  forges Shield of Achilles, 122–5, 158, 173, 181
Hera, 17, 19–20, 31–2, 39–40, 57–8, 71, 87–9, 93–4, 103, 126
  as matriarch, 88, 93, 122, 279
  seduces husband Zeus, 88–90
Hermes, 130
  guides Priam, 156–7, 160

  tells Calypso to release Odysseus, 190, 203–206
  protects Odysseus from Circe, 221, 228
Poseidon, 49, 52, 81–3, 90, 138, 190
  Odysseus and, 190, 202–203, 206, 220–1, 224–6, 230–1, 234, 267
Thetis, 11, 12, 19–20, 41, 53, 57, 63, 70, 92, 109, 114, 116–18, 122, 124, 126, 156, 159

Greek heroes, 28

Achilles, 17–9, 59–65, 125–63, 165–82, 215, 231, 262, 268–9, 276, 283–6
Agamemnon, 12, 17–19, 21–2, 28, 33–4, 43, 50, 56–7, 59–65, 71–3, 88, 90, 126–7, 152, 153, 166–9, 175, 177
  in the *Odyssey*, 190, 196, 268–9
Ajax [the Greater, son of Telemon], 21, 28, 33, 46, 50, 60–4, 72–4, 76, 79, 81–6, 90–3, 95–7, 108–12, 114, 150–1, 153–4, 166, 199, 231, 282
Diomedes, 33–4, 36–40, 42–3, 55–6, 61, 66–70, 72–4, 87–8, 153, 168–70
  v Aphrodite, 131
Idomeneus, 33, 77, 81–6, 166, 169
Machaon, healer, son of Aesculapius, 33, 71, 74
Menelaus, 10, 26–7, 29, 32–3, 38, 43, 50, 66–7, 74, 86, 90, 109–10, 112, 114, 150, 154
  in the *Odyssey*, in Sparta, with Helen, 186, 192–9, 269
  in tradition, with Helen, 276–7, 282

Index B

Key Greek Words

Index C

Contents